The Museum at the End of the World

The Museum at the End of the World

Encounters in the Russian Far East

ALEXIA BLOCH AND
LAUREL KENDALL

PENN

University of Pennsylvania Press

Philadelphia

Copyright © 2004 University of Pennsylvania Press
All rights reserved.
Printed in the United States of America on acid-free paper

10   9   8   7   6   5   4   3   2   1

Published by
University of Pennsylvania Press
Philadelphia, Pennsylvania 19104–4011

Library of Congress Cataloging-in-Publication Data
Bloch, Alexia.
    The museum at the end of the world : encounters in the Russian Far East / Alexia Bloch
and Laurel Kendall.
        p. cm.
    Includes bibliographical references and index.
    ISBN 0-8122-3799-4 (cloth : alk. paper) — ISBN 0-8122-1878-7 (pbk. : alk. paper)
    1. Russian Far East (Russia)—Description and travel. 2. Bloch, Alexia—Travel—Russia
(Federation)—Russian Far East. 3. Kendall, Laurel—Travel—Russia (Federation)—Russian
Far East. I. Kendall, Laurel. II. Title.

DK771.D3B59 2004
957'.7086—dc22   2003070534

To Those Who Do the Work of Culture

Contents

Figure 1. This scene from a mural by Valery Alekseevich Istomin portrays a pilot
delivering books to a Native woman in an isolated village, just as Soviet period civil
servants saw themselves bringing culture and enlightenment to distant places. The
mural is on the wall of the public library in Anadyr. (Photo by Laurel Kendall)

Preface

The Museum at the End of Whose World?

New York, American Museum of Natural History, March 24, 1900
I herewith appoint you to take charge of the work of the Jesup North Pacific
Expedition in northeastern Asia. . . . The object of the expedition is an ethnological
and zoological survey of northeastern Asia. . . . [Since] Mrs. Jochelson and Mrs.
Bogoras are going to accompany the expedition to the field, and thus form part of your
party . . . all scientific work of the ladies must be considered as part of the results of
the expedition.

—*Franz Boas to Waldemar Jochelson*

March 26, 1900
The principal object of your work will be a thorough investigation of the Koryak,
maritime Chukchi, and eastern Yukaghir from all points of view—ethnological,
linguistical, and somatological. You will use every effort to collect as full information
and as full collections as possible from these tribes. . . . You will endeavor to represent
fully in your collections objects that are new to science. You will also make special
efforts to obtain a good collection of anthropological photographs and plaster casts.
You will make studies and collections among the [neighboring tribes] . . . if
opportunity should offer.[1]

—*Boas to Jochelson*

At the end of the nineteenth century, Dr. Franz Boas of the American Museum of Natural History organized the most ambitious expedition in the history of American ethnology. Two teams of researchers, one on each side of the Bering Strait, would conduct parallel and comprehensive research to determine the historical connections between the Native peoples of easternmost Siberia and the northwest coast of North America. As part of the Siberian team, he commissioned two rehabilitated revolutionaries, Waldemar Jochelson and Waldemar Bogoras, and an ivory-tower philologist, Berthold Laufer. Jochelson and Borgoras, friends who had sustained each other with a lively correspondence throughout their years of exile, returned to Siberia accompanied by their wives. Their party also included a young field assistant, Alexander Axelrod, and Norman Buxton, an American zoologist. Laufer would work without such companionship; an American archaeologist, Gerald Fowke, accompanied him in the first months of his travels but the two did not get along, and Fowke returned home early.

While the expressed goal of the expedition was never fulfilled, the work of ethnologists was monumental. Traveling by horse, dogsled, skin boat, and raft, and camping for long and short periods in Native villages, Bogoras, Jochelson, and Laufer gathered data for a shelf of ethnographic monographs, including some "classics," substantial archives of photographs and correspondence, wax cylinders of songs and stories in Native languages, head casts and body measurements, and uniquely comprehensive collections documenting the lifeways of the Native peoples of the Russian Far East.[2]

It was the age of heroes, the time of ancestral ethnographers who were larger than life. More than a century later, one cannot write these words without irony. The anthropologist as hero borrows from the image of the white male explorer penetrating the frozen wastelands. Scholarly writing over recent decades encourages us to think of these works as part of a larger imperial project; we have learned to view the business of recording, classifying, collecting, and exhibiting in museums—whatever the ethnographers' expressed respect for Native cultures—as an affirmation of racial, cultural, and political domination. We should also have learned by now, however, that the bashing of one's disciplinary ancestors is both a cheap shot and a partial truth. In recent years, Native scholars of the Chukchi, Koryak, Nivkh, Sakha, Yukaghir, and Evenk people have come to New York to examine the Jesup Expedition collections, photographs, and archives at the American Museum of Natural History. They are self-consciously using these fragments from their great-grandparents' world in the work of reconstituting a sense of "us" that the twentieth century tried mightily to destroy.

Vladimir Etylin, a Chukchi scholar and activist, told us, "Much of our history is in this museum, and our young people are very interested in it. They can't go to the museum, but they should be able to see this through photos, videos, and writings." Through conversations with Etylin and with similar encouragement from other Siberian visitors, we—a curator and a postdoctoral fellow—went to the Russian Far East as representatives of the American Museum of Natural History. Our aim was to develop collegial contacts with museums in areas where members of the Jesup Expedition had worked one hundred years ago. In August 1998, we traveled to Chukotka, Kamchatka, and Magadan in the Kolyma region, and Khabarovsk on the Amur River, carrying CDs of the collections in New York and exhibition catalogs of expedition photographs. We already knew that images of century-old artifacts would be useful not only to scholars but also to local artisans who were reviving traditional handicrafts. A few years previously, the American Museum of Natural History

Figure 2. The Jochelsons in their tent. Glass plate negatives are on a rack to the right of the photograph. A Koryak basket is to the left, beside a teacup. (AMNH Library 2A13549)

had commissioned a pair of gloves and a pouch designed by a Sakha master artisan, Anastasia Yegorovna Sivtseva. Anastasia Yegorovna was using motifs found on artifacts collected by Jochelson, designs she had seen in slides of our collections brought back to Yakutsk by two visiting scholars. An expedition odyssey could come full circle through acts of visual repatriation.

This is an account of our journey through a landscape made known to us from old ethnographies but subsequently transformed by Soviet efforts to bring "civilization" to the Northern periphery in the form of towns, schools, government stores, museums, and Houses of Culture, a landscape now shaken by that system's collapse. It is a travelers' tale about museum workers, Native scholars, performers and artisans, and a great variety of ordinary Russians and indigenous Siberians whom we encountered on buses, on streets, and in markets in Chukotka, Kamchatka, and in the border town of Khabarovsk.

We did not go to the Russian Far East with the intention of writing a travel book. *The Museum at the End of the World* took shape from our encounters with many different kinds of people as they lived day-to-day in the wreckage of an ambitious but overextended Soviet infrastructure. From Chukotka to Khabarovsk to Kamchatka, a story took shape in our journals and after more than a month of travel, in a spa outside Petropavolvsk, the "travel book" was suddenly present in our conversations. Neither of us might have written it alone. *The Museum at the End of the World* is the product of a particular synergy. On this journey, Laurel is the more innocent traveler. As an anthropologist, Laurel has worked in Korea over more than a quarter century and has also spent time in the "Confucian socialisms" of China and Vietnam, but she speaks no Russian and was totally dependent on Alexia's translations. Laurel masked her insecurities in anthropological fashion by writing in her notebook. Alexia, in contrast, is fluent in Russian and has a personal historical horizon that extends back to Soviet times. Although this was her first visit to the Russian Far East, Alexia studied Russian in what was then Leningrad in 1988 and has done fieldwork in central Siberia in the Evenk Autonomous Region since 1992. Traveling together, Laurel's sense of the surreal caused Alexia to regard the now-familiar with fresh eyes. This dialogue enabled a travel narrative: the intensity of a first encounter tempered by an informed reading of a time and place and energized by the motion of a journey. This play between freshness, even naïve discovery, and a perceptive point of view is the flour and yeast of travel writing.

In Paul Fussel's much cited aphorism, "The explorer seeks the undiscovered, the traveler that which has been discovered by the mind working in history, the tourist that which has been discovered by entrepreneurship and prepared for him by the arts of mass publicity. The genuine traveler is, or used to be, in the middle between the two extremes."[3] That, we thought, was us. Our Jesup predecessors had ventured not into uncharted space but into the unrecorded lives of Chukchi, Yukaghir, Koryak, and Nanai: "An investigation by Mr. Bogoras of the Chukchee [*sic*] happens only once in an eternity, and I think you owe it to science to give us the results of your studies," Franz Boas wrote to a tardy expedition author.[4] That wasn't us. We were, after all, carrying CDs to the descendants of these same Chukchi, with the accurate expectation that the disks could be played.

But if our travels were not a replay in the footsteps of early expedition anthropology, or even of fieldwork in the region today, neither were we tourists. Tourists do visit the Russian Far East. We actually met two. Previous numbers had been sufficient to have generated at least two guidebooks, both woefully out of date by the time of our trip. In Providenia, at the start of our journey, when we found ourselves enfolded into an excursion arranged for the two tourists we encountered, we flourished our notebooks and scribbled incessantly. In retrospect, it was an insecure assertion of our identity as anthropologists distinct from tourists. Following Fussell, "Travel is work. Etymologically a traveler is one who suffers travail."[5] Or in Mary Louise Pratt's words, "The itinerary itself becomes the occasion for a narrative of success, in which travel is a triumph in its own right. What are conquered are destinations, not kingdoms. . . . The travelers struggle in unequal battle against scarcity, inefficiency, laziness, discomfort, poor horses, bad roads, bad weather, delays,"[6] or more bluntly, from travel writer Paul Theroux, "The worst trips make the best reading."[7] As travelers, we would grumble about the absence of hot running water and describe our periodic quests for a vegetarian meal in a land of fish and potatoes; this was part of the subjective condition of being "us"—two academic women from New York—in another place. Even in confessional ethnography, this would be whining, self-indulgent, and not very useful prose. But if our understanding of the genre was encouraging us to be more literally, even banally, present, our searches for vanishing air transportation and our attempts to second-guess a fantastically shrinking currency revealed the exigencies of daily life in the Russian Far East in 1998 not only for visiting anthropologists but for those who live there.

In our professional lives, we are both writers of ethnography, Alexia in central Siberia and Laurel in Korea. *The Museum at the End of the World* is not an ethnography. Travel writing and ethnography have had a close and sometimes problematic relationship. In a well-known essay, "Fieldwork in Common Places,"[8] Mary Louise Pratt reveals how early ethnographers, writing a mix of personal narrative and objectified description, were setting themselves down on tropical beaches—and on paper—in the manner and style of those very explorers and travel writers from whom they would distinguish themselves as objective scientists. The ambivalence of Lévi-Strauss, "I hate traveling and explorers. Yet here I am proposing to tell the story of my expeditions"[9] was in no way unique. Distinguished lineages of anthropologists have borrowed the devices of travel writing to establish a sense of place (distant) and authenticity (I was there). And once Pratt had said it, it suddenly seemed so obvious.

Pratt's aim, in concert with other contributors to James Clifford and George E. Marcus's 1986 *Writing Culture* anthology, was to liberate ethnography from the chimera of pure objectivity and from the necessity of sustaining this illusion through the encumbering prose style of natural science. Pratt could not have been more blunt: "How . . . could such interesting people doing such interesting things produce such dull books? What did they have to do to themselves?"[10] *Writing Culture* was a cry of liberation, a call for an experimental turn in anthropology. Genre-bending new writing by Amitav Ghosh, Kirin Narayan, and Michael Taussig, among many others, borrowed freely from other forms, including travel writing. Clifford would claim, "Indeed one way to understand the current 'experimentalism' of ethnographic writing is as a renegotiation of the boundary, agonistically defined in the late nineteenth century, with 'travel writing.'"[11] But if we have seen a successful return of the repressed, if the mode of the travel writer enables more interesting prose, what then of the reverse? What happens when two anthropologists engage in a work of travel writing, not a field narrative, but unabashed travel writing? Some of the old ambivalences rear their heads.

When anthropologists write a travel narrative, a "how we got from point A to point Z and whom we talked to on the way," is the result no less an ethnography? Should travel writing be considered inadequate, flawed, but more readable ethnography? We were only there for six weeks and in no one place for longer than a week—as long as a week only because the airport was fogged in or the flight out came only once every seven days. Shouldn't that disqualify us? What measure of time makes an ethnography? A year? Two years? Nine months? In the early twentieth century, before solitary residence in a single village became the rite of passage for an anthropologist, Jesup Expedition ethnologists moved across the landscape, from encampment to encampment, until the exigencies of weather and transportation forced them to ground for several months at a time. Some, the cultural critic James Clifford foremost among them, have challenged the seemingly arbitrary boundaries of legitimate fieldwork. Is an anthropologist ever not an anthropologist? We might turn this presumption on its head. When anthropologists cross borders to produce a travel narrative, are they not, in some basic sense, "doing fieldwork"?

For Laurel, the distinctions were obvious. In Korea, she speaks the language and draws on three decades of acquaintance. In the Russian Far East, she could not talk her way out of an airport. Writing was therapy. She made notes of every conversation and encounter and laboriously transcribed them into a handwritten journal, the three handwritten notebooks that, combined with Alexia's notes, became the backbone of our travel narrative. Alexia wrote her notes into a laptop but Laurel preferred the handwritten journal, which she could pull out of her backpack during long waits in cold airports, a Linus blanket offering security in the task of purposeful writing, a sense of "doing something" that sharpened her perceptual abilities in a near frantic desire to record all minutiae. And Laurel wrote with several pairs of imaginary eyes over her shoulder, the linguistically adept and physically and emotionally intrepid anthropologists now working in the Russian Far East—Russian, Western, and Native scholars—several of whom offered advice as we planned our trip, hospitality during our travels, or reality checks on our return. In Laurel's eyes, these are the "real" ethnographers of the Russian Far East from whose work her own presumption to write must be sharply distinguished as another genre entirely. "Travel writing" salvages all that scribbling from being merely superficial, bad, or even bogus ethnography.

Alexia's position is more ambiguous. This writing extends her interest in documenting what the aftermath of socialism in the Russian Federation means for people in the North. While this journey brought her to new places, she has deep knowledge of Siberia, has experienced its recent history firsthand, and is well acquainted with the legacy of Soviet institutions and the emergence of missionary activities that inform the post-Soviet life of towns in the North.

When Alexia has a conversation with a kindly Christian woman on the flight to Anadyr and hears about the devil's latest mischief in the woman's small village, it is an extension of other, similar conversations many hundreds of miles to the west in Evenkia, a fragment in Alexia's composite portrait of charismatic Christians in Siberia. Must this conversation be bracketed off as "not Evenkia," or is Alexia's field, as Clifford and others have suggested, a more mobile and elastic place, perhaps a field called "post-socialism"? *The Museum at the End of the World*, however, is not so much the description of this field as the recounting of a journey through it. The tale is in the travel.

We spent six weeks in motion, traveling by plane and microbus and inveigling a ride on a privately chartered helicopter. We did not travel by sled, on horseback, or atop a huge, tank-like tundra vehicle, although such means of transportation are often a necessity for anthropologists doing fieldwork in the region today. Our target destinations were local museums in cities and small towns, not fishing villages and reindeer camps. The very possibility of such a trip as ours illuminates the contrast between the vicissitudes of travel in the Russian Far East of Bogoras, Jochelson, and Laufer's day and the ubiquitous cosmopolitan comforts of our own, despite present day irregularities of transportation and the paucity of heat, hot water, and sometimes food. We bracket our narrative with selections from the Jesup Expedition field correspondence and intersperse expedition photographs with our own to highlight not only the difference between the rigors of early expedition work and our own relatively quick and easy trip but also the magnitude of transformation in this region over the twentieth century. Much of what we see and experience today is the product of an ambitious, sometimes draconian effort on the part of the Soviet state to remake frontier society in its own image. Our conversations with local residents explore the tremendous costs of that history, but our interlocutors also lament benefits that have now disappeared and a sense of socialist morality that has been negated by the rise of new wealth. The juxtaposition between "then" and "now" also marks a contrast between Native peoples as ethnographic subjects and today's Native intellectuals, curators, and culture workers who discuss the meaning of tradition and critically evaluate works of early ethnography. Finally, we keep the Jesup Expedition visible because it is the common frame of reference for many of our conversations.

The Museum at the End of the World has a dual meaning. It evokes an older genre of heroic travel writing, of adventure stories whose authors have gone "to the ends of the earth." From the perspective of Moscow and St. Petersburg, the Russian Far East was a distant extension of empire, but a frontier that was to be filled with "culture" (*kultura*), as the imperial and then Soviet state understood the term. In Soviet times, the result was "culture" for the masses in the form of comprehensive art collections, ballet instruction, libraries, schools, and "luxuries" such as spas established across the country and extending into areas like the Russian Far East. At this putative end of the world, museum curators poured us tea. Many of our encounters with "Natives" were reunions with true cosmopolitans whom we had first met at conferences in the United States and Europe during their own research trips or when their dance troupe performed at the American Museum of Natural History in New York (the museum at the end of their world?). These reunions, this sense of connection rather than distance, are also a part of the story we tell.

"End of the world" can be understood temporally rather than spatially, alluding to the *Soviet* world that began coming apart more than a decade ago and about which so many of our conversations revolved. These dialogues reflect the pessimism, often black-humored, of post-Soviet times in 1998. As we journeyed, in August and early September, the ruble teetered toward collapse. In museums, we met curators who had not been paid for five months and who mustered considerable ingenuity over small but necessary matters such as how to replace burned-out light bulbs in their exhibition halls. We were continually amazed and humbled by our Russian and Siberian counterparts who would wake in cold apartments, dress themselves with courage and panache, and go to work in cold offices where they would discuss with us their hopeful plans for future projects. As museum people, our logical frame of reference and point of connection was with other museum people, with professionals like ourselves. We are concerned with the particular fate of museums as one locus of ideas and representations in a world that has been redefined. An ambitious state-supported system brought museums to far-flung communities and carried traveling exhibits on the backs of trucks and in the hulls of helicopters to distant villages. Originally intended as a pedagogical tool of the Soviet state, museums have now been forced to rethink their mission in light of shrinking financial support, revitalized claims for Native identity, and the discredited grand narrative of Soviet history that once shaped the content of their exhibits. They have come to recognize the need for showmanship if they are to draw a new public inside. At the same time, the Native peoples who have been portrayed as the subjects of so many static museum displays—frozen manikins in fur—are issuing their own dynamic statements about identity, culture, and a possible future. The end of a world is thus the beginning of a new one, built on the legacy of Soviet times, and the times before that, as recorded by the Jesup Expedition.

This book is the product of two journeys, one in the Russian Far East and the other from a very rough idea to a published book. As will be evident in the following pages, we owe a tremendous debt to those who helped us along the way. It would be impossible to list here all of the museum personnel, scholars, performers, and casual acquaintances who offered us hospitality and insight from Providenia to Petropavlovsk.

Our travels were supported by a grant from the Trust for Mutual Understanding; we are particularly grateful to Richard Lanier, TMU director, for running a creative and broad-minded program. We would also like to ac-

Figure 3. Natalya Pavlovna Otke, director of the Anadyr museum, holds aloft two volumes of Bogoras' monumental study, *The Chukchee,* the classic study of her own people. (Photo by Laurel Kendall)

knowledge the Henry Luce Foundation for its support of Alexia's postdoctoral fellowship at the American Museum of Natural History. Patricia Gray, Nelson Hancock, David Koester, Ingrid Summers, Jennifer Syron, Alexander King, and Christina Kinkaid generously shared information about places they knew intimately through fieldwork. Patty, Nelson, David, Ingrid, and Jennifer also gave portions of our manuscript useful critical readings, as did Igor Krupnik and Bruce Grant. At the American Museum of Natural History, Barbara Mathé shared her deep knowledge of Jesup Expedition photography, Kristen Mable and Belinda Kaye aided our work in the Anthropology Department's archive, and Bridget Thomas produced our map. Kevin Devorsey provided us with his good-humored expertise in computer systems, including in multilingual software and troublesome laptops. Kenneth Mobray provided expertise on physical anthropology and Sarah Nelson on the archaeology of the Russian Far East. Nancy Goodwin, Marie Lowe, and Anthony Scheirman transformed Laurel's handwritten travel journal into typescript; Jennifer Yu assisted in additional research. Their enthusiasm for our story was tonic to our work. Milind Kandlikar aided Alexia in transferring her electronic travel notes and integrating them with Laurel's; Milind's passion for traveling and travel writing was critical at several points when the project was in need of encouragement. Homer Williams provided background information on Koreans in the Russian Far East. An anonymous reviewer for the University of Pennsylvania Press gave us many helpful comments. Peter Agree, our editor, had faith in this project when its authors were at risk of succumbing to doubt. Noreen O'Connor helped us produce a more readable book.

Note on Transliteration

The system used in transliterating Russian terms is adapted from that of the United States Board on Geographic Names. Diacritical marks are omitted. In cases where there is a common English version of a word, such as Moscow, the common spelling of the word rather than the transliteration is used in the text. When foreign terms, such as Russian, Yupik, or Japanese words, are used in the text, they are italicized and explained with first usage. While we have chosen a single system of transliteration, given the historical nature of the material, some ethnonyms appear in slightly different variations, such as "Chukchi" and "Chukchee."

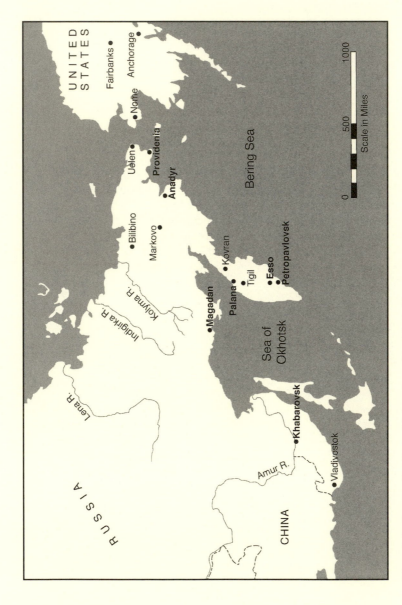

Map of the Russian Far East with locations visited in bold.

Chapter 1

Across the Bering Strait and Through the Looking Glass

St. Petersburg, October 30, 1898
For my part I will make a journey to the coast of the Arctic Sea, and from there to the Bering Strait.

—*Waldemar Bogoras to Franz Boas*

On the morning of August 8, 1998, we are at New York's LaGuardia Airport awaiting take off on the first leg of a six-week journey to Chukotka and Kamchatka, the Russian Far East. Our suitcases hold a minimum of clothing, a maximum of English-language reading material, trail mix, and chocolate (food might be scarce), a large package of Korean dried seaweed (green vegetables will definitely be scarce), an assortment of small gifts, a dozen exhibition catalogs, and eight CDs with images of the objects in the Siberian collection of the American Museum of Natural History (AMNH), collections made a century ago by the Jesup North Pacific Expedition. The catalogs and CDs are the raison d'être of our journey.

In contrast, members of the Jesup Expedition went to the Russian Far East equipped with the best scientific equipment of their day, no matter how bulky. They recorded songs and stories on wax cylinders when the cold weather did not freeze their equipment to inactivity. Waldemar Bogoras and Waldemar Jochelson used a professional large-format view camera that required a tripod and a separate glass plate for each exposure. In addition to this cumbersome rig, they carried the necessary equipment and supplies to develop their work in the field. Calipers for taking head measurements were a tool of early anthropological fieldwork. Dina Jochelson-Brodskaya, Jochelson's wife, put hers to good use and later wrote a doctoral dissertation based on her measurements of some 720 men, women, and children. Berthold Laufer, on the other hand, seemed to share his subjects' squeamishness at the prospect of his actually using the calipers, and the plaster of Paris with which he was to make head casts seemed always to arrive at a port of call just after his departure.

Alexia, a veteran of Siberian fieldwork, has reassured Laurel that the sum-

Figure 4. Reindeer teams transport Waldemar Jochelson's equipment across the Verkhoyansk Mountains. Jochelson and his party often traveled through uninhabited terrain where they were forced to rely on their own provisions. In addition, they carried a bulky camera and tripod, equipment for developing photographs in the field, a wax cylinder recorder, and plaster for making head casts. (AMNH Library 4206)

mers in Siberia are "not really cold." Laurel learned a few days before departure that Alexia had grown up in a part of Vermont that was also "never really cold." Recalling bone-chilling Korean winters several latitudes to the south of Siberia, Laurel rethought her packing. Laurel, a mid-career anthropologist, has read a great deal of ethnography about Siberia during the Jesup Expedition era, but she has no idea what to expect in the post-Soviet world. She is anxious about the reported perils of Russian air travel, the so-called Russian mafia, and making a fool of herself. Today also happens to be Laurel's wedding anniversary. Alexia is less anxious about this trip than Laurel is. Over the past decade she has spent a total of nearly three years living in Russia, first as a language student and then as an ethnographer, most recently just over a month before. She feels at home in Russia; she enjoys the general pace of life, and she has an idea of the challenges ahead. Alexia is very much looking forward to returning to Russia, and particularly to visiting the Russian Far East. Her decision to become an ethnographer was partly inspired by *Dersu Uzala*,

Akira Kurosawa's film featuring a Nanai trapper in the region bordering the Amur River.

Everything seems in order for the journey, including accommodation in Alaska, Chukotka, and Kamchatka and contacts and phone numbers for local museums; even the flights across the Bering Strait, the flights to Magadan and Khabarovsk, and the flights to and from Kamchatka are confirmed after months of arrangements. There remains the unforeseen problem of our Kamchatka visa, something we'll have to sort out by long-distance telephone. At the airport we check our baggage through to Nome, Alaska, before boarding our flight. In Nome, we will pick up a charter flight across the Bering Strait to Providenia.

Our journey will take us to Chukotka and Kamchatka, the northeastern-most edge of the Russian state, so far east that people in Russia generally distinguish this "Russian Far East" from Siberia proper. With only the usual red tape, we are holding Russian visas with permission to visit Chukotka, a place that was, in the recent Cold War past, a high security area. Like much of Siberia, Chukotka was closed not only to foreigners but also to Russian travelers. Officially, a Russian visa is now sufficient to travel anywhere in the country, but for Chukotka one must obtain letters of invitation indicating the specific locales to be visited. We have the required letter issued by the governor of Chukotka to present along with our Russian visas indicating that we can travel to Anadyr and Providenia.

The Kamchatka visa had seemed a sure thing; our letter of invitation from one of the regional museums, received well in advance of our application, was supposed to do the trick. But the regulations changed and the local museum in the town of Palana no longer has the authority to invite us. We are at risk of losing half of our itinerary. Our friend David Koester, who has done extensive fieldwork in Kamchatka, tells us that we can easily secure the required letters of invitation through a travel agency he has worked with in Kamchatka. David produced an e-mail address for the agency and Alexia sent off an urgent request; all we can do is wait to hear back from the travel agency. Alexia takes this in stride. Laurel tries to.

Our visa uncertainties are minor when compared with Laufer's predicament in 1898. As a German Jew, he was barred by Russian law from entering Siberia. When his request for a visa was denied by no less than the Minister of the Interior, his prospects for doing fieldwork seemed dark indeed. The U.S. embassy in St. Petersburg prevailed upon Vasily W. Radloff, then head of the Russian Academy of Sciences, who prevailed upon Grand Duke Constantine, the titular head of the academy, who prevailed upon his nephew, the tsar himself. Permission was forthcoming.

As Russian citizens, Bogoras and Jochelson had no visa problems. Recommended by the Russian Academy of Sciences, they traveled with letters from the Ministry of the Interior encouraging local officials to support their efforts in the field. But this was only half the story. Still suspicious of their revolutionary backgrounds, the Ministry of the Interior issued a secret order to the governor-general of the province of Irkutsk withdrawing all promise of assistance to the scientific expedition and requesting that Bogoras and Jochelson be kept under the strictest surveillance. Only years later, when Jochelson himself published a newspaper account of the incident, translated and sent to New York, did Franz Boas appreciate the full measure of difficulties that Bogroas and Jochelson had faced in the field.

En route to Nome we stop off in Anchorage. The airport is filled with boisterous outdoor types in hiking boots. A cool breeze is blowing through the summer clothing that we donned for a sultry New York August morning. We ask the ticket clerk for a restaurant recommendation and take a taxi to Gwennie's Alaskan Home Style Restaurant, where Alexia tries the reindeer sausage and eggs. We wondered whether there might be a trans-Pacific traffic in venison from Koryak, Chukchi, and Even herds, but the meat comes from Seattle.

On the way back to the airport to board the plane for Nome, we strike up a conversation with the driver, Nikolay, a bearded man in his forties. He is from Kodiak Island, at the top of the Aleutian chain, closest to the Alaskan mainland, a place that was very much a part of Russia before it was sold to the United States in 1867. Nikolay's parents speak Russian, and he describes a "stern" upbringing in the Russian Orthodox Church. Hearing of our itinerary, Nikolay tells us he has never been up to Nome, but his wife had gone there to see the Iditarod dogsled race, the biggest annual event in Alaska.

We wondered later if, with his dark hair and eyes, Nikolay is not at least part Aleutiiq. The Aleutiiq belong to the Eskimo cultures extending from Prince William Sound on the Pacific Coast of Alaska to the Bering Strait, and nearly six thousand miles north and east along Canada's arctic coast and into Labrador and Greenland. The Aleutiiq have inhabited the area of the Aleutian Islands and Kodiak for centuries. Until the late nineteenth century the Aleutiiq hunted sea mammals from skin-covered kayaks equipped with sophisticated harpoons and wore elaborate clothing, including waterproof parkas stitched from seal intestines and delicately decorated hats in the image of seabirds intended to assure a successful hunt. In the late eighteenth century the Russians arrived, seeking furs and sea mammal products; they brought disease and colonial oppression. When the Russians left Alaska in 1867, the Aleutiiq population had declined from nearly 9,000 people at the time of contact to just 3,000. The Aleutiiq resistance to Russian colonization is legendary, but the legacy of Russian ventures into the region persists in the form of geographical and personal names and religion. Today Russian Orthodoxy is widespread on Kodiak Island among the Aleutiiq.

The flight to Nome touches down in Kotzebue, a town just above the Arctic Circle, and Laurel has her first glimpse of a tundra moonscape. In Nome, Laurel discovers that one of her bags has been left behind in Anchorage. It is traced only through the persistence of a ticket clerk, who tells us we can pick up the bag tomorrow. We spend the night in the Ponderosa Hotel, a sprawling cheap construction that smells of fiberboard and mildew. The furnishings are basic and the nearest telephone hangs on the wall in the hallway. Even so, Nome hotels benefit from a sellers' market and we are paying $115 a night for this room. By the time Laurel manages to place a call to her husband, it is already 1:30 A.M. in New York and he is half asleep. Early the next morning, the persistent ring of the phone in the hallway wakes Alexia and spurs her to unlock the door and pick up the receiver. She is glad to hear her partner's voice carried from the other end of the United States. One of the itinerant oilmen, or maybe a gold prospector, peeks out from his room across the hall, apparently also expecting a call.

Later that morning, a quiet Sunday, we find raisin bagels at the Happy Swede, a coffee shop that also sells postcards and Native beadwork to tourists. We buy postcards and go into the local grocery store to buy stamps. On the way in, a drunken woman in a parka latches on to us and tries to cadge cigarettes. Neither of us smokes. In the distance, we can see the cold gray expanse of northern ocean.

While waiting to claim Laurel's bag at the airport, Alexia notices an older Yupik-looking woman and a young man among the people milling around. The woman is dressed in the "traditional" bright flowery cotton tunic with a fur-edged hood and a ruffle around the bottom. We will see this same garment on elderly Yupik women on the other side of the Bering Strait. This friendly pair smile; Alexia smiles back, noticing that like many rural Siberians, the old woman is missing most of her teeth.

At the Alaska Air counter, Alexia asks the woman on duty what people do here for fun, noting that she had seen ads for five liquor stores on the town's official web site. The woman says, "Yes, there's that, and also nine churches for a population of 4,021." Nome's Web site also mentions a bingo hall, a library, a volunteer fire department, two radio stations, fishing for tourists, and three agencies that assist gold prospectors. It will not be so different on the other side: subtract the bingo hall and maybe the public gold prospecting, and add that adaptable survivor of Soviet life, the House of Culture, an institution we will visit frequently.

We go outside and hail a cab to take us and our bags to the nearby Bering Air terminal. Alexia strikes up a conversation with the cabbie, who had once worked in the oil explorations on the North Slope. He has also flown over Russia, but never landed. He thinks that from the air the towns in Russia look like Alaska thirty years ago, before the oil boom. The Bering Air terminal is small but commodious. Sofas encircle the airport's tiny waiting area, creating a homey atmosphere. And a good thing, too, since travelers in the North may spend hours or even days waiting for a postponed flight. On the sofa at the far side of the room, three fair-haired children are playing with a fluffy toy polar bear and seal while their parents chat. The mother teaches elementary school and the father is a high school math teacher; they are going home from vacation to Teller, a small town about one hundred miles north of Nome. Teller is a tightly knit community; the teacher says there will be just four seniors in the school that year, if all the juniors pass. There are twelve students entering the ninth grade so the numbers could increase. The teachers and a Yupik schoolgirl sitting across from us discuss which students might not be returning when school starts next week and which ones will be late. They have all read the police register in the local newspaper and they are trying to decipher the published initials of boys cited for fights and other infractions that might keep them out of school.

We are joining a tour group's charter for the flight across the Bering Strait, the only way that we can get there from here short of chartering a flight ourselves. On checking in for our noon flight, we learn that there is bad weather in Providenia. The plane will take off only if there is a clearing by 4 P.M. If the weather does not clear, we can try again tomorrow. If there is no clearing tomorrow, the charter will be cancelled. We turn to our books, a murder mystery set in Spain and an ethnography of spirit mediums in Bahia, Brazil, worlds far away from the daunting Nome weather. Are we reading about sunny places to fortify ourselves?

At the flight desk, we meet two of our fellow travelers, Tom, the mustachioed planner of itineraries, and Bob, the quieter member of the duo, from Arizona. The rest of their tour group was unable to secure visas; they are the only ones who will be making the trip to Providenia. "I just want to see it," Tom tells us. Comparing notes, we soon realize that their tour group contact in Providenia, Vladimir Bychkov, is the same museum director we are going to visit. Tom and Bob entertain us with stories of their travels to other cold spots (an island owned by Norway but shared with Russia and Greenland for mining) and warm places (the Cook Islands in the South Pacific, where Tom spent a year on sabbatical). Our paths will intersect for the next several days, as so often do the realms of tourism and anthropology.

At two o'clock, Kim, the Bering Air ticket agent and cordial queen of the waiting room, informs us that the weather is still "down" and we will probably not fly today but that she will call the airport in Providenia again at three, just in case. At 3:20, Kim announces that the bad weather has lifted and that we will all go to Providenia at 4. "All" includes Bob and Tom, Nadezhda (a Yupik woman in a pink snowsuit who is the director of the Providenia Town School), and us. Nadezhda is checking ten boxes of fresh fruit and vegetables onto the flight, at a shipping cost of $200, for the schoolchildren. She is assisted by a local woman who is a retired college teacher and an imposing, silver-haired Volga German man who teaches in Nome. We learn from her friends that Nadezhda is one of only three staff members in her school who have been paid in the last several months.

The Volga German condenses his eventful biography into an airport encounter. His ancestors moved to Russia in the late eighteenth century when
Catherine the Great sought to establish European settlements in what is now
southern Russia. When World War II broke out, the Volga Germans found
themselves near German-occupied territory and were suspected of being col-
laborators. Many were relocated to Kazakhstan—his family's fate—or exiled
to parts of Siberia. He moved with his family to the Russian Far East in 1956
when it was permitted. A veteran of multiple relocations, this Volga German
is shipping a pile of flattened cardboard cartons to Providenia—where they are
in short supply—to pack up the contents of his apartment as he relocates to
Nome. On learning our destination, he treats us to a tirade on how bad things
are in Russia. We must never drink the vodka in Providenia. Foreign products
have ruined the economy. It is silly that telephone calls must be routed through
Moscow and take three days to reach their destination (as if Bering Air had not
been getting through to Providenia on an hourly basis to check on the weather
conditions). His bombast is galling to Alexia, who keeps suggesting politely,
"That hasn't been my experience." She mutters under her breath to Laurel,
"Perhaps he's been reading a little too much Solzhenitsyn this week."

After our luggage is weighed, each of the passengers also steps onto the scale
so the exact weight of the "cargo" can be taken into account for the flight. We
squeeze into the Piper Navaho nine-seat plane, which is one seat short for the
number of passengers; the seats on the side opposite the pilot have been folded
up to make room for the cargo. The pilot beckons to Alexia to sit in the co-
pilot's spot next to him. At 4:22 P.M., after hours of waiting and two cancella-
tions, we are finally in the air, flying over the Bering Strait, just two hundred
miles to Providenia, Russia.

Nadezhda sits in front of Laurel. She has limited English but is very friendly.
She is returning from the Inuit Circumpolar Conference (ICC) held in Nuuk,
Greenland, the week before. The ICC convenes representatives of the 115,000
speakers of related Inuit languages who span Greenland, Alaska, northern
Canada, and Chukotka; the Yupik in Russia joined the ICC the previous year.
During the flight the school director scans a resolution calling for assistance "to
Inuit and other indigenous peoples in the former Soviet Union." Technically,
there are no ethnic Inuit in the former Soviet Union, but the Yupik, together
with the Inuit, were once subsumed under the blanket term "Eskimo." "Inuit"
makes a broad claim for ethnic solidarity using a Native, not a white man's,
word.

It is a remarkably smooth flight, the more so for a small aircraft. The plane
descends into a beautiful fjord swathed in clouds with patches of snow on the
steep hillsides. We approach the landing field past toy-like rows of light planes
and helicopters, each bearing a red star. Military men and women, border
guards, stand at attention on the runway, young, slim, with rosy cheeks, in uniforms that have a 1940s look. This retro theatrical image is compounded by

the women who wear their almost invariably red hair bound tight at the temples under their military caps, but full and wavy in the back like World War II pinups. Laurel recalls an episode from *The Twilight Zone* where the airplane bursts through the cloud cover to a landscape several decades back in time. Have we come not to Providenia but through a time warp? In fact, in crossing the Bering Strait we crossed the International Date Line, so with a flight lasting eighty minutes we are now a day later, twenty-two hours ahead of Nome time.

The plane touches down and Nadezhda, knowing that this is Laurel's first encounter with Russia, smiles at her and says warmly, "Welcome." Alexia quickly warns Laurel about filling out the customs forms; specifically, we must not declare the full amount of cash we are carrying to pay for the many flights in our itinerary. If it seems like a lot, the customs officials might crave some. We settle on a plausible-sounding $500 US apiece. In order to clear customs, we are required to declare each piece of inexpensive jewelry we are carrying.

Vladimir Bychkov, bearded and darkly handsome in a duffel coat, greets us on the other side of the barricade. He tells us, half apologetically, that he is also here to greet some tourists. We reassure him that we have already met them, that Tom is a professor and that they are "good guys." He greets Bob and Tom and hands them over to the care of the slim blond man we will come to know as Yura, but that introduction is for later. Vladimir tells us that at present there is neither heat nor hot water in the city of Providenia owing to repair work. This is a common occurrence throughout Russia during the summer, the time for the annual maintenance of water and heating pipes.

Vladimir will put us up in a vacant apartment in his own building. The local hotel is always awash with drunks and he tries to keep visitors, especially women visitors, away from it. Tom and Bob have a home stay in another building.

Vladimir also explains that unlike most government institutions back in the Soviet period, the museum does not have a car of its own. He normally uses a vehicle belonging to the Department of Culture, but today the driver has gone fishing. Fishing, we will learn, is a major source of subsistence. Tomorrow's breakfast will feature some of Vladimir's catch. For the present, we take the bus. It is a brief but bizarre journey through a spectacular landscape of ocean, mountains, and tundra, scarred by moldering concrete buildings that loom at the side of the road. Many seem to be abandoned. An occasional lighted window, a bit of curtain, or a plant belies the impression that we are traveling though a derelict industrial park. The buildings are, in fact, apartments, and many are empty. The town has lost half of its population since 1990 as European Russians have left the North. More vacancies are temporary, owing to the civil servants' summer travel to warmer climes. Two thousand people live here now, many on the verge of pulling up stakes.

Departures, we will learn, are a common topic of conversation. Europeans,

Russians, and Ukrainians flooded the North in the 1970s and 1980s as mineral exploration, gold, diamond, and quartz mining, and the subsequent expansion of administrative centers took hold. Civil servants in the North were paid twice and sometimes three times what they were able to earn in southern cities. They also escaped the common anxiety of Soviet citizens who often waited years for an apartment. Civil servants in the North had what were spacious apartments by Soviet standards. For many young men in particular this was an opportunity not to be missed. But now the boom has gone bust. According to Vladimir, for the past six months, no one in his museum has been paid the "triple hardship" remuneration they are entitled to for serving in the Russian Far East. They haven't been paid at all.

The bus makes several stops as it crosses this desolate landscape. Passengers get on, women with bright red hair and blazing, fresh makeup, dressed in colorful hues, a surprising contrast to the drab buildings from which they have emerged. The young woman who takes our tickets boarded the bus down the road from the airport. Nothing distinguishes her from any other brightly painted passenger. She is wearing a stylish long black skirt, slit open to mid-thigh, a denim jacket, and a black beret set at a coquettish angle. A little white rat with pink eyes sits on the seat beside her and jumps onto her shoulder for a trip down the aisle to collect our tickets.

Vladimir's apartment building is at the end of the line, the far end of town. Built in the 1950s of wood rather than concrete, it is better insulated than the new constructions. He points this out with pride. But this building is slated for destruction; the shrinking population is being consolidated in the newer buildings, something our hosts do not look forward to. The wooden apartment block was once painted pale pink with lime green decorative trim surrounding the window frames. We climb to the second floor via a dimly lit stairway redolent of dry rot, a scent that will become familiar in our journeys up the steps of old apartment buildings.

Vladimir opens the door of his apartment to reveal a large, sunny space, the walls freshly painted and wallpapered. Masses of fuchsias and begonias bask in the long light of a northern summer day. There are a few well-chosen examples of local handicrafts on the television stand, ivory carvings and beadwork. A huge print of a Swiss mountain decorates one wall and a sealskin rug another. This sealskin mosaic of geometric forms is a modern take on the standard rug affixed to walls across the Russian Federation. Vladimir commissioned it in a nearby village. This is his local variation on the hanging "Oriental" rug, often among a Russian couple's first major purchases.

Vladimir serves us mushroom soup, fresh bread, and a green pepper salad. He brings out a huge jar of caviar, known in Russian as *ikra*, after its Japanese name, *ikura*. Laurel has paid a great deal to consume small, tangy mouthfuls of *ikura* in New York sushi bars, savoring the salty astringency of each orange egg as they pop, one by one, inside her mouth, and here is a whole jar of it, with instructions to slather some on our bread. This is Vladimir's own store of ikra, extracted from fish he has caught and then cured at home. Throughout the Russian Far East, we will encounter refrigerators filled with jars of orange fish eggs. A luxury item in the United States, they are a nearly ubiquitous staple along the northeastern coast of Russia.

As we eat this delicious meal, we ask Vladimir about his museum. It was begun in 1986, initially to preserve the work of local artists. By 1990, the museum had gained official recognition as a far-flung local branch within the state hierarchy of museums. Vladimir has been director since that time, coming to the position after a series of teaching jobs. He has a staff of seven including maintenance people. As director, Vladimir is, by necessity, a jack-of-all-trades: curator, photographer, artist, exhibit designer, and preparator. He employs a registrar, a collections manager, and a photographer artist. In summer, they are down to a staff of three. It is the vacation season, although most of his colleagues are just hanging out in town; in the absence of pay, few can afford to travel to European Russia. "But how do you all live without pay?" He smiles. "I'll tell you the 'big secret'." Government employees are all subsidized in the state stores where Vladimir receives up to 500 rubles monthly credit, about a fifth of his overdue monthly pay. He pays his staff's salaries out of income from the summer tourism business, about which we will learn a great deal in the next few days.

After lunch we settle into the cozy apartment we will occupy during our stay in Providenia. A radio program, *Good Morning Chukotka*, is being rebroadcast and gives a sense of the current issues in the area. There is the standard report on the local health department's spring work in one village outside of Anadyr, the capital of Chukotka. After the winter, the good townspeople have been cleaning up the garbage emerging from the melting snowbanks. The health department reports that it does not expect too many health problems; the weather has been so cold this summer bacteria have not had a chance to multiply. The radio program continues with national news items: foreigners invested $40 million US in Russia in 1997; Russian inventors came up with only 114 patents over the past five years, even though prior to 1990 there were at least as many patents issued each year; Russians should be ashamed to be building monuments to German World War II victims just to make money off of German tourists. All of this grist for our curiosity mill pours out of a wobbly, Soviet-era white box affixed to the wall. In a few weeks, an interview with the two anthropologists from New York will also become a sound bite for *Good Morning Chukotka*.

The apartment has the feel of living spaces in other Siberian towns where Alexia has spent months on end. Tools and outdoor wear fill the entryway, and advertising stickers are affixed to available surfaces. Over the sink a sign in English reads, "The kitchen is the heart of the home." The kitchen has totem Western luxury goods: empty Pringles potato chips, Folgers coffee, and Tang containers, all stacked in a towering pyramid. The bathroom is painted a mustard color, accented with long white streaks.

We walk to the museum along the harbor, down the town's muddy main thoroughfare and only road, passing a statue of Lenin gazing pensively out to sea. Providenia is similar in some ways to the town in central Siberia where Alexia has done extensive fieldwork. And yet the towns are different in significant ways. For one thing, Providenia has running water. And cruise ships full of affluent tourists visit every summer.

Vladimir points out a scorched patch where the town's Russian Orthodox church was decimated in a recent fire. The church is being rebuilt. The Baptist church also had a recent fire. Although Vladimir makes it quite clear that an electrical fire destroyed the Orthodox church, he agrees that the burning of two churches in the town in a short space of time is an odd coincidence, possibly even suspicious. In addition to a significant Orthodox community and the Baptists, there is an avid group of Seventh-day Adventists of whom we will hear much more. At this moment in time, it would seem that Providenia has become, like Nome, a northern town where God and drink provide the primary means of recreation.

As we walk, Vladimir gives us a potted history of Providenia, such as he might deliver to a visiting tour group. The town is new, established as an administrative outpost in the 1920s and developed in the 1940s when this northern coast was a well-watched frontier in the Cold War, but the area has figured in the history of northern shipping for a very long time. An English sea captain named Thomas Moore sailed into the harbor in 1848 or 1849 and the coast was a stopping-off point for American whalers. At the height of the whaling industry—from the early to mid-nineteenth century—Yupik and Chukchi men sometimes worked on American whaling vessels as harpoonists. Between 1875 and 1879, merchant ships heading to Vladivostok would use the bay as a transfer point for coal from Kamchatka, but there was no real port. The Alaska trade connection that was particularly active in the mid to late nineteenth century was revived in the early 1990s.

At the edge of town stands a monument to Vitus Bering, a Danish explorer in the employ of the Russian navy. While the seventeenth-century Russian explorer Semyon Dezhnev may have been the first European to explore and map these waters, it was Bering who in 1725-30 determined that there was, in fact, a body of water between the Asian and American continents. In a later expedition (1733-43) Bering mapped the coast of Alaska. Bering's ship was the first European vessel to sail around the northeast corner of Asia, this same point on which we now stand in Providenia.

Throughout the Soviet period and up to the year of our visit (1998), the town has been sustained by shipments of coal and food that must all be unloaded before the harbor freezes over in November. As we are to learn later in our travels, this lifeline of supplies is in extreme danger all over the North this year. Providenia has been in decline for the past several years. As the population shrinks, many local enterprises have shut down. A construction company, a meat and dairy processing plant, and a hide processing and leather factory are gone. Now only a hydroresearch center and a bread factory remain. Freshly baked bread, a critical component of daily Russian cuisine, will appear at every meal. Fish, reindeer, and sea mammal products are less available in the town than in the past since the Yupik and Chukchi who supplied these commodities now depend on them for their own subsistence. In the late Soviet period, fox fur was an important export; every village had a fox farm, feeding the animals surplus fish and reindeer by-products. Most significant, the yearly supply of goods that the Soviet government sent like clockwork each fall was severely cut back beginning in 1991. Communities have been surviving on food and fuel reserves stockpiled over decades; reserves were stretched to provide for the last six or seven years, but the supply crisis has reached a breaking point across the North and it is a real question how communities will make it through this winter. There are no more reserves. (A few months hence, Chukotka will require the assistance of international relief agencies, including the International Red Cross.)

The museum is a box-like wooden building recently painted lime green. The structure dates from the 1950s but the museum has inhabited it only since 1995 when its smaller former residence became the ill-fated Baptist church. The signs are all in Russian and English; the museum plays a big role in the local tourist trade, and tours of Providenia routinely begin here with an orientation lecture. Tom and Bob, our traveling companions on the flight over, got the lecture and a Native dance performance while we were eating our soup. They were then taken on a walking tour of Providenia, more ambitious than our own but crammed with similar facts.

The administrative offices of the museum are freshly painted a sparkling white and furnished with basic blond veneer furniture of a late Soviet vintage that we will subsequently encounter all over town. Vladimir runs a tidy ship. The carpenters' shop and photography lab are immaculate. Vladimir shows us a well-maintained accession log documenting the thousand or so objects the museum takes in over a year. We note that, as in the United States, "confiscated items"—objects made from the tusks and pelts of endangered sea mammals and consequently removed from the luggage of international travelers—are given to the museum. A recent contribution of a harpoon point, toggle, and carvings were a family's gift of personal mementos. Although systematic collecting began only in the 1980s, donors have provided family artifacts from past times, some dating from the 1920s and 1930s. All acquisitions are carefully evaluated and reviewed by a museum committee; the procedure is familiar to us.

One tiny room is dominated by a wooden cabinet of many small drawers originally designed for library catalog cards. The drawers are labeled with the

Figure 5. Vladimir Bychkov shows us a recycled library catalog. Each of the drawers holds the archaeological gleanings of a "lost village," a community that was resettled to accommodate state policy. Old people who once lived in these sites visit the museum and help to identify the contents of the drawers, fragments of a lost way of life. (Photo by Laurel Kendall)

names of "lost villages," whose inhabitants were forcibly relocated, consolidated into larger communities beginning in the 1950s and again in the 1970s. Across the North, the Russian government sought to streamline production and economize by not supplying so many small hamlets. In fact, the consolidation was extremely disruptive for settlements that had sometimes occupied a given site for hundreds of years; the amalgamated towns experienced unprecedented social ills, in part because of underemployment for many Chukchi and Yupik. The drawers contain the remnants of this history, the household flotsam that museum teams have retrieved from village sites with names like Avan, Kivak, Tyfliak, and Ungazik, known to whalers and Russian ethnographers as "Cape Chaplino" or "Indian Point." Today old people who once lived in these places are invited into the museum to pore over the drawers' contents and recall a way of life in fragments, a lost sense of place.

As this is a museum of "local history," broadly defined from nature to art, its collections are more eclectic and consequently more representative of the complexities of life than those in the vaults of most North American anthropology museums. Among his recent accessions, Vladimir shows us a crumpled tin pan, American-made, once used by a hopeful gold prospector; a glass knob from an abandoned power station; and a paddle bearing the English legend: "Kayaks across the Bering Strait." A life preserver, part of the collection, does double duty as a press for flat art objects.

An extensive collection of photographs is stored in carefully labeled envelopes, each with a photocopy of the image on the outside, but these are ordinary high acid content envelopes that will eventually damage their contents. If the archival quality storage materials that would preserve this otherwise carefully tended collection were available, the museum could not afford them. Vladimir is well aware of the unavoidable limitations of his operation. He casts a melancholy gaze toward the wall thermometer. The museum staff monitors climatic changes but has no means of maintaining a steady temperature to prevent damage to the collection from precipitous changes in heat and cold.

The sun has set and it is chilly inside the museum when we go upstairs to the exhibit area. For most of the year, the museum is a resource for schoolchildren, but in the summer it functions as a visitors' center for North American and European tourists. The exhibit begins with an orientation panel, "Where is Chukotka?" Presumably the schoolchildren would already know this. The walls are covered with photographs, some by Vladimir, a montage of local flowers, landscape, wildlife, and Native peoples.

We wander through a gallery of local artwork. We will come to appreciate the ubiquitous presence of local artists throughout the Russian Far East and note that their landscape paintings are routinely integrated into local museums. Another gallery is ethnographic, with hunting and fishing artifacts artistically displayed in sparkling glass cases. The arrangement is Vladimir's touch; he tells us that he enjoys designing cases to produce a pleasing effect. While Vladimir has a degree in history, his museology is more or less self-taught with the benefit of some correspondence courses and seminars, visits from the museum staff in Magadan (hundreds of miles to the south) and in recent years his participation in natural and cultural resource management conferences on the Alaska side. A Chukchi *yaranga* (hide tent) dominates the last room. It is set up so that the visitor can go inside and sit beside the hearth. Sometimes Chukchi prepare food inside the yaranga as part of an active program of cultural performances where native peoples demonstrate local handicrafts and elders describe their traditional way of life. The yaranga is a

Figure 6. Yupik yaranga at Indian Point, 1901. The fur-lined yaranga is a common symbol of traditional life in the far North, and a Northern museum will usually have one on display. (AMNH Library 1343)

central feature of Chukchi and Yupik nomadic life and consequently of Chukotkan life.

Vladimir takes us to what he describes as the town's least raucous café for our dinner. Yura, the English-speaking guide, is waiting for us with the affable guys from Arizona. The café could be anywhere—slightly threadbare, dimly lit, and decorated with strings of Christmas tree lights. We order white wine and cheese, and do our best with the sweet sherry and processed American cheese that arrives. Tom and Bob fill us in on their adventures, describing the coddling they are receiving in their home stay. They have already become fast friends with Yura, whose English is surprisingly fluent.

A schoolteacher, Yura works for the museum during the summer tourist season. He speaks warmly of the new notebook computer he has recently been able to buy with his earnings, "more important than flying to Moscow for my vacation." As we get to know him, he will reveal that he feels estranged from his family in the capital. Yura seems a lost soul. In this first conversation, he tells us he studied Chinese in the 1960s in Beijing. We are astonished—he would have been there after Sino-Soviet relations began to sour in the late 1950s. Yura admits that he was special, that he was being trained for defense intelligence. He and Laurel exchange pleasantries in Chinese but their accents are mutually incomprehensible. We speculate that Yura must have messed up big time to have landed in this isolated Northern town as a schoolteacher/tour guide. Of course, he could still be a spy, gathering intelligence from the tourists, but would it be worth the effort? And were this the case, would he have mentioned his prior training?

In the dim bar, our imaginations begin to run riot. Who are Bob and Tom anyway? If we are in the middle of a spy story, then aren't they the ones who will turn out to be the spies? They seem so nice and normal. Shoudn't this make us suspicious? Who, after all, would take a vacation in Providenia? To complete our growing sense of the unreal, we walk out of the café and find a black 1940s Ford touring car, in mint condition, sleek and shiny, like a contented cat from *Master and Margarita*. Vladimir says it belongs to the proprietor of the restaurant who had it shipped to Providenia by barge from Vladivostok. It must have had a colorful former life.

The next morning, we go to change money in a tiny bank in the basement of one of the anonymous blocks of concrete buildings, making our way down the dim hallways decorated in the light pinks and off-greens apparently found in such abundance only in formerly socialist institutional settings. Alexia has seen this same color scheme all across Russia, Eastern Europe, and in parts of China. We pass the regional archive, social welfare office, and the office for the Bering Sea Region (of which we will hear more later), before we come to the Agroprom bank. While waiting to exchange money Alexia examines the certificates on the wall verifying this as a legal exchange bureau; an Anadyr bank issued the certificate and lists an address and telephone number for consumer complaints. A copy of *Investment*, a glossy new Russian magazine, sits on a corner table.

The man who is ahead of us in line informs us that in some places, smaller denominations of dollars are now preferred to hundred-dollar bills. This produces a ripple of anxiety since, following past wisdom, our supply is almost exclusively in hundreds. The man is carrying a Salem cigarette bag, the relic of an airport duty-free shop, and Laurel speculates that he must have flown in from Alaska. This is not necessarily so, for strong plastic bags are cherished and can have long and eventful lives. A heavy-duty DataVision computer supply bag Alexia once packed with gifts from New York to Moscow later traveled from Moscow to Krasnoyarsk with some books requested by a friend, and then with some fruits and newspapers from Krasnoyarsk to Tura, Evenkia. From there the plastic bag made its way to Ukraine packed with fish for a friend's brother. Who knows, perhaps the bag has made it to Turkey or China with the active cross-border "suitcase" trade in small goods and textiles. Russians are resourceful. When waxed milk cartons first became available in the late 1980s, Alexia's friends flattened them to carry important papers and even cash.

Vladimir has invited us to join a day trip that is part of Bob and Tom's tour package. The excursion vehicle is a large, commodious jeep-like bus with very thick tire treads for potholed or icy roads, as well as muddy absences of roads.

This sturdy and functional transport has been painted bright red, blue, and yellow like a circus van, something that might have driven out of an old Fellini film, in Laurel's view. At first Alexia does not notice the painting on the truck, which is part of a familiar Soviet imagery found in bright murals on bank walls, gymnasiums, and libraries in other Siberian towns. It will not be the first time in these travels that Laurel's heightened perceptions spur Alexia to take a second look.

Inside the flamboyant vehicle we meet Vera Ivanovna Popienko, a warm and animated Chukchi who emphasizes her points with enthusiastic hand and arm gestures and laughs a great deal. She seems to be amused by us. It strikes Alexia that indigenous Siberians are usually not so forthcoming to outsiders, but then Vera is working as part of this entertainment brigade. Vera is married to a Russian man, Vladimir Zhuravkov, the museum photographer. Today, he is on a shoot near the town of Lavrentia, to the north of Providenia. From there he was hoping to get to Little Diomede Island, but despite the blue sky the planes have been grounded since early morning, Vera says.

Vera has studied Spanish. There is so much English around, she says; she wanted something different. A Mexican tour group came through last week and she was called upon to interpret, she tells us proudly. Vera is a teacher of Chukchi language and dance in the school for special education in Providenia; she also directs a children's music and dance ensemble.

We both have our notebooks out, jotting in response to odd bits of conversation. Tom asks if this compulsive scribbling is typical of all anthropologists and we respond that for many of us, it is a sort of reflex action. Perhaps they will now wonder if we are the spies; anthropologists are often seen this way and a very few have been.

We pass an overturned vehicle by the side of the road. "Driving while intoxicated," Yura somberly intones.

At the pit stop, it is men to the left and women to the right, all backs discreetly turned. On the tundra there are absolutely no bushes to hide behind. Vera tells us that this has been an unusually cold year; she sees none of the edible plants and berries that were in evidence when they came out this way in August last year. Vladimir has also told us that times are extremely tough in the smaller villages outside Providenia; people are going without electricity, and heat and food are scarce.

We stop near a shanty with a prominent weathervane on its roof and a splendid view of the sea. A large husky dog guards the premises. This is an outpost for the museum's bowhead whale observation project, a Chukotkan component of a larger effort initiated by the U.S. Park Commission for the Bering Sea Region and administered from Barrow, Alaska. Local sea mammal hunters report spotting bowhead whales in exchange for ammunition and supplies, and the project has equipped the museum with its laptop computer and a fax machine. Vladimir confers with the man who lives in the shanty; this is not the last time that we will see him cannily mixing other museum business with tourist excursions.

Our final destination is the village site of Avan, continuously inhabited for several centuries. Before 1942, when the entire village was relocated, it was one of the largest Yupik whaling settlements. Once the site was abandoned, it was almost immediately excavated by an archaeological team that unearthed relics of ancient Yupik culture, including underground dwellings and whale skulls. We receive this information in the course of a hike over hilly ground covered with wet and slippery grass. Vera and the driver remain behind to cook lunch.

There is a spectacular view of the sea and the promontory. We look out in the direction of the whale outpost and a more distant radar station run by the border guards. Vladimir and Yura point to some bouncing specks in the ocean which, through binoculars, they identify as three walruses and a spouting whale. We peer through the binoculars and see the walruses turning in the surf, then what just might be a whale clearing the surface of the ocean. Up the hill, we come upon an old rusted barrel with "Made in the U.S.A." imprinted on it; Yura describes the barrel as the "symbol of Chukotka." He tells us that there are mountains of them here, a sign of the region's historical dependency on trade with the other side of the Bering Strait. In his tourist patter Vladimir describes this barrel as an artifact of the Chukotka/Alaska trade dating from the days when whalers laid anchor off the coast and hired Yupik harpoonists for their whaling teams. In *The Chukchee*, Bogoras describes the enthusiastic trading that he witnessed further up the coast in the spring and summer of 1901. From the middle of March, dog teams and reindeer caravans arrived on the beach, ready to trade furs and walrus ivory for flour, biscuits, granulated sugar, molasses, muslin, hardware, knives, and beads. When the snow melted in July, the would-be local traders resorted to skin boats. In the past, as today, American goods carried across the strait were far cheaper than similar commodities transported from the interior.[1]

On this August morning one hundred years later, we are suspicious that this particular abandoned barrel has been left precisely in this space to dress the set and illustrate the tale. We will be similarly suspicious of two femur bones, ever so slightly exposed, in one of the hillside graves. A little later on, in a description of sea mammal hunting, Vladimir flourishes a walrus skull opportunely left behind a small hillock. The prop is a bit hokey, reminding us of Vladimir's delicate balancing act between tour operator and museum director.

Vladimir is into his lecture with Yura smoothly translating. With hand gestures, Vladimir maps the site, indicating where whalebone poles on the beach would have had skin boats tethered to them. We pass a couple of meat pits, dug into the permafrost as communal refrigerators. Some six to eight hundred years ago, a communal house was built on the hillside, with walls from the ribs of a bowhead whale, and "here the elders would instruct the young with tales of sea mammal hunting. The entrance always faced the seashore and the whale jaws were placed at the entrance."

We visit some gravesites, one to two hundred years old and excavated in the 1940s and 1950s. Vladimir repeats as tourist patter something he said to us the previous night, that as on St. Lawrence Island on the American side, local residents have been excavating and selling artifacts. This site has not been immune to plunder. Uphill, the more recent graves have been looted; Vladimir and Yura suspect the border guards. Gravesites are usually marked with a large stone cover. A few old ones are still untouched, their locations known to Vladimir and Yura but emphatically not shown to tourists. Yura says they have had a problem in Providenia with teenagers looting the local graveyards and selling skull ashtrays to sailors. "They should realize that someday this might be their own situation, that their own vulnerable skulls will be in some graveyard."

Vladimir calls our attention to a stark contrast in the landscape, a green band of lichens and tundra plants at the lower levels of the hillside and bare rock above. The green, they tell us, is the fertile product of all the animal refuse discarded on this site over the centuries. Yura speaks of a contrast between life and death; the graves are in the bare rock up above. We pass a rusted bedspring and a swath of bare earth. Because this soil is so fertile, people travel here from Providenia to collect soil for their houseplants and modest plots of potatoes. They use the bedspring to sift the soil. As we walk along, Yura finds a very red mushroom which he says can be eaten as is; it is a *syroezhka*. His work as a translator does not deter him from scanning the ground for mushrooms and berries.

Down below, Vera has set up an elegant lunch. A fish and mushroom soup is bubbling in her big kettle. A long picnic table covered with plastic is set with china and flatware. There is champagne (intended for the "ladies" and very good) and the inevitable vodka. Vera feeds the spirits, pouring a shot of vodka onto the hillside in a manner that reminds Laurel of picnics on Korean family graves, a little something for the mountain spirit who governs the place. Vera has no objection to being photographed while she feeds the spirits. We talk about holidays. Most people acknowledge Russian Orthodox Christmas (January 7) and Easter. Tom asks about the anniversary of the October Revolution that brought the Bolsheviks to power. The driver responds with a gesture of absolute dismissal. But what about the Lenin statue in the town? Vera says, "We can't take it away because it's part of history."

Laurel thinks of Teddy Roosevelt in bronze, riding his horse outside the main entrance of the American Museum of Natural History in New York, with a black man and a red man in attendance at ground level. This statue causes much embarrassment to those who work at the museum today. Would we be so forthright as Vera in acknowledging the awkwardness of our own history?

Figure 7. Before we begin our tundra picnic, Vera Ivanovna Popienko feeds the spirits by pouring a libation of vodka. (Photo by Laurel Kendall)

As vodka and champagne are consumed, Vladimir goes on at great length about the dangers of bottled Russian mineral water; the mineral content is said to affect the kidneys. He drinks his vodka and, in another mood, observes that Waldemar Bogoras of the Jesup Expedition worked on the opposite side of the hill just behind us in 1901. The swarthy driver asks, "Who is this guy Bogoras?" and Vladimir tells him the story of Waldemar Bogoras, a.k.a. N. A. Tan, the unlikely father of Soviet anthropology. As a student in the early 1880s, he had been a revolutionary, a member of the underground organization Narodnaya Volya—the People's Will—and was arrested in 1882 for his participation in student protests. Arrested again in 1884 for organizing what he described as "a pretty nice strike,"[2] he was incarcerated, then exiled to Siberia. In later life, he would dryly observe that the two arrests and political exile set the course of a long career in ethnology.[3] He and his fellow revolutionary exiles, Waldemar

Jochelson and Lev Shternberg, discovered that studying the languages and customs of native peoples was an antidote to the boredom and intellectual stultification of exile: "I am now flirting with ethnography. I traveled through the area, lived for seven months with the Chukchi, goddamn them, rode on reindeer back, went downstream on rafts—well, this is hardly interesting to anyone but an ethnographer."[4] The tsarist authorities who encouraged this work as useful to their own mission recruited them into the Sibiryakov Expedition where they diligently gathered statistics and recorded the conditions of Native people. Their unique ethnographic knowledge brought them to the attention of the Russian Academy of Sciences and paved the way to rehabilitation after ten harsh years in Siberia. When Franz Boas contacted the academy, looking for scholars who could work on the Siberian side of the Bering Strait, Bogoras was euphemistically described as "a gentleman . . . living in Eastern Siberia."[5] Surprised by the turn his life was taking, Bogoras noted dryly to his fellow exile, Shternberg, "Ah this is what the Acheans went to conquer Troy for! So that they could afterwards take apart Chukchee [Chukchi], Yukaghir, and Gilyak and other texts."[6] An illustrious scholarly career was ahead of him.

Vera, a proud Chukchi, complains that foreigners who visit Chukotka seem to care only about the "Eskimos," the Yupik people that Bogoras would have studied in this village. We tell her, with great relish, that thanks to Borgoras's work in Chukotka, the Chukchi are well represented in a permanent exhibit at the AMNH in New York. A proud Chukchi warrior in armor there strikes the fierce pose that the manikin-maker took from an expedition photograph. Vera chuckles and strikes the warrior's pose herself.

Vera boils up a "tundra tea" of sweet grasses she gathered as part of the lunch preparations. We sip our warm and fragrant tea as the ocean fog rolls in and covers the tops of the hills in mist. It is time to leave. On the way back we continue our chat with Vera. She recalls how, when she was in school, the teachers would bring the children to excavate old village sites. She did not appreciate what they were doing at the time—it was simply a part of the school routine—but now many items from those digs are in the museum.

Talk turns to the Baptists, who are an active presence in Providenia. They run camps for children, support a children's dance troupe that performs in the House of Culture, and have taken local children to the United States on a dance tour. When we drive past the airport, the locals recognize the missionaries in the crowd outside the terminal, returning with their charges from a Baptist camp in Mexico. Vera tells us that her son has attended the Baptist camp; she considers it a good opportunity. Talk turns to religion and Vera asks Alexia, "What is your religion?" Alexia mumbles something about atheism, and then poses the same question to Vera. Vera first replies, "*drugoé*" or "other," and then says in Russian "*yazychestvo*," a word usually rendered in English as "pagan"; these are awkward translations for Chukchi beliefs in a vast spirit world.

Figure 8: With a proud tradition of warfare, the Chukchi had been subjugated by the time of the Jesup Expedition. This Koryak or Chukchi man in armor, circa 1900, was probably a model for the posed manikin who displays Chukchi armor in the American Museum of Natural History's Hall of Asian People. (AMNH Library 1559)

Back at the museum, we show images of our Chukchi and Yupik collections on the CD that we have brought and then we all have tea in the staff room and discuss museum business. After tea, Vladimir takes us to the security bureau to register, as visiting foreigners are required to do within three days of arriving in Russia. He introduces us as his museum colleagues from New York. The security officer is a thin, blond, intense type. We expect a bit of a grilling.

Alexia introduces Laurel, telling the security officer that she researches shamanism in Korea. He registers surprise, "Do they have shamans in Korea? Are people harmed by them?" "Shaman" is clearly an active category in his imagination. He asks if we go to church. We do not know where this conversation is leading and answer honestly, negative. He tells us, "Well, I read the Bible," and asks, "What is the Korean shaman's attitude to eternal life?" Laurel gets on an ethnographic hobbyhorse, speaks of the power of human memory and the difficulty this makes in accepting the absoluteness of death. She speaks of shamans as addressing human need by bringing the voices of the dead into conversation with the living. He tells us he finds his own answers by going to church. Laurel tells him that she thinks Christianity offers good and true teachings but that there are other ways of looking at things that are also good. He says that he finds peace by going to church and not thinking too much about these matters. Sensing that this conversation has run its course, we tell him that we are happy he has found peace. He thanks us, smiles, and goes back to work.

Laurel has had this conversation before, usually with Korean evangelicals, but it is not what she expected of an interrogation in a Russian security office, not under a portrait of Lenin, Christ-like and pensive, bowed over an empty table, a Last Supper from which all guests have departed. Seeing our amusement, Vladimir tells us that the security officer is an avid Seventh-Day Adventist who gets into trouble with his superior because he always spends too much time talking religion with the people who come in to register. Vladimir now suggests that we drop in on his friend, the army recruiting officer. "Is he religious, too?" Vladimir says no and we all share a chuckle.

The army recruiter has the big-boned good looks of a movie star war hero. His desk bears a curio from Wrangel Island, off the Chukotka coast, a signpost indicating 4 kilometers to Alaska and 6,480 kilometers to Moscow, a wry comment on Chukotka's place in space. He describes a military that is haltingly moving toward an "American" system where professional training is given in the course of military service. Because there are few benefits left for those who live in Chukotka, the Chukotka regional administration has successfully obtained the right for enlisted men to serve in the immediate region. They can avoid the real hot spots, like Chechnya, and can claim this privilege even if they have gone away to study. Those who still wish to serve in the wars of a crumbling Russian empire can request to do so, but he considers it his duty to discourage them. When Laurel registers surprise, he confronts her gruffly,

"Aren't you a mother?" Laurel, both a mother and a pacifist, simply did not expect to hear these sentiments expressed by the man behind the desk.

The recruiting officer describes the young men as having a romantic notion of war. As a twenty-year military man who came through the ranks, he knows what the experience is really like. He does not want their deaths on his conscience. When they report for conscription, he is the one who shakes their hands. Should anything happen to them, he is the one who would have to deliver the report to their families. He tries to discourage them, but he is not always successful. In the course of this conversation, we learn that Vladimir's father was an officer. We also realize that resourceful Vladimir has made this social call to have his military friend provide our transportation to the airport tomorrow morning. This successfully arranged, we leave, Vladimir calling out to his friend in cheerful cynicism, "Our great patriotic army marches on."

On the street outside, Vladimir shares a bit of biography. As the child of a military man, he spent his early years in small towns in Chukotka before his parents relocated to the Baltics. His parents and in-laws live in the city of Kaliningrad on the Baltic Sea and he and his wife still have an apartment there. As we walk, once again, down the long muddy street of the town, he opens up about his situation. He does not know how long he can hold on in Providenia without pay. He likes living here, with the possibility of going around to the Native villages and photographing and sketching. He regrets that so much of his time is taken up with administration. He also recognizes that he is very good at what he does and that he is unlikely to find such a favorable position in the intensely competitive job market of European Russia. He speaks with pride of the whale observation project and of a new study of polar bear migrations that would draw on the local knowledge and bear lore of Native communities. But he needs to feel that his work is appreciated; the lack of pay since the past April does not suggest that the higher-ups value what he is doing. He also has a strong sense of time passing. Vladimir is thirty-four years old, and thirty-five is the cutoff for a great many entry-level positions. He will hold out until November, when he is scheduled to take a leave and go home to Kaliningrad, and then make his decision.

That night, at the café, Vladimir's wife, Svetlana, or Sveta for short, tells us that she is going home in October. She finds life in this small Northern town just too difficult and she has no desire to return for another winter. Svetlana is a warm and charming woman, and she and Vladimir seem to be very close as a couple. We begin to appreciate the full complexity of Vladimir's situation.

Our evening in the café is meant to be a farewell party. There are toasts. Bob and Tom give Vladimir a radio. Yura speaks nostalgically about wanting to teach in China, but tomorrow, in the clear light of day, he will tell us that a stint in China would not fill his financial needs. It would just be an experience and a chance to improve his spoken Chinese. We leave Bob and Tom with promises of "meet you at the plane." The vintage Ford is again outside the café.

On Wednesday, August 11, we awaken to the sound of rain. The town is socked in with deep gray fog that dims our prospects of flying out this morning. At the museum, Yura gallantly plugs in his small space heater for our benefit. We are hopeful of an afternoon clearing. We sit cozily at unoccupied desks and write in our journals. Alexia is surprised to find copies of Stalin's works on one of the desks next to a vintage telephone; it is unusual but highly appropriate for a Russian local history museum to be documenting the Soviet past on par with other typically "ethnographic" topics like human settlements and hunting practices. Vladimir says these are for an upcoming exhibit on a historical theme. He is amused when Laurel takes a photograph.

Yura tells us that the rain and fog are a "weather cycle" and that we might not be able to fly out for two or three days. We naively assume that he is teasing us. All in all, this seems a more interesting place to be stuck than, say, Nome, although it would be wonderful to be able to take a hot shower. It will be a while before either of us can enjoy a hot shower.

Chapter 2

Chukotka
At the Edge of a Crumbling Empire

Mariinsky, April 1, 1901
We will leave in a week or so with seven dog teams and proceed northwards, probably as far as Indian Point. We will not be able to return with dogs and will have to wait till the coming of the steamer. . . . I sent a letter to Vladivostok asking the postal steamer to call on Indian Point for the sake of the expedition. . . .

—Waldemar Bogoras to Franz Boas

Indian Point, June 18, 1901
I am going to leave Indian Point tomorrow morning for my journey back to Anadyr. Since no steamer could be induced to take me back [to Anadyr], I had to construct a skin canoe of a moderate size and try to make the trip myself with my men. It was not very convenient, since I had to dispose of 100 dogs with considerable loss of value. . . . [since they could not go in the small boat.]

—Bogoras to Boas

Still thinking that we will spend the night in Nome, we consider the delay a fortunate turn of events, because now we will be able to visit Vera's school for special education. We are curious to see how Vera's enthusiasm for teaching about Chukchi culture is realized in such an institution. When Vera invited us yesterday, we had assumed that it was a casual offer, but when we placed the call, we learned that Vera and her director had been waiting for us for the last hour. "Where were you?"

Schools for special education exist throughout Russia, even in far northern regional centers like Providenia. For decades the schools have provided education for children who are considered retarded; in the Providenia school children study basic reading and writing and learn beadwork and sewing, working with local animal products. The children sew seal and walrus skin to create slippers, mittens, and tall boots. The caregivers in the school will tell us that the number of children in need of such specialized attention has increased in recent years. Alexia's research on residential schools in another part of Siberia has made her aware that more than half the students in schools for special education in the

Figure 9. In this image of the beach at Indian Point, the sea is visible just beyond the line of yarangas. Bogoras came here in May of 1901 and spent the summer in Yupik villages, like this one, observing the lively summer season of seal hunting and trading. (AMNH Library 1346)

late 1990s suffered from fetal alcohol syndrome. These schools continue to teach children some basic skills, but they can also be sad places where caregivers are dispirited and children long to be home in their villages.

Providenia's school for special education is a large mass of concrete. Alexia registers surprise that this is such a solid building, contrasting it with the poorer, shabbier schools in Evenkia. Inside, murals brighten the foyer wall: jolly Natives are depicted engaging in sea mammal hunting and reindeer herding. Chukotka's mineral wealth seems to ensure that the town has infrastructural amenities, such as this solidly constructed school and municipal running water, not found in many small towns in the North.

Vera ushers us up the stairs and introduces us to Nina, the director, an enthusiastic, stout, blond woman in her sixties. Nina wears a brightly floral chiffon scarf around her shoulders like a shawl—the style of an older Russian woman; it softens and adds sparkle to her stylish black suit in a manner thoroughly consistent with her character. She seems to be extremely dedicated to her Native students, who need a sense of their own history, she tells us. Her view that human beings cannot live by scientific principles alone, that they need some intuitive, emotional knowledge, is a common opinion in the post-Soviet era. Many of the people we will meet in our travels describe the Soviet Union's primary fault as one of hyperrationality; the system was rulebound and did not allow for human variability. Nina comments that it was the Soviet imposition of rigid ideas and forms of economic development, like consolidating Native people into settled villages, that caused such hardship.

Vera stands by quietly while Nina is speaking, but then begins to describe the curriculum for the students in the school. Vera has already told us that the school offers Chukchi language for only three hours a week. She considers this inadequate since the children's primary language is Russian and they are often embarrassed to speak Chukchi in public. This is a familiar story among the Native peoples of Russia, North America, and many other places, but it is a marked contrast with the proud Chukchi of one hundred years past who, in Bogoras's time, did not assimilate readily: "Whenever they come in contact with another tribe, they do not learn its language, but force the other to learn theirs. . . . The Chukchee [Chukchi] are so self-sufficient that they prefer to make words of their own for new objects coming from the civilized world, rather than adopt the foreign names."[1]

Vera's own life story is a mix of resistance and capitulation. Vera was born in 1958 in a Chukchi yaranga, a nomad tent. Her sister, born in 1972, also came into the world this way, although by then clinics were widely available. Vera's mother felt that she would "lose" her children if she did not birth them in a traditional Chukchi setting. "But now we have all gone our own way," Vera says, laughing softly at her mother's attempt to keep her children from drifting into the Russianized world of the towns. Still, as a knowledgeable teacher of her language and tradition, Vera has honored her mother's intentions.

Nina is anxious for us to see the small museum that she has made inside the school. On our way down the hallway, we pass a room full of dark-haired children clustered together attentively watching a video. Vera says that these are the orphans, nearly half of the sixty students enrolled, who must remain at school during the summer because they have nowhere else to go. Laurel misses her own dark-haired child, huddled with his friends in front of a video monitor barely a week ago when she picked him up at the end of a session of summer day camp.

The museum is a large, gray room filled with what at first seems like a disorderly jumble of artifacts, tent models, amateur art, books, and photographs. Most elements of a local history museum are crammed together in this single room. Students and teachers at the school contributed many of the artifacts. Nina describes her museum as having an educational function, in the broadest sense, and we see that these modest exhibits have been thoughtfully arranged so as to be accessible to children. Students from other local schools study the collections as part of their ethnography and decorative arts curriculum. Day-care centers also bring their charges here. Nina and her staff give tours, and older people from the community who remember life on the tundra come in and talk to the students. The old-timers are delighted when they see their younger selves in some of the photographs and return with their children and neighbors. Their comments are recorded and appended to the photographic collection—a common museological practice in the Russian Far East.

The museum is a source of great pride to Nina, who points to a certificate on the wall acknowledging its official designation as Local History Museum 6338. The museum began in 1983 in a corner of the school's library. This history reminds Alexia of the early Soviet practice of having a Red Corner, sometimes no more than a bulletin board, in a school or other public institution. In the 1920s and 1930s, before the Red Corner was superseded by the House of Culture—a community center occupying an entire building and dedicated to educational and cultural programs—these small display spaces inculcated Soviet culture, instructing the public on the organization of the Soviet government, sanitary practices, and how to be a good citizen. Sometimes they were also used to promote literacy lessons in Russian as a means of acculturating Native people. It is ironic to see this latter-day Red Corner turned upon itself in a countereffort to revitalize Native cultural heritage.

Nina was an active voice in the movement to establish a local museum in the town. As head of the Department of Culture for the Providenia district she not only set up the museum corner in the school but also made collections in anticipation of the day when the town would have a proper museum. She was disappointed when many of her objects were disdained by the new Providenia museum as duplicates or inferior works. Relegated to a subsidiary status, these pieces now sit in her school's museum, officially on extended loan from the Providenia museum.

We examine these treasures: featherwork ornaments made from walrus bladder to decorate waterproof parkas, two small ceremonial baskets made of whale baleen, a hide pouch with the face of a watch worked into its design, a pair of seal fur boots with a decorative band at the top embroidered and beaded with what seem to be European-inspired patterns of birds. The boots were stitched tight with sinew, covered with fat to make them watertight. In the far North, this precise stitching could be a matter of life or death, staving off crippling numbness and frostbite. Nina shows us the boots' fur inner soles and the straw for insulation, as she would instruct a group of visiting schoolchildren. She points to a display of Yupik balls, decorated hide spheres that symbolize the sun and are given as gifts to celebrate a birth. These are familiar to us from the examples collected by Bogoras for the American Museum of Natural History one hundred years ago. He described lively games of kickball, girls on one side, boys on the other, or "more frequently they all run about, trying to catch the ball as it flies from side to side."[2] Today, schoolchildren learn to make balls in Native arts classes. We will see the Alaskan version of these popular souvenir items for sale all over Anchorage.

Nina begins to describe the use of different kinds of snow beaters, flourishing a long curved stick with a knob on the end. The large beaters are used to beat snow off a tent; Vera remembers the vigorous pounding from her child-

Figure 10. Chukchi girls dancing at Indian Point. Some of these children could be the great-grandparents of the children seen in Figure 11. (AMNH Library 1344)

hood. Nina flourishes a smaller beater: "This is for beating snow off of clothes—it's made from reindeer antler." Vera affably corrects her: "It's for children to beat snow." Nina shows us snowshoes, which were "necessary in the deep snow." Vera corrects her again; on the contrary, in the dead of winter it was easy to walk on the packed, frozen ground. The snowshoes were needed to navigate the softer, slushier snow of spring. Not missing a beat, Nina continues, telling us that children today prefer skis and will not wear Native snowshoes. Vera's corrections are friendly, and Nina takes them in that spirit, praising Vera's knowledge of tradition. The mutual respect of these two pleasant, confident women, one Native, the other Russian, is extraordinary, something Alexia saw only rarely during her fieldwork with residential schools. Nina's genuine enthusiasm toward Native cultures is also unusual. Nina has even tried to learn to speak Chukchi, albeit unsuccessfully.

An entire shelf of the museum is dedicated to various carved renderings of the elf-like *pelikan*, the big-eared, big-bellied mascot of Chukotka. "Pelican?" Laurel ventures. "Not 'pelican,'" Vera corrects her, "Pel-ee-kaan." The original image supposedly came from San Francisco, and local ivory carvers began to replicate it. The ancestral *pelikan* might have been a long-eared, big-bellied Buddha statue from Chinatown.

One wall is devoted to memorabilia from local history. There is a photograph of a young Soviet doctor who froze to death in the line of duty in an isolated coastal village. The region's first emissaries of the Soviet state were idealistic young Communists, eager to live among the people and learn Native languages. Like Bogoras and Jochelson, who arrived in northeastern Siberia in the 1880s as political exiles, these young Soviet volunteers also wrote from their firsthand knowledge of Native life. As some of the earliest graduates of the Faculty of Ethnography at the Geographical Institute in Leningrad (precursor to the Institute of the Peoples of the North) in the early 1920s, these Soviet enthusiasts became teachers, doctors, interpreters, census takers, and administrators across the North. With encouragement from these cultural emissaries, in 1926 Native Siberian students began to attend university in Leningrad and return to work in their home villages. Images of locally recognized personages celebrate this journey from the Bering Sea to the metropolis and back.

There is a photograph of an old, lean-faced Yupik woman wearing spectacles. Vera explains animatedly that this woman, Ukhsima Ivanovna Okhsima, was a renowned Yupik activist as well as an actress and playwright. She was the first Yupik Komsomol (the Communist Party youth organization) leader, and her father is said to have been a harpoonist for American whalers. In addition, Ukhsima Ivanovna was a hero of Sovietization, a propagandist who organized Native women through sewing cooperatives. Even when she was old she continued to work with children, and "she was always very kind," Vera adds with admiration in her voice. This is a story from a moment in time when the Native peoples of the North had been encouraged to see their needs as a central concern of the Soviet state. Activists like Ukhsima Ivanovna are held up as local heroes for their part in that federally supported effort to "educate" and care for minority groups like the Yupik and Chukchi. In the late 1990s, these sentiments are a comment on the present, when the state's declining investment in the region means curtailed aviation, scarce and expensive foodstuffs, and inadequate heat and electricity. People are also aware of the repressions of the past and the suffering caused by the collectivization and relocations in the Soviet period, but many people, especially those over forty, often have nostalgia for their lives in the Soviet Union.

The exhibit skims over the painful periods of collectivization and relocation in the North, as well as the resistance to Sovietization in its early period. In the tumult of the early 1930s, Chukchi and Yupik, like others across Russia, were coerced into joining what were called collectives (*kolkhozy*), consolidations of private holdings that came to be owned by the state. Historically, indigenous Siberians like the coastal Chukchi and Yupik were seasonally nomadic, depending on the needs of reindeer herding or sea mammal hunting. Ultimately, the collectives established among the Chukchi and Yupik by the 1950s all but required them to become employees of the state. Instead of hunting, fishing, or herding to support their families and communities, they turned their products over to the state. In exchange, they would receive a regular paycheck that remained the same, regardless of the catch. By the late 1990s many local Yupik and Chukchi were returning to traditional economic arrangements as the state collectives crumbled. These roller-coaster elements of local history are nowhere to be seen in this exhibit, which tells an optimistic story of Native revitalization without a destructive protagonist—the onslaught of Sovietization. This history may be too immediate and unresolved to include in a school museum.

Books are scattered throughout the exhibit to encourage the children to read. A special section of children's literature and textbooks about Chukotka includes a Chukchi reader, a textbook in Yupik, and a work of folklore by an early ethnographer who was a long-term resident in the region. Nina concedes that reading the children's literature on natural history and folklore is beyond the ability of the special education students who attend this school but that the books might spark interest among the visiting students.

Next, Nina takes us to her "Alaska room," a space set aside to commemorate renewed contact across the Bering Strait since 1988. Pointing to a wall of newspaper clippings from the early 1990s, Vera reminds us, "In the past, we always went back and forth." Her words underscore centuries, even millennia, of contact between Northern peoples around the Bering Strait that were suspended by the Cold War.

Nina's display holds the flotsam of more recent encounters between Providenia and Nome: a Sunday school bookmark ("and God so loved the world") rests next to an old Estee Lauder compact; there are odds and ends of plastic toys, Alaska souvenirs, and a full shelf of Christian literature for children. Missionary philanthropy is "where the money comes from," says Vera with a chuckle. Postmodern critics of "artificial" ethnographic museum categorizations would most surely love this place for its random kitchiness, a fair recreation of sporadic and fragmentary meetings.

We examine Nina's memorabilia from the Iditarod dogsled race, which was established to commemorate the heroic team of Chukchi dogs that brought diphtheria medicine to Nome in 1924. Was she aware that a statue of the lead dog, Balto, was erected in New York's Central Park? Oh yes, she says, she saw it when she was visiting her son who lives in New Jersey. Here the conversation swerves to the personal. Her son immigrated to New York via Israel. When he first left the Soviet Union, they spoke frequently on the telephone, but she soon realized that the line was tapped. The authorities told her that her son was "disloyal." Her indignation at the memory of those conversations melts into grandmotherly pride when she takes out a photograph of her New Jersey grandson at a dance performance, a smiling child in miniature dress shirt and black tie.

Vera and Nina recall the pervasiveness of anti-American propaganda during the Cold War. In these changed times, sometimes these attitudes persist. When Vera's mother saw a large American woman embrace Vera, she initially thought that the tourist had attacked her daughter and was going to stab her. We have a laugh over this, but the anecdote reminds us of how deeply distrust of Westerners was ingrained. In the past an "Alaska room" celebrating cooperation and the building of trust between residents of the United States and Russia would have been difficult to imagine.

Our last stop is the bright, sunny school library, where Nina has cultivated huge plants—begonias, philodendrons, and piggyback ferns—in the light that pours through the windows. "She has so many interests," says Vera. The teachers use this pleasant space as a common room. Some children wander in while we are talking, and one little girl, an obvious favorite, gets a long hug from Vera.

We ask what the children do after they graduate from this school at age sixteen. Nina and Vera first mention successes; the most outstanding was a girl admitted to a technical sewing institute. They also tell us that some students are misdiagnosed and sent here by mistake. Some are quickly transferred out once the error is recognized, but those who remain receive a practical education, despite their mislabeling as "retarded." Of course, they admit, the severely retarded go on to do menial work, often as janitors.

Vladimir catches up with us on the path back to the museum. He tells us that there will be no flight out this afternoon and suggests that we have lunch in "the Baptist café." It is warm and cozy, and the food isn't bad—cabbage and carrot salad and pelmeni, meat-filled Siberian dumplings in a broth. We chat about the active Baptist presence in this Siberian town and the New Age religious curiosity about Siberian shamans in the United States. Vladimir encountered an American neo-shaman on one of his Alaska trips, a white man bearing tattoos from the South Seas. Vladimir was amused to arrange a shamanic competition between this braggart and a Russian ethnologist friend who had mastered several Chukchi shaman songs.

Vladimir's talk about Western seekers of exotic spirituality reminds Alexia of her own encounters with the New Age religious interests that began to surface in the late 1980s in the Soviet Union. As a student of Russian language in Leningrad, Alexia frequented a café recently opened by Hare Krishnas (*krishnaity*). In those early days of Perestroika, local police often shut it down, citing minor infractions of municipal restaurant codes. There was also a group of Roerichites (*rerikhity*), followers of the early twentieth-century artist and Theosophist Nicholas Roerich, known for the mystical paintings he made during his treks from Central Asia to the Himalayas. This group of young people made frequent pilgrimages from Leningrad to the Altai mountains bordering Central Asia where Roerich was said to have located a source of spiritual energy in the form of the "white waters" (*belye vody*). In the post-Soviet period, the widespread interest in New Age, alternative, and revitalized spiritual pursuits seems to be a natural outcome of a system that had denied and repressed such beliefs and practices for so many decades.

As we will not be flying out of Providenia this afternoon, Vladimir has arranged an excursion to a Yupik village for his tourist charges. After lunch, we pile into the van again with Yura, Bob, and Tom, the driver's wife, and the director of the House of Culture. The director is a striking blond, dressed in black with a leather coat in a knockout shade of coral and a broad-brimmed black felt hat. She must be the most fashionable woman in Providenia.

Our destination is the village of Novoe Chaplino, a settlement built in 1958 on the site of the former seasonal settlement of Tkachen. Novoe Chaplino was created from the consolidation of other villages declared "unsustainable" (neperspektivnye) and relocated. As we heard earlier in the museum, such was the fate of many villages across the North in the 1950s and again in the 1970s. This government policy also applied to villages in other parts of Russia as the Soviet state sought to streamline its supply lines to outlying populations. According to Lyudmila Bogoslovskaya, who spent years researching the history of settlement on the Chukotka Peninsula, including the history of these "lost villages," Ungazik, one of the villages resettled in this place, had been the largest whaling settlement on the whole peninsula. At its height in the nineteenth century Ungazik had a population of nearly five hundred and was known as simply "Cape Chaplino."[3] Bogoras and the American whalers who helped make it the center of American trade on the Chukotka Peninsula called it Indian Point. Bogoras came to Ungazik in the spring of 1901, a trip postponed from the previous summer when a measles epidemic had raged in the northern villages and no guide could be induced to travel north from the mouth of the Anadyr River. In winter, the blizzard-pounded tundra was impassable. Bogoras, with his assistant Axelrod and four "Russianized Natives" carrying provisions and trade goods for barter, reached Indian Point in May, in time to observe the lively summer season of seal hunting and trading. Bogoras and his party spent a month in Yupik villages in northern Chukotka and crossed over by boat to St. Lawrence Island on the American side, observing Yupik and Chukchi life, taking measurements and photographs, and collecting objects for the museum.

By the time Ungazik was officially closed in 1958-59, supposedly owing to erosion of the shore, it had about two hundred inhabitants, predominantly Yupik with some Chukchi and a few non-Natives. Most of the Ungazik population moved to Novoe Chaplino at this point. People were forced to choose between remaining in their ancestral homes or having a local school, access to some storebought foodstuffs, and basic medical attention. Sometimes there was no choice; in both cases, these dislocations caused great hardship for families. Removed from their ancestral lands, the elder generation had difficulty passing on local knowledge of the landscape and ritually important sites. Today young people are often unfamiliar with hunting and fishing practices, and, as Vera explained, they do not fully appreciate the rich array of mythology associated with the landscape.

Although the village of Novoe Chaplino is no more than half an hour's drive from Providenia—walking distance for most inhabitants—it bears the official designation of a "remote Native village," one of eight that remain after the relocations and consolidations of the region's twenty-four Native villages that existed here in the 1950s. Novoe Chaplino is home to nearly five hundred people, more than half of whom are Yupik, with the rest comprising equal numbers of Chukchi and non-Natives. Except for the few who are teaching or working as local administrators, people get by as sea mammal hunters and fox farmers. A gravel road to the village, accommodating the bus from Providenia that runs out here twice a day, is an amenity gained by the village's proximity to a military artillery range.

Our first stop is at the village's fox cages, built on high platforms so that they will not be snowed in. Fox farms were started all over the North in the 1950s and 1960s as part of the government's efforts to render semi-nomads into sedentary people within the Soviet system. Many cages are empty, but small dark creatures with glittering eyes lurk in some corners. The cages reek of fishy excrement. Yura provides tour patter. There used to be two thousand foxes in these cages, but now there are only two hundred. The fish and sea mammal meat once used to feed them is now desperately needed by the human popu-lation. Novoe Chaplino is still officially considered a "state farm engaging in sea mammal hunting," but no one has been paid by the state for three or four years. The demise of this industry is a mixed blessing. The village lost its prin-cipal means of support, but fur farms did not sit easily with the community since people hated to see the meat they hunted go to feeding foxes. Vladimir has told us this before; it must be part of a standard tour script.

Novoe Chaplino seems more viable than the Native villages Alexia visited in central Siberia. Built in the 1980s, the government-constructed houses are newer by at least a decade and are more solidly constructed, with foundations that raise them off the frozen ground. There is electricity in the village and we see several television antennas, but some services, such as heat, are available only in Providenia. The driver mutters that there is nothing for the villagers to do in Providenia once they move there, and he says a few other things about drunken Natives.

We spend nearly an hour at the village store with its Soviet-era prices. We had thought that the simple boredom of a summer's day in half-deserted Prov-idenia had caused the driver's wife and the director of the House of Culture to join our excursion, but it was the range of cheap goods that had lured them. The village store is an odd enterprise, a dark, cavernous array of shelves sparsely stocked with hideous fabric and other random merchandise that hap-pened to land in Chukotka. There are bags of herbs and spices with English-language labels (including "laurel"), turkey wings, powdered cappuccino mix, bags of yeast, a carton of eye-ridden potatoes, and, Yura points out, a large stock of medicinal tea used to discourage alcohol consumption. As to our tee-totaling friend's past familiarities with this tonic, we can only speculate. Alexia buys a large notebook with marble-patterned covers to use as a travel journal. Vladimir buys a supply of light bulbs for the museum, smiling as he cradles the parcel in his arms.

There is the feel of another era about this place. A huge Chinese-style aba-
cus seems at home on the cashier's stand. Elsewhere in the Russian Federation,
they had largely been replaced by pocket calculators by the early 1990s, but we
have seen them all over Providenia. A poster on the wall announces a village
cleanup campaign. A large black complaint book hangs on a string by the
counter, but the entries all seem to express such sentiments as "Congratulations
on all the fine work you ladies are doing—International Women's Day, 1996."

Outside the door, children gather. When they ask if we want to buy "slippers," Alexia tells them no. Vladimir reminds his charges that the seal fur used
to make this lovely, warm footwear will not pass the border control. A man
with an athletic bag over his shoulder approaches and on his behalf, Vladimir
asks if we want to buy fur medallions, which proliferate on the Northern
tourist trail. We say no and wave him in Tom and Bob's direction—"They're
the tourists."

Further down the village lane, we meet a robust blond woman carrying professional camera gear, animatedly talking at a group of Yupik children. She
sprinkles her nonstop English with volleys of Russian and Yupik words as she
urges the children to inflate dozens of colored balloons in the chill wind.
Vladimir introduces us to Saunders McNeil, a photojournalist from Anchorage who has been staying in the village with an interpreter. Her aim is to pho-

Figure 11. Supplied with balloons by a visitor, children in Novoe Chaplino pose for a
photograph. The grandparents and great-grandparents of some of these children
would have grown up in Ungazik, Bogoras' "Indian Point." (Photo by Alexia Bloch)

tograph Yupik families on both sides of the Bering Strait. She has lived with the St. Lawrence Island community, on the American side of the Bering Strait, but it took her two years of planning, negotiation, and grant-writing to reach their cousins on the Siberian side of the strait. She draws us all into the act, and we find ourselves trying to inflate somewhat resistant balloons.

Vladimir disappears for a brief while. We later learn that he is making arrangements for rehearsal space for the Yupik dance group scheduled to perform on Sunday when a tour boat will call. The resourceful Vladimir accomplishes a great deal while providing an excursion for his marooned charges.

Vera has invited us to her Native dance group's rehearsal in the House of Culture later that afternoon. Back at the Providenia museum, we mention this to Vladimir, who telephones the director of the House of Culture. At Vladimir's urging, she invites the entire group for tea after the rehearsal. The House of Culture is a large, imposing structure. There is even some marble in the foyer ("Soviet infrastructure at work," says Alexia). Like so much else we have seen today, this House of Culture is in better repair than others Alexia has visited. Since the mid-1990s the commodious auditorium and adjoining café have accommodated groups from the tour boats throughout the summer season, in addition to regular cultural programs for local consumption.

We spend so much time paying our respects in the director's office that when we finally make our way upstairs to the dance studio, we pass Vera, drum in hand, descending with her students and their parents. We have missed the rehearsal. The director borrows Vera's drum, and Vladimir uses it as a prop while he gives us all a lecture-demonstration in the dance studio. We begin to realize that travelers are routinely stranded here and Vladimir is adept at pulling cultural rabbits out of a hat for their amusement.

Later, over tea in the director's office, Yura says that he has not been paid for his teaching job for a year and a half. With a wry smile, he describes himself as better off than employees in the state farms who have not been paid for several years. Yura is considering the prospect of a teaching job in Novoe Chaplino. He is well past his mid-thirties, when someone with his special linguistic and computer skills could still expect to be recruited into the new companies. In the village, the pay would be better than at his current job and a steady diet of marine products would be guaranteed. One drawback: a small stove would be his only source of heat during the Arctic winter.

Yura's mother and sister are in Moscow, but he is content enough to spend the summer in Providenia working the tour boat season. Yura tells us he gets along far better with Vladimir and his colleagues and "you guys" than with his own family. We speculate that Yura is a man with a colorful past, but the moment of exchanged confidences passes and Yura slips back into tour guide patter.

Back on the rainy street, feeling tired and wet, we decline further socializing and leave the others with damp wishes of seeing each other on the plane tomorrow. We suspect that Vladimir must be just as happy as we are to have time off.

The sky is overcast on Thursday morning and the planes are still grounded. By way of entertainment, Vladimir offers a visit to his friend, the town dentist. We beg off in favor of a morning spent updating our journals and meet Vladimir later in the Baptist café for lunch. He reports that there is no chance of our leaving today. This afternoon we will visit the library and this evening, if we really want it, his wife, Svetlana, will take us to ladies night at the *banya*, the bathhouse complete with scalding sauna. We assure him that we really do want to visit the banya.

We meet up with Tom and Bob at the museum. They have been sharing their home stay with a Japanese documentary film crew that is recording human global migration in reverse; the Japanese have just "gone back" across the Bering Strait from North America. Yura arrives, smiling like the cat who has eaten the canary. "I have just enriched my vocabulary with another English expression, 'sugar daddy.'" We go to the library which, like the museum and Vladimir's apartment, is freshly painted and wallpapered and very pleasant. Here, too, plants including cilantro and cucumbers flourish in the sunlight from a large window. Some of the cilantro will appear with our tea. Two fair-haired young men occupy one of the reading room tables. One is poring through a stack of *Soldier of Fortune*-type magazines. The other is engaged with a magazine that resembles *Popular Mechanics*. Pushkin and Sholokhov look on from the wall.

Galina, the head librarian, is a woman in her late forties or early fifties. With her wild, wiry silver hair, she could have walked out of any library in New York City. She begins what is probably a standard rap for stranded travelers and visiting bureaucrats about the current state of the library now that the cost of purchasing new books and shipping them has become prohibitive. Galina laments that people no longer have time for reading; so many of her patrons are taken up with plans and preparations for leaving Providenia. She does try to stock newspapers since people can no longer afford to subscribe at home. In the past, interlibrary loans were free and people could get any book on request. Now, the library requests books only for people who are taking correspondence courses; law and accounting classes are hugely popular. The subscribers cover the cost of shipping themselves, so in effect there is no longer an interlibrary loan system.

The current literature table includes translations of popular mysteries by Nicholas Blake and Mary Higgins Clark, *Jaws*, and a copy of Charlotte Brontë's *Shirley*. Detective novels are in demand now. There were few in Soviet times, but soon after translations from English came onto the market, Russians began to write their own. Thrillers with lurid covers are in such demand that borrowers pay fifty kopeks a day to borrow them, while there is no fee for other books. There is also a stack of paperbacks in English, supermarket fare, including Judith Krantz and the like. These are a contribution from the Bering Air representative in Providenia, Daizee, a local personality whom we will finally meet on our flight back to Nome and Anchorage.

Another table holds sale books contributed by people preparing to leave town. Galina notes that since everyone in the town used to belong to the same book clubs, they all seem to have the same books. These are two rubles apiece (less than twenty-five cents). These discard books include classic works in translation by Flaubert, Dreiser, and Hugo. Yura pulls out the diary of a wealthy Russian Old Believer, Morozov, who supported the arts and the 1905 revolutionaries, committing suicide after that abortive effort. With dry Russian wit, Yura comments, "Of course everyone is interested in him now because he was rich." Alexia finds an anthology by the Chukchi author Yuri Rytkheu. Vladimir quietly palms it and walks away. Later he asks Alexia if she wanted to buy it. She asks if he intends it for the museum, and when the answer is yes, she says that she didn't really want it. She finds instead a novel in English by Nabokov, *Bend Sinister*, and a collection of Brodsky's work in Russian.

Writers such as Marina Tsvetaeva and Sergey Esenin are back on the shelves. Until the late 1980s, these authors' works were considered "anti-Soviet" and were available only in unofficial (*samizdat*) versions. Galina says with sorrow that they were published briefly after Perestroika, but they are out of print now. The publishing market is in detective novels. A gaunt Tolstoy looks on from the wall.

Galina launches into a heated discussion about changing tastes. She herself has no stomach for contemporary writing; she can barely read through the abridgments in journals. Raised on the classics, she finds the contemporary style too simple and the subject matter too crudely realist. Literature should make people feel more erudite and worthy. There is no sense of wonder in contemporary popular works. Hemingway looks on from the wall.

Material conditions have changed, Galina says, and so has the way that people think about the world. They used to have a sense of heroism—they were involved in the conquest of the expanse of stunted northern forests and lichen-covered plateaus—now they look on the past with cynicism. She gives the example of the trans-Siberian gas line as something that people living in the North all felt they had a hand in, something that gave them a common sense of accomplishment, but now this work, and the Soviet era generally, has been discredited. A large color photograph of Sakharov looks on from the wall.

In a lighter voice, Galina acknowledges that some people do like the new writing, and tastes will continue to change. She tells us we can call it "the literature of a lost generation" or "the literature of changing times." Galina tells us that she doesn't read fiction now so much as history to try to understand the present through the Russian past. She reads detective novels for pure relaxation. A gaunt Solzhenitsyn looks on from the wall. Galina says she can't stand him.

Galina goes off to see if the tea is ready. Lidia, her sturdy assistant, describes a book club that has been in existence for twenty-five years. The members meet once a month to discuss common favorites such as Chekhov. In the early 1990s, in the glow of Perestroika, these meetings used to include serious political discussions, but in these troubled times the gatherings are more social. They also have holiday celebrations with food and liquor. Laurel mentions that her book group in New York has wine at every meeting. "You can have more intense discussions that way," Lidia observes.

Galina and her staff have prepared a high tea with white wine, vodka, potatoes, a beautiful cabbage salad garnished with herbs from the library flowerpots, similarly garnished tomatoes, little sandwiches with melted cheese and luncheon meat, stacks of blini—Russian crepes—and dishes of honey to dab them in. We begin our festivities with everyone talking about where they or their ancestors came from. One of the librarians is a Volga German and, most surprisingly, Vladimir claims a half-Nivkh grandmother from the indigenous people of Sakhalin Island, north of Japan, and some Tatar blood. Yura, though all Russian, was born in Poland "during the 'liberation' or the 'occupation,' depending on how you look at it." Alexia finds this assortment typical of other towns in the North. We talk about how "Americans" often claim that they don't distinguish background in such precise ways, but then discourse at length about their polyglot immigrant genealogies anyway.

We eat and drink and more intense discussions ensue. After several glasses of vodka Galina reveals that her daughter is living with a forty-year-old New Russian in Irkutsk. She begins a tirade against the New Russians (*novye russkie*) which Alexia, with equal rapidity, translates: "Yes, socialism oppressed our people but it also gave them a common sense of purpose. These days, the New Russians are rich because they are corrupt, because they have unjustly seized monopolies by grabbing state enterprises. Wealth given to the top never gets to the miners" who have been striking for several months. "I'm poor, and someone else is rich at my expense."

Tom offers encouragement, saying that things will get better, that it took the United States a long time to develop its own economy. From her reading of history, Galina considers this developmental perspective simplistic. "Russia is too old a country to follow the evolutionary path of American capitalism. Industries have existed in Russia from before the Revolution. The Hapsburg Empire was great once upon a time, and the Roman Empire too, but now they're gone. Who knows what the new world order will be. We are living through a moment when everything is being shaken." Galina's comments reflect the growing widespread despair in Russia in the late 1990s. The common sense of purpose created in the Soviet period is strikingly missing in this era, where the socialist maxim of "From each according to his ability, to each according to his needs" is nowhere to be seen.

Yura pursues a running argument with Galina over the definition of "New Russian." In his view, doing business is a necessity and can be distinguished from large-scale exploitation. In Galina's view, any entrepreneur is necessarily corrupt; there is no room for compromise. Vladimir and Yura, working with the tourism industry, are in their own small way entrepreneurs. When we discuss this encounter with Vladimir a few days later, he does not share Galina's view of the Soviet past. We cannot resist asking him about Galina's background: "Was she a prominent Communist?" He becomes taciturn, simply stating that he does not agree with her. They are, after all, close friends, living together in a small town. She hosts tea parties for his stranded travelers (ours was not the first), perhaps in the hope of garnering support for her library. Even the righteous Galina has her tenuous ties to Providenia tourism.

With visions of auditoriums, dance studios, museums, and book groups dancing in her head, Laurel is beginning to see the Russian frontier as a place infused with culture, a contrast with the American West where the school-marm and the librarian have been portrayed as threats to a wild and wooly man's world. Isn't Providenia a bit like some Jane Austen village, cultured people living in an obscure place? Alexia does not see the parallel and reminds Laurel that the non-Native types are all temporary residents. Even without the current wave of departures, civil servants generally retire to European Russia at the age of fifty (women) or fifty-five (men). The hill stations of the British Raj, brought to life in *The Jewel in the Crown*, are a better literary analogue.

In the evening, Svetlana takes us to the banya after warning us that it will be crowded and not clean. Relative to Korean public baths, where Laurel has been scrutinized in cheek-by-jowl tanks of hot water, the banya is not too crowded, there are no more than ten bathers inside the bath area, only a few women share the common sauna at one time, and no one stares. It is also very clean, although everyone seems highly conscious of potential dirt, wearing rubber sandals and placing their clothing, soap, and sponges with care. The steam room smells of old wood. Plump Svetlana, looking like an alabaster odalisque, swats our backs with a bundle of birch leaves that drip scalding water. It is a good, hot pain, and the persistent ache in Laurel's lower back utterly vanishes. In the changing room, Alexia chats with a woman who has made her own face mask from a complicated recipe that includes oats and honey. They talk about using salt to abrade the skin—as some pricey American spas do—and other potions which, when applied to the scalp, produce thick, lustrous hair. Alexia says that in other banyas she has visited, women are more inclined to use commercial preparations. We sleep very well that night.

On Friday, August 14, we wake up and anxiously scan the gray sky. The airport will be closed on Saturday and Sunday. If we don't get out today, we will be stuck here until Monday, miss the flight from Anchorage to Magadan, which runs only on Saturday, and lose an entire week. Vladimir has told us that if the Kaldun, the "Sorcerer's Mountain" opposite the town, stands out clear in the harbor skyline, the weather will be fair for flying. Gray clouds hover at the summit. At breakfast Vladimir reports that the dispatcher gives us a 60 percent chance of getting out. The wind is blowing in our favor.

During breakfast, Svetlana receives a telephone call from a friend who has just returned from Khabarovsk with a shipment of dairy products which she sells in a rented space under the movie theater. Svetlana, who is on her way to work, asks us to pick up what we want. Our first task, though, is to do laundry, using Svetlana's heating coil in a large plastic bucket to heat the water.

On our way to buy dairy products, we stop to exchange currency in the basement of the bank. We arrive twenty minutes after the exchange window has closed for the day, but they open up again just for us because two hundred dollars is considered a significant transaction. We leave with 1,200 rubles. On the bulletin board outside the bank, most of the postings are of things being sold off by people who are leaving the North. The offerings include furniture, a computer, a chandelier, and a fur coat. Svetlana has told us that some of her pieces of furniture are choice discards. There are several ads for spas, a venerable Soviet institution that, according to Svetlana, is now better organized with more amenities, such as fortune-telling. Of course, now one pays. The ads offer specialties. A spa in Anapa, on the Black Sea, tends respiratory problems, digestion, circulation, gynecological ailments, and allergies. In Vladivostok it's the urinary tract, gynecology, joints, and digestion. These treatments probably have more to do with the specialists on staff than with any relationship between ailment, cure, and climate. Digestion and respiratory problems are the most common complaints in the North.

Elsewhere on the board a computer printout with a dot matrix rose congratulates women employees on the thirtieth anniversary of the social welfare department. This message is "very Soviet," not in the sense of politics but as a familiar element of the shared culture of the Soviet experience. An announcement for the Orthodox church is prominently displayed in the center of the bulletin board. This is unusual; in other northern towns where Alexia has been, such church announcements have usually been placed off to the side or torn down.

We ask directions to the theater, and Alexia tells a helpful woman about the arrival of the dairy products. After bumbling into a video rental operation, also located under the theater, we find a small room full of cheeses, butter, milk, and many eager customers. We stock up on these prized items for ourselves and for Vladimir and Svetlana, buying blocks of cheese from Belarus and Estonia. We also stock up on several flavored yogurts and consider the Russian milk and sour cream.

Alexia is disappointed that the shipment does not contain any kefir, *tvorog*—Russian farmer's cheese—or *prostokvasha*—a close approximation of plain yogurt. While living in the Soviet Union and post-Soviet Russia she developed an insatiable taste for traditional Russian whole-milk products. Although the new products offer their own variety, it seems too bad that the old ones are so rarely produced now. Alexia reflects that she may not gain the ten pounds that she usually puts on living in Russia.

As we move on to search out the baker, where fresh loaves are being taken out of the oven, Alexia compares the local situation with the area in central

Siberia where she conducted research throughout the 1990s, and most recently just a few months prior to this trip. Stores here are better stocked, with just about all the foodstuffs imported from the United States, particularly Alaska, a revival and elaboration of the lively trade in flour and molasses that Bogoras witnessed one hundred years ago. But there are many other differences. There is running water in this regional capital; in the Evenk Autonomous Region's capital, with a similar population, households lug their water, bucket by bucket, from barrels on the street. A town truck transports the water from a pump station on the river to the barrels each household depends on for its weekly supply. At the telephone office here in Providenia, the villages have direct dial telephone lines; the codes for dialing are written on the cabinet doors of each booth. In the Evenk Region, as of summer 1998, villages do not have direct dial lines; people communicate mostly through word-of-mouth, but there is also the remote radio, *ratsia*, for emergencies. This system is not very reliable. Alexia remembers the day when a young boy broke his leg while herding in the taiga. The remote radio was not working properly and no one could get through to the town hospital to call for a medical emergency helicopter. After a couple of hours the connection was eventually made and the helicopter located the child and transported him to the district hospital.

By noon, it is raining again. There will be no flights out until Monday—if then—and we are contemplating a possible escape by German cruise ship when it calls at Providenia on Sunday. Vladimir is surprised that we have not planned on traveling straight through to Anadyr, just over an hour's flight from Providenia. Friends familiar with travel in Chukotka had warned us about the unreliable flights to Anadyr from Providenia. But what could be more unreliable than this?

Bogoras's problems in attempting to leave this part of the world were the reverse of our own. It would have been logical for us to continue on to Anadyr, but the rest of our gear is in Alaska. It would have been most expeditious for Bogoras to continue on from St. Lawrence Island to mainland Alaska, and from there to New York, where Boas expected him to write up his material, but Bogoras's wife, sixty additional boxes of collections, and some unsettled accounts awaited his return at Mariinsky Post (present-day Anadyr). He was able to ship his Chukotka collections to Boas on an American whaling steamer, but no passing steamer was willing to take him south. His only recourse was to purchase the frame of a Native skin boat and have it covered with walrus hides. In this risk-ridden craft, his party made a thirty-two-day journey back to the mouth of the Anadyr River just ten days in advance of the annual steamer that would take the researchers and their crates of collections on to Vladivostok.

Vladimir gives us soup for lunch from the big kettle on the stove. We wring out our laundry and hang it up, then write for a while and go for a walk. Our first stop is the international telephone exchange next to the post office. Alexia places a call to the recommended tourist agency in Kamchatka, where a friendly voice assures her that they can give us the needed visas that were denied on the eve of our departure. We also try to call home. At first the operator is reluctant, "We can only call Alaska. We can't call the rest of the United States." We assure her that if she can call Alaska, she can call the rest of the United States. Her response is indicative of a Providenia worldview: "Alaska" is a critical reference point; New York is off the map. The calls go through but neither of our men answers.

We visit the graveyard at the far end of town on a point high above the sea, a fitting image of finality. The path leads us past the large anchor that is a monument to Bering's explorations. On our way up, Alexia spots a child waving to us from the window of a house and beckons her to follow us. The little girl, Lena, is twelve but the same height as Laurel's nine-year-old son. Lena tells us that she moved to Providenia when her grandmother was allocated an apartment by the regional authorities in 1996. The whole family moved from Enmelen, a predominantly Chukchi village to the northwest of Providenia along the coast; Lena points in the direction of the village. Alexia asks if she has any relatives buried in the cemetery, and Lena takes us to the gravesite of her uncle who died in 1991.

This is Laurel's first visit to a Russian graveyard. Having lived in Korea, where ancestors receive feasts and families picnic on grave mounds after paying respects to their dead relations, Laurel is no stranger to ancestor worship. She suspects that her Korean shaman friends, who routinely communicate with the dead, would appreciate these Russian graves equipped with tables and benches, some very elaborate, to accommodate the living who bring their loved ones vodka and bread on the anniversary of their deaths.

These graves have their own cultural twist, a porcelain cameo portrait of the deceased adorning the center of each metal tombstone. Soviet hammers and sickles are more prevalent than Russian Orthodox crosses. One striking tombstone, with a bright red metal fixture jutting out against the background of the Kaldun mountain, turns out to be that of Ukhsima Ivanovna Okhsima, the Yupik actress and Komsomol leader we heard about at the school museum.

Walking back to town, we search for bottled water, a quest that leads us into most of the town's small shops, hidden away in the bowels of dank buildings behind windowless metal doors. The heavy doors, intended to withstand winter storms, give grocery stores in Providenia the air of a speakeasy. Inside these establishments, we marvel that so many products are available and that so many things for sale are foreign; although Russia is again manufacturing foodstuffs, significant quantities do not yet reach Chukotka. One little shop is filled with candy, gilt foil creations in various shapes and sizes. In several shops a purple velvet-covered collection box for the local Russian Orthodox church is attached to the wall; the church is raising funds to rebuild.

In one of the shops, Alexia spots two unmistakable New Russians sporting stylish haircuts and well-cut wool coats, one with a laptop computer slung over his shoulder, the sort of people that Galina was damning just yesterday. They look so much like New Yorkers that Laurel does not register their strangeness here. The New Russians, who played the Soviet Union's collapse to their own advantage, are widely disdained by everyday Russians for their underhanded get-rich-quick tactics and their assumed connections with organized crime. Throughout Russia today the New Russians are easily distinguished from the majority of the struggling population by their expensive cars and sport utility vehicles with tinted glass, designer clothing imported from the United States and Europe, and gigantic brick houses in the suburbs of cities.

The sky has gotten bluer and bluer throughout the afternoon, but now Gambell on St. Lawrence Island in the Bering Strait, the pilots emergency backup landing point, is out of commission. Resigned to missing our flight to Magadan tomorrow, we dine on bread, cheese, and some halvah garnered during our late afternoon shopping expedition. We write and read.

Saturday morning brings patches of sunlight on the water, a particularly beautiful sight after days of overcast skies, but the wind is blowing strong and cold. Vladimir is in a good mood, a combination of sunshine and Saturday we surmise. He calls the airport and tries to get us a flight: "You people are paid to fly, why aren't you flying?" But any departure from Providenia would involve the customs officials, and it would take an order from the Chukotka capital in Anadyr to get them to work today. In addition to being Saturday, this is one of the many minor holidays that clutter the post-socialist calendar. Vladimir thinks that he can get us out of Providenia on the German cruise ship tomorrow.

We chat about museum work and have another conversation about future prospects for collaboration. Laurel envies Vladimir's easy access to Native artisans. When rats chewed part of the yaranga in his exhibition hall, he called an old Chukchi woman, who was happy to come and mend it. As in many other museums, freezing is a common means of pest control, but it is easily accomplished here without any equipment. The other Vladimir, Vera's husband the photographer, shows us a stack of black-and-white prints and tells us that we can take what we like. This is an exchange for several rolls of film, but never so explicitly stated. We choose nine images that portray Chukchi and Yupik peoples in the context of contemporary Providenia, a complement to Bogoras's century-old images. We tell Vladimir that his work will be preserved in the American Museum of Natural History's archive for one hundred years. He says, "Only a hundred years?"

Our host is impatient to be off to a place called Flower Bay where he intends to photograph. The driver brings his daughter—young and sweet—and a very large black dog—not so sweet. Yura and Vladimir's friend the Tatar dentist is also with us. The sparkling bay is absolutely gorgeous in full sun. The rough coastline recalls a northern California unblemished by human invasion, at least at present. Between 1946 and 1990—the duration of the Cold War—this was the site of a military barracks, but all traces of it have vanished. Until the early 1960s nearly 30,000 military personnel were stationed here. Now there is only empty tundra.

The dentist pulls some leafy seaweed from the surf and we all chomp on the chewy, tasty spines. Yura bundles a healthy bunch of seaweed into the plastic bag that he has brought along for foraging. Berries are abundant but not quite ripe, although we sample a few. Yura tells us that all over Russia people pick berries, but here in the North they are officially encouraged to do so because food is scarce and berries are one of the few available sources of vitamin C. Mushrooms are sparse today, but people pick what they find, exhibiting seemingly encyclopedic knowledge of the edible and inedible varieties of plants that grow on the tundra. We climb the rolling tundra hills in search of *zhizhiga*, blackberries growing close to the ground, and again *syroezhka*, the mushrooms that one can eat raw or lightly salted. We also spot wild rose plants, whose roots the Yupik and Chukchi use to make a tea or to flavor meat, and a rhododendron and birch tree, both stunted but tenacious. We are not inclined to spend a great deal of time in this fiercely cold and windy place, despite its beauty.

At the foot of the hill we survey a pile of whale bones at the edge of a windswept meadow. Vladimir tells us that this area has had several occupants over the past fifty years. After World War II it was a marching ground for the military, which was housed in barracks located close by. In recent years a French-Canadian film crew used it to make a movie with a Yupik hero. The whale bones were dragged up onto the shore as part of the set; these withstand the rigors of time and maritime climate beside a less durable concentration of rusting metal cans.

On the way back to town, Yura points to a few solitary dairy cows, the remnants of a once substantial state-subsidized herd. There used to be a pig farm as well, but the pigs are long gone. Why hasn't private enterprise taken this over? It is simply not profitable to maintain meat and dairy herds here. This was part of the Soviet state's ambitious project to supply the far North. When state funding disappeared, these enterprises went under; they lacked the money for even the animals' winter fodder. Alexia remembers the same situation in central Siberia, where the local dairy farm was barely able to produce enough milk for the town's toddlers in 1994; by 1995 the farm disbanded, the remaining cows were eaten, and the babies were fed formula marketed by multinationals like Nestle.

Vladimir spots some ducks flying overhead. With great excitement, he has the driver pull over to the side and reaches for his rifle. We did not realize that he had brought it along, prepared for any eventuality. Vladimir unsheathes his rifle, takes aim through the hatch in the vehicle roof, and blasts away at the distant ducks. It's a long shot and he does not score a hit.

After a late lunch, Vladimir plays his videotape of Latvian filmmaker Andris Slapinsh's Siberian documentary completed after Slapinsh's heroic death in Riga in December 1991. We have seen Slapinsh's film, most recently at the American Museum of Natural History, but there it was a film of a distant place, the first contemporary footage of Siberia to reach the West. Laurel was introduced to this work, then incomplete, at a shaman conference in Seoul in 1991, little more than a week before the end of the Soviet Union. The Soviet delegation, themselves a remarkable presence at such a conference, had brought a copy with them, and the rest of us crowded into a small room around a video screen used by the hotel staff for their English-language training tapes. On tape, an old man went through the motions of a dance, a pale evocation of the magic that Bogoras evoked with his description of bird calls and animal cries echoing through the darkened tent.[4] Here in Providenia, the film takes on the aura of a home movie. Some of the participants are known to Vladimir, and several old people who address the camera are now dead.

Inevitably, talk turns to Slapinsh's death; he was shot by Soviet troops while filming the seizure of the Riga television transmission tower in Latvia. Fatally wounded, Slapinsh passed his camera to his assistant shouting, "The bastards have got me, keep filming!" The assistant cameraman and several others opposing the Soviet guards also died. In retrospect, some say that it was not necessary to defend the television tower against the force of Soviet arms; the Soviet system would have fallen even without this act of resistance. But, Alexia reflects, perhaps martyrs caused the system to collapse more quickly.

Later in the afternoon, Laurel curls up in front of the space heater to read and write, relishing the warmth and solitude. Alexia goes off to play tennis with Vladimir and Svetlana, a Saturday ritual for the Bychkovs. At the gym just down the road, four of their friends join them. They have all just recently learned to play, but they are much better at getting the ball over the net than Alexia, who has not played in fifteen years.

The tennis match reminds Alexia of how newcomers, the temporary residents of former Soviet towns like this one, struggle to create a separate space from a relentlessly cold and temporary environment. Many people seem to rely on structures that are familiar from a Soviet past for ordering their lives, even if these structures are mere shadows of that secure time. The Soviet infrastructure once extended from sea to sea (Black Sea to Arctic Ocean to Bering Sea to Caspian Sea), even to small villages in the North, imposing its own institutional regime. For today's newcomers, such remnants of Soviet infrastructure as the library, House of Culture, museum, or gym are still key to maintaining balance and meaning in their lives.

After the tennis match, it is again ladies' night at the banya. Once more we accompany Svetlana to enjoy the steam and the sensation of using an abundance of hot water to get thoroughly clean. This time Laurel knows the rituals of hanging clothing in the proper wooden cubbyholes, swatting with birch branches to encourage circulation, and then cooling down in the tank. Alexia decides to really steam in the sauna. A solid woman in Teva sandals asks her whether she goes to the banya in New York. Alexia tells her of one on the Lower East Side of Manhattan run by a Ukrainian man and his ex-wife. The ex-wife runs the banya on certain days exclusively for women, and the man on alternate days exclusively for men. Alexia can feel the chill of Providenia dissipating as she sits on the top of the three-tiered wooden shelves and roasts until she can no longer stand it.

In the changing room, we meet Saunders, the photographer, and Svetlana invites her to join us for tea at the Bychkovs' apartment. Drinking sweet tea after returning from the banya is part of the proper Russian way of doing things. We add jam to our cups and hear about Saunders's experiences in Novoe Chaplino, where she stayed in a house without windowpanes. Remembering the chilly wind that blew through the village, Laurel shivers, despite the warm tea and the aftereffects of her steaming bath. The possibility of food shortages during the coming winter is a very real concern. Now that people again depend heavily on sea mammal meat, the supply may not be adequate. "What does whale meat taste like?" someone asks. "It tastes like chicken," Saunders volunteers, and the three Americans giggle. Vladimir, a connoisseur of sea mammal meat, offers a disquisition on the relative merits of this cuisine; walrus meat is too oily, but the flippers and the ribs are tasty.

Sunday morning is bright and almost warm. Looking out the window at the harbor, we catch sight of a whale frolicking near the surface of the water. It spouts, then flips up its tail and dives beneath the water. It seems so close. We take this as a good omen. Perhaps we will sail out of Providenia today.

By the time we leave the apartment for the museum, the Hanseatic tour boat has docked. We meet the Tatar dentist on the path—he has letters for Alexia to pass on to his friends in Brooklyn—and together we watch the approach of the tourists. One phalanx—the group with an English-speaking guide—is approaching down the long street, all wearing identical red parkas, perhaps because, like primary school children, they will be easier to spot in this garb and less likely to get lost. We catch the lilt of the tour guide's speech. "British," says Alexia. "Australian," says Laurel. The dentist is surprised that we can make these distinctions.

In Vladimir's office, we meet up with Tom and Bob to negotiate with a representative of the tour boat. The tour would take us back to the United States for $700 US apiece; en route to Anchorage, the boat will stop at Little Diomede and St. Lawrence Island, weather permitting. Tom and Bob jump at the chance to leave; Bob's prescription medicine is running out. For us, however, this is a lot of money. We decide to take our chances on a flight out on Monday. Daizee, the Bering Air representative in Providenia, has told us that the three-day forecast is favorable and we could be on the first flight out on Monday morning, maybe by 10:30.

For the last time, we swap impressions with Tom and Bob. They went to the banya on Friday night with Yura, their first visit. "It was really something, all those naked men," says Tom with a chuckle. Bob is more equivocal: "Oh, it was all right." But six days in Providenia have had their effect on Tom. "You know," he says, "this is all so conspiratorial. Vladimir, he's the one who gives the orders around here. No one can do anything without his OK. They had to call Vladimir before they could change our money in the bank." It was hardly a matter of Vladimir's dark controlling presence; the bank needed someone to vouch for two strangers who could not communicate in Russian.

Groups from the tour boat are being guided through the museum. We want to observe the tourist routine and hasten upstairs where Yura is lecturing. He displays a walrus skull with a flourish. The tourists have been staggered to accommodate the crowd; some are gathered around Yura, while others sign the guest book and examine the contents of the souvenir stand—mostly beaded leather pendants and postcards. The makeshift souvenir stand is operated by the museum assistant, Alexandra. A can for donations has been placed beside the open guest book with an English-language sign inviting visitors to support the work of the museum. "It's gotten so commercial, even here," we overhear one of the tourists muttering. Later that night, over another farewell dinner, Vladimir will reveal that the souvenir stand garnered a much-needed $200 for the museum's coffers.

We follow the tourists to the House of Culture where tables of local handicrafts, most not very well made, have been set up in the foyer like a church bazaar. In the middle of these exhibits is another can for donations, with another English-language sign inviting visitors to help support the preservation of cultural heritage in the region.

Laurel buys a modern version of a Chukchi ball, in blue suede with a powder blue trim as ornate as a Fabergé Easter egg, for twenty dollars. The artisan, Lyubov Nikifronovna Damlinko, learned how to sew leather from her Yupik mother (her father is Ukrainian). Although "all the older women sew here," her mother's fur slippers had been very much in demand. Lyubov had herself worked for the dressmaking collective—once a ubiquitous Soviet institution—and when it closed down she joined the staff of the House of Culture as a resident artisan. Her leather handicrafts are sold at the museum and the House of Culture.

Nina, the director of the special education school, has set up a stall out on the steps. She is vending Soviet-era magazines, medals, postcards, and memorabilia flea market-style, which reminds us of the jolly jumble in her Alaska room. It makes us sad to see this intelligent and energetic woman bundled up in the cold wind, hawking the flotsam of another time.

Once the red-parka throng is settled in the spacious auditorium, the glamorous head of the House of Culture introduces the program. The emcee role is a frequent aspect of the job. The performance alternates a children's group, Raduga (rainbow), in folkloric Russian costumes with the Yupik group, Solnyshka (sun), from Novoe Chaplino. The children are predictably cute and competent. Their costumes are stage-classical Russian; they would not be out of place in *The Nutcracker*. Their repertoire includes a dance accompanied by "Kalinka," a standard Russian folk song. The direc-

Figure 12. Lyubov Nikifronovna Damlinko, a local artisan, displays a Yupik ball she has made following traditional techniques, but using blue suede. She has set out her wares in the House of Culture in Providenia in the hope of attracting customers from a passing tour boat. (Photo by Laurel Kendall)

tor makes much of this on the assumption that many in the audience are already familiar with this song. The audience is invited to "Take our Kalinka to your friends and family at home." The children's group is supported by the local Baptist church. Through the director's interpreted remarks we learn that the children "travel a lot and have many friends." It is not unusual for a local House of Culture to have such a troupe. Conservatory-trained dancers often end up teaching in such places. By an odd twist of

fortune, with the collapse of state support, the work of the once quintes-
sentially Soviet House of Culture is sustained by the Baptist church, with
some help from global tourism.

The adult Yupik group has been performing together for thirty-five years. In
the last half of the Soviet period, folk dance, song, and other elements of "traditional" culture were widely supported by the government. In the 1980s every
House of Culture in the North had at least one dance troupe, and sometimes
several, as well as space for crafting traditional leatherwork and beadwork.
These activities brought elders and young people together, preserving some
traditional cultural practices. The performance groups were often called upon
during Soviet holidays and when important guests visited the region. In the
post-Soviet period renowned groups perform for the opening ceremonies at international symposia on indigenous rights. Local groups continue to perform
for holidays and for visitors, only now their paychecks are no longer guaranteed by the local Department of Culture; in Providenia, they are almost entirely dependent on tour boats docking in town.

The costumes are a bit overdone, trimmed with huge, puffy bands of fur for
theatrical effect, but this does not get in the way of a spirited performance.
Yupik dance is primarily the work of the upper body, of forcefully graceful
movements of the arm and shoulders. We are initially pleased to see so many
old folks in the troupe—it makes for better transmission—but later Vladimir
will tell us that the younger Yupik do not have time to rehearse dances; hunting and fishing take precedence as matters of survival.

The dance groups alternate numbers. The Yupik ensemble has the finale,
when "according to the tradition of the group" members of the audience are
invited to dance with them on the stage. No one budges. "Last time half the
group was on stage," the director says as she tries to shake the audience out of
their passivity. A plump blond woman mounts the stage to applause. She is followed by others including one bespangled girl from the children's troupe.
Some of the tourists follow. Saunders joins them, casting a disappointed glance
in our direction when we hold back. The performance is hailed as an "Eskimo,
Russian, English, German, American" experience.

It is very chilly outside. We learn that because of a steep rise in portage fees,
the group is hastening their departure. Yura sees off Bob and Tom. Later, in
the museum, he tells us, "I miss my guys." He admits to having shed a tear
when they sailed. He also complains that the new portage fees are bad for business. Most immediately, the museum did not earn the additional $40 US that
would have come their way had they been able to present their standard slide
show briefing on Chukotka that is usually a part of the tour boat package.

Because the slide show is set up, they show it to us instead. Vladimir the photographer is particularly anxious that we see his work. The images are a pas-
tiche of border guards, scenery, Native people, the gym, the school ("students
have gone from here to study in the United States"), and ice floes that close the

Figure 13. The director of the school for special education in Providenia chats with Alexia Bloch. The director has set up a souvenir stall on the steps of the House of Culture. The architecture in the background is typical of Providenia; the Kaldun peeks from beyond the concrete blocks. (Photo by Laurel Kendall)

port from December to June. Yura delivers the narration in florid prose, with just a touch of sarcasm: "Arctic flowers—they raise their delicate heads where no other plants have managed to get a foothold. . . . From time immemorial Natives produce the timeless art of ivory carving. . . . As the sun sets over the harbor," and for a group of walruses sunning themselves on a rock, "a unique band of sunbathers enjoys the beach."

Back at Vladimir's apartment, Svetlana asks us if we want to go on a tundra picnic to celebrate the end of the tour boat season. It is so cold that we are not tempted. Svetlana tells us that because they are utterly immobilized at home during the long winter, they make the most of even chilly days. We wave them farewell and enjoy another afternoon of reading and writing beside the space heater.

By suppertime, we are fogged in and wonder if we will ever leave Providenia. We visit the Baptist café where we see Alexandra, the museum assistant, at another table. She tells us that a storm is predicted and that it might snow. It is raining fairly heavily when we leave the café and the fog has rolled halfway down the Kaldun's peak. It is close to ten in the evening when the Bychkovs return from the tundra picnic. Alexia joins them at the disco café and talks and dances until one in the morning.

On Monday morning, we race to the window. The Kaldun is covered with a sprinkling of snow but the mountain is clearly etched under a cloud cover. At nine in the morning, Vladimir says that we "might" be able to go; in fact, barring problems, we can plan on it.

We settle our telephone bills and offer Vladimir an additional sum of money for the extra days of food, heat, and hospitality. He has anticipated this, or perhaps the telepathy was Alexia's, for when we arrive at the museum, having agreed on an appropriate amount on the way over, he has the receipt all ready for us. Vladimir the photographer gives us beaded leather medallions, a "traditional Chukchi gift" from Vera. We give him a gauzy scarf for her, postcards for him, and colored markers for the children in her school. Vladimir asks us to join the staff sitting solemnly around the table in the common room. We observe a moment of silence, a small Russian ritual intended to wish us a safe journey. Alexia says that according to custom, this moment of silence is usually observed while the traveler sits on a packed suitcase. Instead of the expected tea, Vladimir produces a bottle of very good red wine, a thank-you gift from the tour boat staff. He has thoughtfully brought from home the new "Arizona" shot glasses that Bob and Tom gave him as a gift. We exchange several sentimental toasts before boarding the Department of Culture's painted vehicle for one last ride, first to collect our luggage and Svetlana, who comes along to see us off, and then to drive to the airport. As a final surreal note, we leave town to the music of Boney M singing, "Rah, rah, Rasputin, the lover of the Russian queen," with Svetlana happily bouncing in her seat in time to the music.

At the airport we meet Daizee, the Bering Air representative, an expansive blond in a denim jacket with "Alaska" spelled out in rhinestones across her back. She is in the process of packing up and moving back to Alaska for the winter, and she tells us how her Russian husband will join her soon in Alaska. She will be on our flight; her stepson, Sasha, assists her with her luggage. Vladimir and Svetlana go to the control tower to visit the crew, who serve them tea. This high-security area is closed to us, but Vladimir manages to convey two meat-filled pastries to us in the waiting room. He pulls out the two Arizona glasses from their special box in his briefcase and pours us some more wine, charming and resourceful to the final moment.

We go through customs, which is as excruciating as everyone warned us it would be. Why hasn't Alexia declared her laptop? She tells them, "I couldn't have bought it in Providenia, could I?" They ask if anyone has given us letters to carry, and when she denies it, they tug at the pack of mail Vladimir has given us at the last minute. "Academic papers for our colleagues in New York," she tells them and they desist.

On the flight we have a spectacular view, heightened in the clear cold. Onboard with us are Daizee, some of her worldly goods, and several Yupik Russian Orthodox missionaries on their way to a conference on St. Lawrence Island. As the Bering Air Piper Navaho plane lands on the beach in Gambell, a crowd of townspeople race toward it on three-wheel all-terrain vehicles. The U.S. customs man throws open the door and cold wind whips in. He makes a quick check of our passports, and a little girl and her mother peek into the plane from behind him. The woman tells Alexia that she is Yupik from the Siberian side and came to Gambell Island just three years ago to visit family. She met the Yupik customs official and ended up marrying him and remaining in this Yupik community.

Her husband the customs official gives the passengers a quick scan and says, "Welcome to the United States!" Perhaps he figures that with border control so strict on the other side, the work has been done for him. In just a little while, we are reunited with our luggage in Nome and on our way to Anchorage.

In planning our itinerary, we had seen the Alaska stopover as a respite, a chance to recharge our batteries, and we had planned on a day or two with the guilty air of playing hooky. As we had been stuck in Providenia and missed the weekly flight, we find ourselves with more time in Alaska than we had bargained for. Even so, it takes the better part of a week to change our air tickets and negotiate our Kamchatka visa through a Seattle travel agent. It will all work as long as we submit the requisite forms for overnight delivery on Tuesday, so that the paperwork can be completed by the travel agent on Wednesday, and the visas granted on Thursday, in time to be delivered to us at the airport by express mail before our Saturday departure on the weekly flight from Anchorage to Magadan. Miss a step and we will lose a week of travel. This delicate scenario is nearly derailed on Thursday morning when an anxious call from the travel agent informs us that the visa-chopping machine in the Russian consulate in Seattle is broken. Fortunately, it is running again by the end of the workday, and on Saturday morning, the visas are waiting for us at the Federal Express airport office, along with a package containing Alexia's boots and winter hat which, after her first encounter with Chukotka in August, she had decided that she needed after all. Between urgent telephone calls to travel agents and visits to express mail offices, we have spent our unanticipated holiday soaking in our friend Molly Lee's hot tub in Fairbanks, visiting museums, catching a glimpse of Mount Denali, combing the shelves of used book stores to replenish our stock of emergency reading material, and shopping for small gifts such as fishing lures.

During the Fairbanks respite, Alexia designed a Russian-language name card for Laurel, using the Cyrillic font on her laptop. A few days before our departure, as we were having the cards printed at a copy shop, we spotted a blond man in military fatigues making a color transparency of the map of Afghanistan. Was he on his way there? He described himself as a member of the Pacific Basin Crisis Reactionary Force—"if trouble breaks out, we deal with it." Flattered by our curiosity, he told us how he had won his various medals, described parachuting into Central America under fire, men dying all around him. He added that these experiences have left him with little sympathy for his daughter when she scrapes her knee and cries. The next day we learned of the U.S. bombings of Afghanistan and Sudan in retaliation for attacks against American embassy compounds in Kenya and Tanzania. Years later, as we recall this encounter, with American troops in Afghanistan and Iraq, we can imagine that this career soldier has been very busy of late. But on that sunny Saturday in 1998, we are in motion again, on the four-hour trip from Anchorage to Magadan.

Chapter 3

Magadan
The End of History

I made up my mind to attempt the tundra with pack-horses. . . . We were accompanied by a Cossack, an interpreter and two packers, who also served as guides. . . . Pack-horses as well as saddle-horses became mired and had to be extricated, so that we did not average more than ten miles a day. . . . In winter, nomadic Tungus visit this country, but in summer it is deserted by all human beings. This journey was the most difficult one that it was ever my fate to undertake. Bogs, mountain torrents, rocky passes and thick forests combined to hinder our progress. . . . A heavy rain which fell during the first few days of our journey soaked the loads of the pack-horses and caused the provisions to rot. . . . [When] we reached the upper course of the Korkhodon River . . . our horses were exhausted . . . and the cold was increasing day by day. . . . Haste was necessary if we were to reach Verkhne-Kolymsk before the closing of the river.

—Jochelson as cited by Boas in American Museum Journal, *October 1903*

The city of Magadan did not exist at the time of the Jesup North Pacific Expedition; it became a settlement only in 1929. During the Soviet period some of Stalin's most brutal prison camps were located around Magadan. Waldemar Jochelson's party conducted research in the area and in the Upper Kolyma, farther north, in 1901 and 1902. In August 1901, Jochelson and his wife, Dina, began the fifty-six-day journey from Kushka, at the mouth of the Gizhiga River on the Sea of Okhotsk, over the forbidding Stanovoi Mountains to the upper course of the Korkodon River. Fashioning a raft, Jochelson's party descended the river "made dangerous by numerous rapids and short bends, by the rocky banks and by jams of driftwood."[1] Although their guides had estimated that the journey would take only two days, they spent a full nine days on the raft with only three days' provisions; the rest had been left for the three Yakut guides who traveled overland with the horses and baggage. "For the last six days we had to be satisfied with forty-five pounds of flour, or an allowance of two cups a day for every person and a little tea without sugar."[2] After four days in Yukaghir settlements on the Korkodon, and now well supplied with fish, they continued down the Korkodon and Kolyma rivers by boat. The river

Figure 14. A Yukaghir woman in front of her tent. The composition of this photograph may have been inspired by images of Native Americans. Jochelson worked with the Yukaghir during his exile and persuaded Boas to allow him to return for further research during the Jesup Expedition. In the winter of 1901–1902 he found Yukaghir encampments suffering from a severe famine. (AMNH Library 1682)

froze up at the end of their journey, forcing them to leave the now useless boat and continue on foot for two more days, eventually reaching Verkhne-Kolymsk, near a tributary of the Kolyma, on October 9. The guides who had been left with the horses arrived two months later.

Jochelson was already forty-six years old when he made this trek to the Upper Kolyma. Like his younger friend and colleague, Waldemar Borgoras, he had been an ardent supporter of the underground movement People's Will. He worked at the movement's printing house while studying social science and economics at the University of Bern. Trying to enter Russia in 1885, he was arrested at the border. After two years in solitary confinement, he was exiled to the Russian Far East where, over ten years of exile, he became an expert on the Yukaghir, a small population of reindeer herders. Anxious to continue his research, Jochelson persuaded Boas to include the Yukaghir within the scope of the expedition, but when he returned to the Yukaghir he found them in the middle of a famine: "I assisted them as far as I could, and sent a messenger to Sredne-Kolymsk to request the assistance of the government. In the spring of 1902 the inhabitants of three Yukaghir tents on the Omolon were found starved to death. Even in Sredne-Kolymsk the fishing had been a complete failure, and the people were compelled to kill their dog teams because they could not feed them."[3] It was a difficult trip in every respect for, as Boas later related: "Mr. Jochelson does not state in this report that on his whole journey overland . . . certain Russian Officials, following a secret order issued by the Minister of the Interior, did all they could to hinder the progress of the expedition and to thwart its success."[4]

Although Magadan is a major city with a population of about 110,000, the airport seems to be in the middle of nowhere, surrounded by low-lying mountains of a purplish hue and very young trees beginning to turn color in the fading light of an August afternoon. This is the Kolyma region, the grim location of some of the Soviet Union's most notorious prison camps. Because an American friend who is working in Magadan is waiting for us on the other side of the immigration barrier, we try to position ourselves advantageously in the shuttle bus to the terminal. We miscalculate and end up last in a slow-moving line of fifteen people. The woman at the head of the line is on some sort of Rotary Club exchange and does not have an exit date on her visa. This precipitates great confusion, compounded by her rudimentary Russian and the immigration official's lack of English. Seeing the situation deteriorate, Alexia volunteers to interpret, and the local officials agree to let the woman through since she promises to take care of the paperwork immediately. In any case, the next plane she could take back to Anchorage is not for several days. The line inches forward.

An airport official emerges from the back room and asks loudly in Russian, "Is there someone here who is going fishing? The helicopter is here." A burly American man with copious fishing gear is hustled to the head of the line and out to the waiting helicopter. The rest of the people in line carry laptops. They are most likely associated with the Omolon Gold Consortium, a joint venture mining company with significant investment from Canada. "Omolon" takes its name from the Omolon River, where Jochelson had found the Yukaghir camps decimated by famine in 1902.

In the mid-1990s Omolon established a scholarship as part of the provisions granting it rights to mineral resources near Gizhiga, a town northeast of present-day Magadan, where Jochelson spent time during the Jesup Expedition. Back in New York, several months after our trip, we will meet Andrey Khalkachan, from Gizhiga, who is the first recipient of the Omolon scholarship. Khalkachan is an Even, a descendent of the reindeer-herding "Tungus" and "Lamut" of Jochelson's accouts. At the American Museum of Natural History, he will study the Even artifacts collected during the Jesup Expedition. While Even were encouraged to attend university for nearly three generations in the Soviet period, Andrey is the first Even student to attend the University of Alaska.

On the other side of the barrier at the Magadan airport passport control we meet our friend from New York and are soon speeding to town in a commodious black Land Rover. Along the road, we pass shabbily dressed people lined up in groups of three or four selling buckets of some sort of berries. Solid, scarf-bundled, weather-worn women on the shoulder of the paved highway watch the cars careening past. Alexia registers the strangeness of riding in this extravagant vehicle. When we stop at traffic lights people approach and peer in. Our friend laments at one point, "People here don't have enough money to buy bread and they don't have any space to think about anything else."

Talk turns to the forest fires raging in the region. They are an annual phenomenon, but this year there is no money for containment and the smell of smoke has hung in the city for days. We pass a monument to the victims of the prison camps. Exact numbers are still contested, but it is generally agreed that more than one million people suffered in the labor camps that were established beginning in 1931 in and around Magadan. In the early 1930s more than 130,000 people were imprisoned, and by 1938 more than 300,000 people were sentenced to the hard labor of mining gold and uranium. They were sent by the trainload from European Russia to Vladivostok or nearby stations, then sent north by boat through the Sea of Japan and into the Sea of Okhotsk to disembark in Magadan. Here, there was nowhere to run to and it took all of a prisoner's strength and endurance to survive the brutal conditions in the gold mining camps and the harsh winters of the Kolyma. Thousands died of cold, hunger, and disease. Thousands more died of despair. As Jochelson's field trip evidenced, the Kolyma exacted a toll from disease and starvation even on those who knew the tundra as a way of life. Today the camps are closed and deserted, although there is talk of opening them as tourist sites.

In Magadan today, many government functions have been curtailed as federal funding has disappeared with the breakup of the Soviet Union. As elsewhere in southern Siberia, Chinese traders make their way to Magadan to sell t-shirts, jeans, and plastic housewares, but the local population is leaving in great numbers. Magadan can no longer employ them or guarantee a future for their children; there is little left to sustain the economy of a city founded on prison labor. Although some prison camps reportedly continued to operate in the Soviet Union into the 1980s, these most dreaded labor camps in Magadan closed after Stalin's death in 1953. The Soviet government continued to subsidize Magadan's local economy, particularly the mines. The present market conditions, however, require that these operations show a profit in order to support their employees; government funds are no longer forthcoming. The town's population has shrunk by more than one-third since the early 1990s.

We stow our bags in our friend's apartment and head to the museum. The building is a massive concrete structure with sleek lines and few windows; we learn that it was built just five years earlier under the direction of the Magadan mayor. We have heard a great deal about the Magadan museum, placed high on the hierarchical chain of museums in the Russian Far East. We have an official appointment here tomorrow, but the galleries will be closed, since it will be Monday. Only half an hour remains before the Sunday afternoon closing and the ticket seller is reluctant to let us in for such a short time. At this hour on a Sunday, New York museums would be at maximum capacity, but this museum is empty and the staff wants to head home. We argue that we have come from halfway around the world and that half an hour is far better than nothing. The ticket seller capitulates, sells us tickets for five rubles each (a little less than $1 US), and we race for the ethnology exhibits. We examine cases of Yupik, Chukchi, and Koryak material, and find a copy of Jochelson's photograph of the interior of a Koryak house on the wall, a familiar face in a strange place.

Upstairs an exhibit hall is devoted to the Kolyma camps. Tomorrow, some of the museum curators will tell us how in the first flush of Perestroika in the late 1980s, people began to speak openly about the camps. The researchers went out to the sites and through salvage archaeology collected the physical evidence of prison camp experience—the restraints, the barbed wire, the pick-axes. They photocopied and displayed materials from the KGB archive that had been off-limits previously. They collected newspaper clippings, photographs, and personal documents such as conviction notices, and interviewed survivors. From the information in the archive, they were able to trace prison camp survivors who had returned to European Russia and collect their stories. In the dramatic exhibit that resulted, a looming black watchtower and tangles of barbed-wire fence dominate the room. The victims' stories are witnessed in several rows of carefully arranged cases. This exhibit opened in 1992 and was updated as new information became available. The painstakingly researched presentation effectively evokes the individual identities of those who lived and tragically died in the Magadan camps. We barely notice the presence of museum cases that might otherwise seem to present the material in an overly sanitized format. The women in charge of looking after the exhibits and visitors have graciously stretched the official thirty minutes until closing to nearly forty-five minutes.

The next morning, we go out early to change money before our eleven o'clock appointment at the museum. It is a sunny day and many of the Art Deco-style buildings in the downtown district are being restored and painted in pleasant pastel colors in anticipation of the city's sixtieth birthday. The range of Soviet architecture surprises Laurel, who expected gray, lumpy, and uninspired structures. It is difficult to reconcile this potentially pretty city with the brutal system of convict labor that built it. In fact, people in Magadan compare their city to St. Petersburg, drawing parallels between the climate (fog and cold) and the architecture. Indeed, the attractive buildings in the city center were designed by architects from St. Petersburg who ended up in the gulag. Ambitious flowerbeds line the major boulevards untended, full of weeds and late-blooming wildflowers, but on a sunny day, the effect is meadowlike and not unpleasant. The only tended flowerbed is in front of the lovingly restored tourist hotel where representatives of the mining company stay. The bank and

Figure 15. Magadan street scene. Older buildings were constructed in an ornate "Leningrad" style by architects from St. Petersburg (then Leningrad) who ended up in the gulag. The sign on the boutique reads "Adam and Eve." (Photo by Alexia Bloch)

some of the buildings in the city center have added elaborate iron grillwork to their Art Deco-style façades. Laurel remarks that there is a resemblance to Prague, while Alexia tells her not to get carried away.

On the way to the bank along Lenin Boulevard, we catch sight of a young man dressed in a sleek black leather coat and dark jeans. Something about him reminds Alexia of a Soviet commissar of the 1920s. When she gets closer she sees a pin bearing a hammer and sickle outlined in red on his lapel. We have been told about a growing right-wing movement in Magadan and apparently there is also an active young communist group here.

In the bank we wait for nearly two hours behind an Australian businessman and his gaggle of local supporters who are trying to convince the bank that it is possible to pull $3,000 US from his account in the British Midland Bank. Once we get to the window, our transaction is easy. As of last week, the ruble is falling again, from six to $1 US when we arrived in Providenia to eight today. We don't pay much attention, thinking a little fluctuation is to be expected, but soon the plummeting rate will become an obsession for everyone, including two travelers dependent on currency exchange.

The delay at the bank puts us behind schedule. We dash to the museum and are warmly received by the scientific secretary, Tatyana Alexandrovna Chemshit, a slim redhead in a chic denim jumper. She invites us to meet her colleagues. We sit in a small multipurpose room and address the museum staff who are not currently on vacation—about ten people—and explain our purpose. The meeting begins on a stiff note. We are facing the staff with a large table between us, as if we are prepared to lecture. We are uncomfortable, and their stoic faces suggest that they feel obligated to be present. What good is the computerized database we are discussing when the museum does not yet have computers? Their problems are more immediate. The staff here has not been paid for five months.

Their museum opened in 1934, and the historical horizon of its exhibits extends back only to the late 1920s and 1930s, when Russians settled in the area, first to exploit the mines and then to run the expanding prison camps. The Magadan museum was established as the regional keystone for Chukotka; museums in Anadyr, Gizhiga, and other smaller towns looked to Magadan for training, traveling exhibits, and financial support. Magadan also collaborated with the local museums for archaeological and ethnological expeditions. In turn, Magadan looked to the next museum along the ladder, in Khabarovsk. The breakup of the Soviet Union in December 1991 and increased regional autonomy severed the familial relationship with the smaller local museums. The government no longer subsidizes travel to these places for advice and staff training, and the other museums are no longer able to bring local personnel to Magadan for training workshops. This loss of mobility is a constant theme in our conversations with museum personnel throughout the Russian Far East. A highly institutionalized system of professional assistance and support, sustained in part by fuel subsidies for air travel over vast distances, is now only partially maintained through personal contacts begun in better times. As the staff explains this to us, a deep voice from the back row offers the wry comment, "We've opened the national borders and closed the internal borders."

Questioned about our structure and our sources of financial support, we explain about government grants, private foundations, and private contributions. They tell us, "Our rich people are not interested in museums." We mention some private foundations that might help them, and pens flash across notebooks. One bright-eyed young woman listens with particular attention and it is she who provides a translation for "Office of Development," a new concept. We describe our volunteer program and start talking about research and how exhibit projects are developed in our respective institutions, a dry discussion of structures and procedures, when suddenly a dam breaks.

One older woman remarks hotly, "It used to be that way for us. We had students. We had pensioners. Now everyone is too busy trying to make a living." Another woman wipes away a tear as she voices exasperation that museum work has lost its foundational significance in a post-Soviet era. Up until the winter of 1991 with the fall of the Soviet Union, museums across the country had a solid master narrative for their exhibits, a story of the progressive march of socialism. Now, everything is up for grabs. The old exhibits sliced history into a thoroughly predictable periodization, from the pre-Revolutionary era to the Revolution to Soviet times. Now that story is discredited, no longer a "valid direction," but what is to take its place? They used to represent the Civil War following on the heels of the Revolution in a heroic, celebratory way, but now they have no interpretative frame. Most of the research staff are historians specializing in the history of Magadan since its founding; they have a rich archive of materials and interview data, but they are at a loss as to how to present it. For example, their excellent historical collection of material from the Komsomol includes an assortment of pins and scarves spanning several decades, but they have no enthusiasm to tell this story. Such an exhibit was well received in Berlin in the mid-1990s, but in Magadan the experience is still too close for an ironic recontextualization. Or perhaps, as Alexia later reflects, in places like Magadan, the breakup of the Soviet Union has led to such extreme poverty and social breakdown that it is difficult for museums to create exhibits with critical distance on the recent Soviet period, which was an economically stable, plentiful, and hopeful time for many, including museum professionals like themselves.

In the early days of Perestroika, museum staff enthusiastically embraced a new story, a critical antihistory that had prompted them to research and represent the prison camps—"the former camps," one researcher is corrected by a colleague. The wry voice from the back row adds, "All the Kolyma is a camp now." Restrained laughter. They tell us that the heady moment when it was possible to produce this exhibit passed into the "unstable conditions" of the present. The future is opaque. Their expert knowledge of the Kolyma's past makes them acutely aware of the danger of too hastily adopting a moral reading of history that is also necessarily a political line. But they seem to be insisting that there is no line, no narrative of the past that would make sense of their chaotic present, no overarching judgment. They have, quite literally, experienced the death of history as they knew it. Where does that leave them as museum professionals? They have attempted to fill the void with pleasant displays of attractive objects, gems and intricately carved ivory in sparkling showcases to draw in the public whose admission fees they now need to sustain their endeavors.

Hard times have also curtailed their research and collecting. One of the researchers smiles sadly when she shows us the photographs of the old truck that used to transport them on research expeditions. Now they cannot afford the fuel. These are serious museum professionals, people who were trained as experts in a comprehensive and well-subsidized national museum system that no longer exists. They are struggling to find new ways to maintain their enterprise. For the immediate future, they tell us, they will focus on the city itself, interviewing longtime residents and prison camp survivors before they die out. They are also sensitive to contemporary developments and are making an effort to collect the new memorabilia of elections. The parameters of this task are uncertain. In the past their collecting was spelled out in a precise protocol with guidelines decreed from above. Now they are on their own.

We have covered a great deal of ground and it is already 2:30 when we plug in Alexia's laptop to demonstrate the CD of the Siberian collections of the American Museum of Natural History in New York. Half a dozen women stay with us, and they are intensely interested. One woman is so intrigued by the patterns on the Koryak aprons illustrated on the CD that she spontaneously pulls out a box from storage so we can look through their examples. And it turns out that there are ways for the staff to access the electronically stored material. The scientific secretary can view our CD at home on her computer, and the library next door to the museum has one. The lack of computers inside the museum is not an insurmountable problem after all.

Although the museum is closed to the public today, we are given a quick tour of the exhibits that we did not see the previous day. The museum staff realized that in the new era, attendance by school groups was dropping off. The exhibits simply did not appeal to children, their primary constituency. In response, they created a new education department and developed special programs for children. With support from the city, they created a luminous biological hall, incorporating taxidermized beasts from the old museum. This was in the early 1990s, when there were still funds for such projects. A menacing-looking wolf and bear at the center of the biological exhibit are the children's favorites.

A new exhibit presents the history of gold mining in the region, beginning with early prospecting and ending with a grinning portrait of the governor of the region clasping a golden brick in his hands, juxtaposed to a sepia portrait of some scraggly geologists from long ago. The young man who leads us through the exhibit is a history student and is full of amusing anecdotes, but there is no grand narrative. We spend some time learning about two early geologists—a husband-and-wife team with movie-star good looks—who were accused, imprisoned, and cleared. Because of this history they left the area in 1940 for Leningrad. She starved during the German siege of the city and he died on the Western front. "Everyone likes to hear that story," our guide chuckled. In this exhibit, there is almost no mention of convict labor in the mines. That story is told upstairs in the hall devoted to the camps.

We examine a room full of ivories carved in the workshops of Uelen, the Chukchi village we heard about when we were in Providenia and will hear of again in Anadyr and Petropavlovsk. Since the 1950s, the carvers have used electric tools, similar to a dentist's drill, to produce extremely intricate pieces. Deer with complex intertwinings of antlers are a favorite theme, bric-a-brac that seems destined for display on some heavy, ornate piece of Victorian furniture. Under the current ban on walrus hunting, some carvers have turned to whale bone, which, unlike walrus ivory, can be exported to the United States. This is a softer medium, far easier to work, but it will not take intricate detail. These new carvings are bulky and abstract, a refreshing contrast to the sometimes overworked ivory.

We take a quick look at the variety of regional minerals and gems in a small but handsome display and return to the ethnology hall with a couple of experts to look at more Koryak aprons. It is now late afternoon. We have not eaten since breakfast and are exhausted from the flood of information and dialogue. Alexia has been translating nonstop. There is warmth in our farewells but we are also eager to move on.

We walk through sunlit streets past vendors of fish, berries, and large crimson radishes to Ariran, the town's Korean restaurant where the Russian waitress immediately disabuses Laurel of the possibility of speaking Korean. The restaurant is a mélange of tacky ethnic restaurant décor. Laurel associates the patterned plastic beaded curtains with Chinese restaurants in Seoul circa 1970. On the ceiling, the plastic grapes could have come from a Greek taverna in New York. The decorations include a Japanese doll in a glass cube and some macrame baskets with pink artificial flowers. This last element would be found in a South Korean tearoom, but not a restaurant. We order soup and several spicy side dishes, but the steamed rice that usually forms the centerpiece of a Korean meal is not available. The soup has sliced purple beets on top, a Russian touch, and the spicing is generally unfamiliar. We have marinated fiddlehead ferns (*paporotnik*), a signature dish of Koreans in the Russian Far East. Laurel feels as if she is and yet is not eating Korean food in a Korean restaurant.

After this early dinner we walk with our friend to a store on the other side of town that is rumored to have received an order of name-brand American toilet tissue. It has already sold out, but the proprietress says that more will be available tomorrow. Alexia catches sight of ice cream being sold in familiar plastic tubs, instead of in the more common ice cream packaging found in Russia with individual portions packed into what look like dixie cups made of grey construction paper. This ice cream is the product of a Russian-American joint venture. At a kiosk outside the store she also spots a brightly illustrated children's book based on a poem by the renowned Soviet-era children's writer and translator Samuil Marshak, and buys it for a friend's new twins back in New York. We walk to the broad harbor, again more picturesque than its history. Some wooden cottages just up from the shore have small gardens. Alexia observes that villages often appear just beyond the core of Siberian cities. We pass a new block of high-rise apartments where a man in a stylish sport coat is lugging a briefcase home. Some children are wobbling along on still-to-be-mastered in-line skates. This street seems far removed from the wooden cottages just over the hill, indeed, from everything else we have seen in Magadan.

Back in our friend's apartment, we have tea and some of the surprisingly creamy ice cream. The travel agent arrives with our tickets for tomorrow's flight to Anadyr. She is a bubbling, enthusiastic woman who equips us with postcards and luggage decals that say "Magadan, USSR" from some bygone overstock. Alexia is relieved that the arrangements made with Red Star Travel have worked out. Somehow, her credit card payment to the travel agent in Seattle has magically resulted in these tickets materializing in Magadan, and even being delivered to our door. At $650 US each this is the most expensive leg of our travel within Russia. Arranging them in advance seems worthwhile in order to keep to our tight schedule.

The next morning, a taxi comes to our door on schedule, just before dawn. We are uneasy during the trip to the airport. The taxi is a recycle from Japan with the wheel on the right-hand side, giving the driver only limited visibility when passing cars and trucks on the narrow, foggy roads. On the way in, our friend had told us that these taxis were the source of much roadside mayhem, but we arrive safely at the airport.

We are too early to check in for our flight to Anadyr, so we stop for tea at a kiosk. The proprietress wears her ample russet hair bound up in a knot on the top of her head. With her vintage coiffure, framed by the dark wood and mirrored backdrop of the concession stand, she could be one of Toulouse-Lautrec's Moulin Rouge models come to life. Laurel takes a photograph. The woman asks for a copy, provides an address, and chats with us. She tells us that she is a Christian and, in the same breath, adds that she spent a month this summer attending a Seventh-day Adventist camp in Magadan. Service with a smile is not typical of airport concessions in the Russian Federation, but Alexia has met many newly proselytized Christians during her time in Siberia, and they tend to be especially affable.

In line for the flight, Alexia finds herself next to another jolly Christian woman in a gray wool coat who claims affinity for both the Baptists and Seventh-day Adventists. The woman strikes up the conversation with the same warm inquiry that bubbled from the Toulouse-Lautrec woman, "Are you Americans?" This conversation will be sustained throughout the flight. The woman asks Alexia to pass on a letter to an acquaintance in Anadyr; a Chukchi man will collect the envelope from our hotel. Alexia suspects that this is church business and agrees to help her out, but does not ask any questions. She recalls the delicate relationship between authorities in the Evenk Region in central Siberia and the new Baptist church there. The security bureau in town continually harassed the church members and, as one woman claimed, monitored their correspondence with other Baptist groups in Russia. Alexia decides that it is best if she remains uninformed about the exact nature of the letter she has agreed to carry.

We hold our breath as we check our bags. Fees for overweight luggage can be exorbitant. We have stuffed our heaviest gear, all our emergency reading material and the museum catalogs we intend to give as gifts, into our carry-on luggage. We leave the bulging bags quietly out of sight as we approach the counter, and we are not alone in this. "No fee," we are told and we heave a sigh of relief. In fact, the "check-in" requires three stages, with separate sets of female airport personnel; first we check in with our tickets, then we weigh and check our bags, and last we go through the passport control. At each stage we are asked if we have the required permission of the Chukotka administration, and each time Alexia reassures them that yes, we have obtained this written permission.

Heading nearly one thousand miles to the northeast to Anadyr, we fly over a mountainous terrain. Laurel spots what she thinks is a long, dry riverbed, but Alexia tells her that she is looking at a solid expanse of ice. The mountain landscape gives way to dry brown steppe with lakes of melted snow and a few patches of green. We fly along the coast with the Bering Sea off to the right side of the plane. We can see the waves crashing against the already frozen banks. It is only the twenty-fifth of August.

En route Alexia finds herself drawn into a lengthy conversation with the church woman, Lyubov, who stood in line with us. Lyubov was born in Norilsk, a major industrial city located above the Arctic Circle in central Siberia. When she was a teenager, her family moved briefly to the Altai and then to a village outside of Anadyr, where her father continued his meteorological research. She returned to the village after completing her studies in music in the western Siberian city of Novosibirsk and has lived there ever since.

Lyubov enthusiastically describes the missionaries' popularity in the region. In brief, people find solace in the church. Lyubov is well aware that there are

several types of Christians. She claims that people think of the Russian Orthodox Church as a "state" or government organization. She describes the
Charismatic believers (*kharismaty*) as people who sing and dance a lot, and the
"Fifty Year" people (*piatidesiatlety*), or Seventh-day Adventists, as more subdued
in their worship. She sees the Baptists as especially strict in their daily practices—strictures against drinking, dancing, and watching television—when
compared with the Russian Orthodox believers.

Lyubov recounts how her daughter was the first in the family to convert to
Christianity. She had been studying in Magadan to become a choir director
and was invited by a friend to attend a Seventh-day Adventist church. As
Lyubov describes it, her daughter joined the church because she was impressed
by all the good will between people in the congregation and by their willingness to share. At first when she told her mother and three siblings about the
church during her periodic vacation visits to the village, the family paid little
attention to what she had to say. Eventually, however, when a young preacher
moved to the village and won a large local following, the rest of Lyubov's family got involved. Although Lyubov had baptized her daughters in the Russian
Orthodox church in the late 1980s when, in her words, "It was stylish to get
baptized," they did not attend church then. Like many people in the post-
World War II generation, Lyubov herself had been baptized as a child. At the
time, her parents did not believe in Christianity, but they thought it was a
"good idea" to have their daughter baptized. Like many Russians in that period, Lyubov's parents probably had strong ties to the ritual practices of their
childhood. Even in the 1940s through 1980s when religious beliefs were the
subject of official scorn, an indication of a "backward" mentality, many people were quietly baptized by parents who still followed these centuries-old rites
of passage. Alexia has met several.

Alexia asks Lyubov if there is any resistance on the part of local authorities
to the widespread conversions today. Vladimir's mention of the two church
fires in Providenia is fresh in her mind. Lyubov does not claim to see any evidence of opposition, but maybe she prefers to avoid making such statements
to outsiders she has just met in an airplane line. Then she revises her statement, acknowledging that in her town "the devil" vandalized some church
property by breaking some windows, relaying this information as if it were a
comment on the weather.

Missionaries are an increasingly common feature of daily life here in the
Russian Far East. Lyubov observes that the majority of the ministers are from
Ukraine, possibly because Ukrainians preserved their connection with Christianity whereas Russians have lost their faith and their traditions. Alexia asks
Lyubov if this new church influence has any impact on women's roles. During
the Soviet period women came to assume they would be breadwinners and
have full-time employment, and the official ideology sought to make them
equal to men in every way, hardly the same philosophy espoused by contem-

porary Baptists and Seventh-day Adventists. Lyubov reflects on the secondary role women play in these movements. Women are never priests or ministers. They sometimes travel with their husbands on church business, but they never read sermons and don't seem to play a primary role in her church. Then Lyubov reels off a list of American evangelists like Jimmy Swaggart and Jerry Falwell, and notes that while the evangelists from the United States are all men, sometimes those from Germany or Sweden are women.

Our conversation turns to the desertion of villages. Lyubov describes the villages around Magadan as ghost towns: "You drive along the highway and house after house is empty, deserted." People have departed for the "mainland" (*materik*), or central Russia, and they have also made their way to America. Now that the social services are gone and schools and clinics have closed, there is no reason to stay in villages; only religion sustains the few people who remain. As we have seen in Providenia, religion also holds the possibility of mobility. Lyubov's own daughter has traveled to Chicago as part of a choir directors' conference.

The plane touches down in Markovo to let off a few passengers and make a pit stop. Markovo is a familiar provenance in the AMNH catalog. Jochelson and his wife camped here, Bogoras and Axelrod passed through, and Buxton, the biologist associated with the expedition, also worked here. Bogoras described the local residents as "Russianized Natives." In Bogoras's time, Markovo had been the site of a summer trade fair and during the measles epidemic of 1900, was a major site of contagion as Yupik and Chukchi traders carried the infection home to their villages.

We hope to get back to Markovo after our stay in Anadyr, but we will have to go by helicopter, the regular plane runs only once a week and it is out of sync with the weekly flight to Khabarovsk. For now, all we see of Markovo is a tiny wooden airport and some vintage planes surrounded by fields of tall grass. We swat an abundance of flies and use a very clean outhouse. Laurel offers packaged hand wipes to Alexia and to Lyubov who says, extrapolating from her prior experience with Americans, "You people wash your hands after everything!"

We land in Anadyr, the capital of Chukotka, the modern Soviet town that has absorbed the old Mariinsky Post we know from another Bogoras encampment. The border guard comes out to the plane and takes our passports, telling us to claim them from an office on the third floor of the airport. We are a curiosity on the Anadyr flight, and Cold War security procedures linger on here, as in Providenia. Alexia has not been subjected to these checks in her central Siberian travels. Lyubov, in a much-appreciated act of Christian charity, offers to watch our heavy bags while we climb the three flights of stairs to the border guard office.

Laurel recognizes the words for the third floor (*treti etazh*), obviously derived from the French. The two familiar-sounding words are surprisingly reassuring

Figure 16. The town of Markovo in 1900 or 1901, a small settlement grouped around a Russian Orthodox church. At the time of the Jesup Expedition, Markovo was the easternmost town in the Russian Empire. Bogoras would describe the lives of the "Russianized natives" living in and around Markovo. (AMNH Library 1327)

amid all the Russian she does not understand in a cold, gray foreign airport where she is bereft of her passport. The security authorities keep us waiting in the corridor for what seems an unnecessarily long time, nearly an hour. When they tell us to wait, their tone is not rude, although Alexia says that in such situations, it can be. The man who returns our passports even smiles when he tells us that our passports have been photocopied; we have not had to produce our letter of invitation from Alexander Nazarov, the governor of Chukotka. Of course, we will still have to register with the local security bureau in Anadyr.

Our wait on the third floor has caused us to miss the four o'clock bus to the ferry that will take us across the Anadyr Estuary. Luckily, Lyubov has our interests at heart. She has been talking to a woman who wears a remarkable long sweeping leather coat with a large fur-lined hood, something that Vivien Leigh might have worn in some 1940s costume drama. Her hairstyle and makeup also recall the late actress, had she lived to the far side of middle age. The woman with the cape has arranged for a taxi to town and asks us to join her. We readily agree since we would otherwise be stuck there for another two hours and then have to navigate the ferry and transportation on the other side on our own. We bid warm farewells to our Christian friend, who goes off to catch her flight to her village.

Our new traveling companion is a judge and the daughter of a judge. She has come to the airport to meet her son, who is studying law in Moscow. When the young man arrives we take off in the large black van of Sergey, a ferocious-looking individual with wild hair and bulging eyes. He and the judge seem very well acquainted. He expresses joking incredulity that she is still collecting hardship pay, three times the usual salary, as compensation for working in the North. In many quarters, "northern pay" has been discontinued and, of course, many civil servants have not seen any earnings for several months. She answers breezily, "They still want to keep the judges happy," then adds that she is counting on this income to help her grandchildren. Sergey, the fierce entrepreneur, says that since he is providing such an important service, he should get triple pay as well. In fact, he charges us each 100 rubles rather than the posted rate of 80, but his is no ordinary vehicle. The van interior resembles the decor of a disco, with white squares of linoleum on the floor of the van and black padding on the walls. Sergey has clearly invested dearly in his taxi service.

The judge is originally from Ukraine but has lived in a small village near Anadyr for the last thirty-two years, traveling all over the region for her work. Once she was riding on one of the ice barges that skate along the frozen surface of rivers and harbors when the ice broke. The passengers all had to climb through to the roof and would have frozen to death in or out of the icy water if another ice barge had not fortuitously appeared. Thoughts of near drowning are very much with us as Sergey drives his large van onto a small and seemingly insubstantial barge. The van barely fits. The barge bounces us across the dark, roiling waters of the Anadyr Estuary that flows between the airport and the town itself. Waves splash high outside the windows of the pitching van. The crossing seems to take forever and reminds Laurel of an ill-advised ride on the lower deck of a Hong Kong ferryboat just before a typhoon.

Eventually, the city of Anadyr rises up on the far shore, a series of large concrete buildings painted in pastel shades and decorated with patterned bands of color. We will later learn that only the buildings visible along the main thoroughfares received this giant Easter egg treatment, in anticipation of some official visit. One of these decorated rectangles is our hotel.

Chapter 4

Anadyr
Tundra Town in Pastel

June 8, 1900, Vladivostok
Mr. Bogoras and his wife left for Anadyr on June 1. . . . The last stop of the ship
"Baikal" on which Mr. Bogoras is sailing, is at the mouth of the Anadyr River
[Mariinsky Post]. His further itinerary couldn't be determined from here, it will
depend on local conditions. . . . All members of the expedition are well, send their
regards and ask to be remembered to President Jesup. My wife arrived here three
days ago.

—*Jochelson to Boas*

We left Vladivostok June 14, 1900 for [Mariinsky] Post at the Mouth of the
Anadyr River, taking the only regular means of conveyance, the Russian mail
steamer, which visits the place but once a year. . . . We arrived there after five
weeks' journey. . . . The Native village is the southernmost settlement of the
maritime Chukchi.

—*Bogoras, cited in Boas,* American Museum Journal, *1903*

When Bogoras and his party arrived in Mariinsky Post in 1900, it was considered the most remote outpost of the Russian Empire, no more than a Chukchi village and the barracks of a small Cossack detachment. Bogoras had anticipated that the annual fair held in Mariinsky Post would be an opportunity to measure a large sample of Chukchi and to purchase objects for the museum, but that summer, an epidemic of measles swept through the Pacific coast of the Chukotka Peninsula, resulting in great loss of life. No Chukchi or Yupik trader from the northern villages ventured south to the fair. Bogoras spent the summer visiting the summer camps of reindeer Chukchi that were close to the shore, putting his camera and calipers to good use.

In October he left Mariinsky Post, traveling by dogsled over the frozen ground to northern Kamchatka. "The winter was still more unfavorable for us than the summer." He wrote, "I can say it was quite extreme such as arrives once in 50 years only."[1] The freeze that set in after the October rains covered the tundra with a sheet of ice and deep snow. Many reindeer starved; their corpses were strewn along the track when Bogoras returned in April. Famine followed in the wake of this disaster.

Through this harsh winter Bogoras's wife, Sofia, remained on the Anadyr River, traveling between Markovo and Mariinsky Post collecting and documenting most of the 2,192 objects from this area that are now in the collection of the American Museum of Natural History. We see Sofia in an expedition photograph surveying the fruits of her labor, a yard full of crates awaiting shipment from Mariinsky Post.

The Soviet era transformed the landscape of Sofia's day, and it is a Chukchi intellectual and museum director who will proudly guide us through collections made in Chukotka, lamenting the objects that were shipped far away in those crates that Sofia industriously filled. Natalya Pavlovna Otke, director of the local museum and our sponsor for our week in Anadyr, is waiting for us in the hotel lobby, resplendent in a coat of artificial leopard skin. She is part Chukchi, part Yupik, and a petite bundle of energy and direction. She had wanted us to wait for her at the airport, as she is responsible for us and seemed unwilling to risk whatever unforeseen events might attend our finding

Figure 17. Sofia Bogoras surveys the crates of collections prepared for shipment from Mariinsky Post (present-day Anadyr). While Bogoras made his long research treks, Sofia traveled between Markovo and Mariinsky Post, assembling extensive collections of Chukchi and Yupik material. (AMNH Library 1380)

our own way to town. She insists that tomorrow we must leave the hotel and move into an apartment that she knows of. She sweeps us off to dinner in a local restaurant called Pizza. As many times as we will eat here (this is one of two restaurants in Anadyr), pizza will not appear on the menu. Tonight, and for several nights to come, we dine on the meat-stuffed Siberian dumplings called *pelmeni* and fresh bread. It is a thoroughly starchy meal, but fresh and good.

Over dinner, the animated Madame Otke—as we quickly come to think of her—tells us that her father was a walrus hunter who became a Soviet activist, local leader, and the first mayor of Anadyr. The town's main street is named for him. In addition to acting as a district governor within Chukotka in the early 1940s, he also served as one of Chukotka's representatives (*deputat*) to the Congress of Nationalities in Moscow for two terms, from 1946 to 1954. Having related this pedigree, Madame Otke speaks of her own travels and makes various pronouncements. She has been to the Anchorage Museum of Art and History but prefers the Yupik community museum in Bethel, which has a more homey feeling. In Bethel, she tells us, clearly savoring the memory, she had declared in English, "My mother was an Eskimo," and received a round of applause. Although this trans-Bering Strait Yupik side of her genealogy was muted during the Cold War, it has become an asset in changing times. The Yupik she met in Alaska do not seem to mind that Madame Otke's self-referent terminology does not correspond with theirs, presumably understanding that politically correct language (Yupik, not Eskimo) often does not transcend borders. She continues to discourse on museums. The Magadan museum is large, but in her view they do not change their exhibits often enough. We try to offer a polite contradiction based on our recent visit there, but she is barreling ahead, nonstop. In a small museum like her own, one has to be creative. She even sews the curtains herself.

She has been to Zurich for an exhibition of archaeological material from a joint expedition with her museum. She prides herself on securing favorable contracts with foreign archaeological teams. These expeditions give her poorly subsidized staff a chance to get to the field. She also makes certain that half of the archaeological material remains with her museum—the glories of past excavations were hauled off to Moscow. When Laurel mentions how anthropologists at the American Museum of Natural History either analyze on site or return material after it has been analyzed, she snaps, "But you took things from Chukotka in the past." We end the evening not quite knowing what to make of the encounter.

Back in the hotel there is hot water, a welcome change from the cold showers in Magadan. We wonder if the renowned geothermal springs or the coal supply in the area guarantees hot water; we learn later that we were just lucky since this is a rarity in August. The room itself is unheated; owing to maintenance work, only half the city has heat and our hotel is in the unfavored half.

After hot showers and with hot tea from the electric kettle, a predictable item in Russian hotel rooms, we have chased the chill.

Wednesday, August 26, dawns clear and cold. A few latitudes to the south, people are still getting sunburned at the beach. Ira, the head of research and exhibits and Madame Otke's second-in-command, calls for us bright and early. She describes herself as a historian of "pre-Revolutionary history," the old Soviet term, and then corrects herself—"nineteenth-century history." She leads us out into town and up a dingy stairway to the security bureau where, as visitors to Chukotka, once again we must register. This marked door, among many unmarked doors, is locked, despite the fact that it should be open according to the posted hours. We have done our best to conform to the letter of the law and will try again later. Ira takes us to her own apartment in the half of the city that has heat, welcome heat sizzling through the pipes.

Ira calls a friend who works in the security bureau. The friend tells us to come back at five. We are saved the second trip when, on our way down Otke Street to the museum, Ira recognizes two women from the security bureau. We hand them our passports on the spot and they tell Ira to collect them at three. On Otke Street, Ira also nods to the director of the local folk dance troupe. We ask her if it would be possible for us to attend a rehearsal. Our request is relayed to Madame Otke who, by the end of the day, has arranged a command performance for which we will be expected to pay several hundred dollars. We tell her, as gently as possible, that we appreciate the effort but that this is not what we'd had in mind when we made our casual request. When we again encounter the director of the troupe, she tells us that she also considered the paid performance an odd idea, but that some members of the troupe would like to meet with us for tea the next day.

We meet another Sergey, this one slim and slightly rumpled, the museums exhibit designer who is also a poet and an author of children's books. He bundles our bags into his van and takes us to his friend's apartment where we will stay for a nominal fee. The family has relocated to European Russia but their beds, chairs, and tables remain; a healthy clump of Swedish ivy is still growing in the kitchen. There are several oil paintings on the walls, the work of the former proprietor. One of these is of a Siberian shaman and some others have Christian themes. Sergey asks if we noticed that the shaman leans his head into his drum as if he were playing a violin. The shaman is an icon of a Siberian past, but it is unlikely that the painter ever saw a shaman perform.

It became popular to depict shamans in the era of Perestroika in the late 1980s and early 1990s. In the Evenk Region Alexia was given a very delicate black lacquered brooch made from reindeer antler and painted with an image of a shaman going into trance. Similar jewelry was being produced and sold by a talented young Russian and even commissioned by the local indigenous rights organization. During the early 1990s many spiritual traditions were no longer sanctioned against as they had been since the 1930s. Also, an interest in

Figure 18. These pastel buildings with their geometric decoration were visible along the main thoroughfares of Anadyr. They had been painted in anticipation of some state visit. Buildings on less visible byways lacked fresh paint and decoration. (Photo by Laurel Kendall)

things spiritual and mystical coincided with the growing public outcry by indigenous Siberians about their dismal conditions. Like many images of Native Americans at the turn of the nineteenth century, these shaman images were tied to a romantic notion of a bygone era but were also an oblique protest against the injustices done to indigenous Siberians in a modern Soviet era. More recently, members of the intelligentsia throughout Russia have begun to hark back to a Russian Orthodox past. Alexia suspects that the Christian-inspired paintings postdate the shaman with the drum.

From the apartment, Sergey calls the charter company to see what it will cost for us to fly to Markovo. It turns out that price is not the issue. There is no fuel (an irony in that this region produces oil) and the helicopters are grounded. Private charter companies are the lowest priority for scarce fuel. The situation could change with a new shipment, or we might be able to hitch a ride on a medical transport. For now, these impediments seem surmountable. In Borgoras's day, it was a difficult five-day journey to Markovo.

The museum is housed in a pair of two-story buildings painted bright yellow, cozy-looking structures in a city of high-rise blocks. Unlike the monolingual Russian signs in town, the signs on the museum buildings are in Russian and Chukchi. We go to the far building, which serves as the administration center with some exhibition space. The near building is entirely given over to exhibits and has the preferred toilet, we are told. It is tea time when we arrive. The collections management staff is celebrating the birth of a six-pound daughter to one of their colleagues. Galina, the motherly looking collections manager, presides over the slicing of a chocolate and wafer cake. We drink tea made from the rosehips that one of the women on the staff gathered during her most recent visit to her home in the Moscow region. People comment on the brevity of this summer. There were only two weeks this year when they could wear light dresses and not bundle into sweaters and long underwear. On hearing that we will be finishing our travels in Kamchatka, they talk about the Kamchatka hot springs that everyone dreams of visiting but no one ever does; when summer comes, they are ready for warmer, more southerly climes. In addition to their northern hardship pay, they are supposed to get a paid vacation, but not this year. They suspect that they won't see it next year either. Ira tells us they are happy to have just received their April pay. She acknowledges that the situation in Anadyr, the capital of the Chukotka Region, is better than most places in the North.

Ira takes us on a tour of the museum's exhibits. We see the inevitable stuffed polar bear and walrus in the natural history section, the anticipated room of ivory carving, much of it dating from the 1940s and carved with electric drills, and the display of handicrafts collected in the 1960s, 1970s, and 1980s. We are introduced to the Chukchi woman who tans and repairs hides for the museum and ask about tanning techniques. She tells us that now commercial chemicals, rather than urine, are used and expresses surprise that the women from the big museum in New York should know about such things or even care to ask.

The museum's oldest ethnographic piece is an apron worn by Even reindeer herders. From the mid-eighteenth century, every governor was to provide artifacts for the Peter the Great Museum in St. Petersburg. For some reason, this apron was never sent beyond Vladivostok and came back to Anadyr when the local museum opened. It was probably a nineteenth-century object, decorated with metal pieces from an alarm clock and bits of a Winchester rifle.

Another section is devoted to archaeological materials dated to the first century B.C., and recognized as belonging to the Ekven complex; the museum has only catalog illustrations of important pieces that were excavated locally in the 1940s but are now in Moscow. The museum takes pride in this national recognition of their local history, but the removal of these objects clearly rankles.

We are introduced to Madame Otke's younger sister Nadezhda Pavlovna, a writer. A representative to the Congress of Nationalities in Moscow from 1984 to 1990, following in her father's footsteps, Nadezhda Pavlovna now heads the "Museum of Literature" (actually a subdivision of the regional museum). The name of this institution is evidence of Anadyr's image of itself as a city; all significant cities in Russia have literature museums. Again, Laurel is amazed by the intellectual strength of professionals in these northern towns.

Nadezhda Pavlovna Otke shows us the lovely exhibit of "Chukotkan stories" that she has prepared for children. Works of local literature appear beside ivory carvings from the museum's collection. There are images of a grandfather and a grandmother telling stories, symbolic representations of cultural transmission. In another case, an elaborate ivory carving illustrates a tale of a wife kidnapped by a bear and rescued by her husband. The curator's work with children includes not only literary appreciation but also instruction in dancing and singing; this continues a Soviet tradition of promoting folklore and performing arts. Other local literature is in an adjoining gallery for adults. Ira tells us with pride that this curator knows all the significant Chukotka writers personally. Sixty years ago writing systems were developed for Chukchi and Yupik; "One can say 'Chukotkan writing' began then," the younger Otke says with both regional and ethnic pride. She lauds Waldemar Bogoras for his role in developing Native scripts and praises the early ethnographers and linguists who painstakingly collected, wrote, and published on Native culture.

In Nadezhda Pavlovna Otke's view, the first generation of Soviet culture workers who came out to Chukotka in the 1920s and early 1930s from European Russia had a relatively positive attitude toward local cultures. Those who followed denigrated it, in large part because assimilation and Russification became the accepted policy beginning in the mid-1930s.[2] At that time the grand narrative of a modem Soviet Union came to rest on evolutionary paradigms espousing the inevitable advance of socialist societies. Following nineteenth-century social science theories, the success of socialism was linked to the transformation of "less developed"—or "less evolved"—societies (e.g., hunters and gatherers and herding societies like the Chukchi and Yupik). In the pursuit of an ideal society, there was little room for diversity. Before these ideas had become fixed in policy, Bogoras had written with a deep respect for those among whom he had lived and worked. Nadezhda Pavlovna points to an inscription on the wall, a quotation from Bogoras: "It is important to remember that Northern people created a unique culture."

Nadezhda Pavlovna speaks of an article she has seen in the Russian journal *Museum World* on the issue of "sovereignty" over artifacts. She asks, "And don't you have a lot of things from us?" Laurel has expected this question and speaks to the purpose of this trip. "It is true that large collections were made one hundred years ago. The question of who owns this material is complex. It is a lawyer's question. But in terms of how the objects should be used, and who can have access to them, our attitudes have changed a great deal. For example, we are here to let you know more about our collections, to share a database with photographic images, and to talk about ways we might work together in the future. We see this as our responsibility." They smile. Ira says that, of course, they all knew of the big collection in New York but never thought that anyone from that museum would come to Anadyr to talk about research access. She seems genuinely moved. This is a warmer reception than museum professionals from the United States are used to.

Ira asks (as everyone does) how our museum is financed and how people like us are hired. That conversation takes us to lunch, a hearty northern meal of fish, instant mashed potatoes, fish roe on bread, tomatoes and cucumbers, and vodka for toasts to welcome us. Madame Otke talks about the Chukotka/ Alaska tumblers she received in Alaska and then hastily adds that she should bring them to the museum, lest it be thought that she has benefited personally from her opportunities for international travel. After the first round of toasts, Laurel makes a formal presentation of *Drawing Shadows to Stone*, the catalog of Jesup Expedition photographs published to accompany the exhibition curated by Barbara Mathé and Thomas Ross Miller at the American Museum of Natural History the previous fall.

Madame Otke wants to discuss Native art. She has seen how many galleries in Alaska guarantee that their ivories are carved exclusively with hand tools. She is proud of her museum's extensive collection of electrically carved ivories from the Uelen workshop, where artisans copy prototypes created by designated master craftsmen. The intricate shapes and designs on these pieces could not possibly be carved by hand with traditional tools. She cannot understand why artisans would pledge to use only hand tools: "Art should develop." Her comment reflects a history of Soviet policies that valued Native cultural productions—handicrafts, music, dance—but saw it as the mission of the state to "develop" them. The handcrafted ivory carvings in the Alaska shops are valued by Western (and Japanese) folkcraft traditions that see an intrinsic "authenticity" in handmade crafts, a romantic link to pre-industrial traditions of artisanship. Very different artistic sensibilities value a tour de force ivory model of a steamship, every detail, down to the portholes and fluttering flags, precisely rendered by electric tools, versus an elegantly simple hand-carved seal, celebrated as "primitive" art. Craft "development" in the Euro-American world is most often associated with improved marketing techniques and the adaptation of older forms to new customer demands. In the Uelen workshops "development" meant, above all, the mastery of a new technology—different traditions, different histories, different notions of "authentic" handicrafts.

In the afternoon, we accompany Sergey and Ira to the studio of Valery Alekseevich Istomin, a local artist whose work has been exhibited around the Russian Far East, in Moscow, and in Alaska. We will recognize a mural of his on the side of a building along Otke Street and more of his work on the walls of the library. Istomin—as he signs his paintings—has lived in Chukotka for twenty-five years, teaching adults at a pedagogical institute and children in the local School for the Arts. His studio is populated with art school relics; busts and figure forms, including reproductions of the foot and ear of Michelangelo's David, share space with whale baleen and other local artifacts.

In addition to his mural painting, Istomin works in linoleum block prints and lithographs and, more recently, has turned to producing unimaginative oil paintings of local scenery. The oil paintings sell well these days, he tells us; people relocating to European Russia want to take a souvenir of Chukotka with them. Istomin uses the English word "nostalgia" and looks to see if Laurel catches it. Birthdays are another occasion when people buy an oil painting. In the past Istomin had a constant flow of commissions from the Department of Culture to commemorate important anniversaries or to decorate public buildings. These images were reproduced as posters, postcards, and textbook illustrations. This is not done anymore. Now he has free time for his own work, without the government orders—but no pay. Laurel asks if his subjects have changed. He says that no, his work hasn't changed; his hands have always just moved to inspiration. Is this possible?

Istomin's prints of life in the North appeal to us. Laurel's favorite is a rendering of an old Chukchi couple in their yaranga surrounded by cultural artifacts of the contemporary moment, such as a shortwave radio. A Mona Lisa hangs on the wall behind them. The title translates as "mulling it over." This one would not be out of place on the pages of the *New Yorker*. Another, of Yupik men eyeing a young woman, her parka blowing in the spring breeze, could be a *New Yorker* cover circa 1945 if the men were sailors and the woman's parka were a polka-dot sundress. Istomin claims never to have seen a copy of the *New Yorker*. In still another print, the fierce and beautiful visage of a black-haired Native woman suggests Soviet poster art, no surprise in that many of Istomin's prints were originally commissioned as Soviet posters. Istomin creates bookplates as a hobby, making designs that would be appropriate for different local and national literary figures; he has traded with collectors in Australia, Japan, and Canada. He enters these in an annual competition and takes a few orders. Do we want some? We scrutinize a fascinating variety of tiny prints, some recalling 1930s poster art and others Japanese folk prints.

Istomin has made several trips to Alaska and has been an artist in residence at the University of Alaska. He has also painted a few scenes of life there. He shows us a flamboyant sketch of two obese Americans sitting on a bench and chuckles as he says that this pretty much encapsulates the image most of the world has of the United States. He would love to visit Alaska again, but says he would have a hard time living where people spend so much time alone, where less effort is invested in socializing with each other. His own son is away in St. Petersburg studying museology. His education is financed by the Chukotka government, and he must work in Chukotka for at least three years upon completing his studies.

The local library is next on the itinerary that Madame Otke has determined for us. The library is dedicated to "Tan-Bogoras (1865–1936)." This is the pen name of the distinguished ethnographer and Jesup Expedition participant Waldemar Bogoras; it evokes his earlier alias, "N. A. Tan," based on his original Hebrew name of Natan. In those years prior to the Russian Revolution, the names of revolutionaries changed often. Like many others, Bogoras took on aliases for the range of genres in which he wrote: novels, revolutionary tracts (for which he was arrested and sent into Chukotkan exile), and ethnography (as a consequence of that exile). A frieze with a distinguished-looking bust graces the library foyer, celebrating this versatile man as a "Soviet writer, ethnologist and public organizer."

A member of the staff gives us an exhaustive and exhausting tour of the library. Exhibits in the foyer situate Chukotka in a larger legacy of once-Soviet culture. In Istomin's mural, above the staircase, a cosmonaut waves his hand as he flies over the town and a Native woman reaches up to clasp books being lowered from a low-flying plane. We see prominently displayed volumes inscribed by notable literary figures, among them the Soviet poet Yevgeny Yevtushenko, who once gave readings in the Anadyr library. Another exhibit celebrates a literary prize bestowed in the name of Yuri Rytkheu, the first Chukchi author, who is internationally known and now resides in St. Petersburg. As in Providenia, the shrinking infrastructure has curtailed the library's once ambitious outreach to a scattered and isolated community, services idealized in Istomin's mural portrayal of a book drop. According to the librarian's patter, the library serves Anadyr's population of 13,000 as well as the nearly 80,000 people (some put the current figure below 70,000) scattered through eighty branches in villages throughout Chukotka. We learn later that only sixty-seven of the original eighty branches remain, as the villages they once serviced are abandoned. The Russians and Ukrainians, who made up more than 80 percent of the Chukotka population in the late 1980s, began leaving by the thousands in the early 1990s. We pass a table of books on sale, titles the librarian selected in Moscow for regional libraries that now cannot afford them or may no longer exist. A book exchange program with Anchorage and Nome, begun with great enthusiasm in the aftermath of the Cold War in the early 1990s, has been suspended.

The library claims to have 60,000 books. It once subscribed to 600 journals, but it can no longer sustain this list and no longer orders subscriptions from a centralized list provided by the library in Magadan. The library collection includes videotapes and CDs and there are several computers but they are not available for public use. Alexia finds works by Brodsky on the shelf. The librarian who is our guide tells us that she "loves his work and can talk about it endlessly." The library has an excellent collection on Chukotka and tries to collect everything published about the region anywhere in the world: travelogues, works by local authors, articles on reindeer—anything relevant to Chukotkan life. When we tell them about the *Drawing Shadows to Stone* catalog, they say that they will order a copy, but even this paperback could be beyond their means. The rare book collection has old journals, such as *Soviet Chukotka*, which ran from 1937 to 1988, two of the three English-language volumes of Bogoras's monograph *The Chukchee*, literacy textbooks from the 1930s, and long runs of a regional newspaper that went out of business in 1995.

According to our guide, the library tries to serve as many people as possible, even conducting a survey on reader tastes. In the past, they say, everyone read the same thing, "If Jack London was published, then everyone read Jack London. Now the market is open to all kinds of things." Their patrons want novels, romances, murder mysteries; women want female protagonists and women's themes. The general public wants light reading and students want to improve job prospects. People want do-it-yourself guides—how to fix a watch, how to grow vegetables in a greenhouse. It is what we had heard in Providenia but without Galina's wounded intellectual passion.

Our guide reels off statistics and describes the library's computerized bibliography. Our eyes begin to glaze over. Our backs ache from standing in one place for so long. And then, like an apparition, Professor Nikolay Borisovich Vakhtin of St. Petersburg walks through the door and folds us, each in turn, in a great Russian bear hug. He had been researching back issues of local newspapers and heard that we were in the building. We had last seen him at a conference in New York the previous November and had no idea he would turn up here. We are amazed and delighted and show it; Nikolay wears his unflappable half smile. Later he observes that even a few years ago, when it was still difficult for a Russian researcher to gain access to Chukotka, he never dreamed that he would be making dinner plans with a couple of Americans in Anadyr.

It has been a long and tiring day and we are beginning to feel frustrated. These have been interesting encounters, but we did not come to Anadyr to visit artists and libraries. Tomorrow, Ira assures us, Madame Otke will be available to examine our database and talk about possible areas of collaboration. She kindly leads us in and out of a bakery and a couple of grocery shops as we assemble the provisions of bottled water, cheese, bread, and yogurt which, combined with our bouillon cubes, dried seaweed, and the jar of salmon roe Madame Otke gave us at lunch, will make a pleasing supper. On the way home, we meet up with yet another Otke sister along Otke Street.

The next morning, we nearly miss Ira because we mistake the sound of the electronic doorbell for the cry of some lunatic tundra bird outside our window. She is forced to telephone us, but seems as amused as we are by our mistake. When we arrive at the museum, Madame Otke is busy with visitors from the local television station. Ira shows us the museum's substantial collection of machine-carved ivory and scrimshaw, an attempt to document the shifting motifs developed by Uelen master carvers.

Since it is evident that the director will not be free anytime soon, we suggest taking care of some errands in the town. At the bank we are the only prospects in line for currency exchange. The rate is now 8.7 rubles to the U.S. dollar. The rumor is that it will go to 12 so we try to calculate our needs very carefully and change no more than is necessary. The bank is full of people waiting for their pensions and child subsidy payments.

At the air ticket office we book our flight out of Anadyr to Khabarovsk. The agents urge us to wait another week, since on September 1, the day after the next scheduled weekly flight, the system of dual rates, with inflated ticket prices for foreigners, will be abolished. It takes all of Alexia's tact to convince them to sell us a ticket without flat-out stating that it is worth a great deal of money to us to avoid an extra week in their lovely city. We ask about supply flights and hospital emergency flights to Markovo, hoping that we can make a short trip to this other Jesup field site during our week in Anadyr, but nothing is scheduled, and nothing will materialize during the rest of our stay. While we wait for our Khabarovsk tickets, Ira asks us once more about fund-raising, training, and other museum matters.

We arrive back at the museum as a schoolteacher from Uelen is delivering several pieces of scrimshaw. He has been pressed into service as a courier because he has business in the town. Every traveler is a potential resource for passing on information or goods. Madame Otke is still busy with her visitors but joins us by and by. We prepare once more to demonstrate the electronic database on Alexia's laptop.

While we are setting up, an elderly man wanders into the room, hands us his resume, and introduces himself as Igor Grigorovich Riga, a history researcher at the museum. He was at neither lunch nor tea the previous day, and this seems odd. Ira tells us he has been here since the early 1950s and was associated with the museum's old Soviet Department. He has the pathetic air of a has-been struggling to keep his dignity, insisting that his substantial local knowledge be recognized and validated, the old professor whose work is now out of vogue and with whom younger colleagues are impatient. It does not take the collapse of a Soviet Union to produce the likes of Igor Grigorovich. Throughout our presentation, he interjects such comments as, "I see you have material from Mariinsky Post. I know a hundred people who used to live there." "Did any of your Markovo material come from Grange Kermou?" He tells us that he has just written a monograph on a geologist in the area who specialized in permafrost. Madame Otke, meanwhile, engages the database, taking notes and suggesting rapid-fire corrections to our notations. We scribble frantically. This is precisely how a shared database should work. In her flush of enthusiasm at finding our errors, Madame Otke discredits each unfamiliar provenance with "Never heard of it." Igor Grigorovich reminds her, in slow and measured tones, that over a century, many villages have disappeared and many names have been changed. We wonder at the working relationship between two such different temperaments stuck with each other year after year.

In the afternoon, we tape an interview for a local television program. Madame Otke arranged this in the morning and presented it to us as a fait accompli. We are both nervous at the prospect but also pleased to have this forum for our project. We are particularly eager for Native people to hear publicly that we have deposited a copy of the database with the local museum. We cover the usual ground in the interview, describing the Jesup Expedition and our desire to share our resources electronically with the people whose ances-

tors made the artifacts. The only curve comes with the final question, something that had not arisen during our warm-up conversation with the inter-
viewer before the taping session. "What do you think people in the North
really need?" By implication, what is the point of museum collections in the
face of serious economic hardship here and with so many immediate material
needs? Laurel struggles for an answer that will sound substantive but noncom-
mittal. "We are following the lead of our colleagues here. We have been told
that Native people in the North want to make connections to their traditions.
As museum people, links to the past through its material artifacts are what we
have to offer."

Once the interview is taped, a technician asks to film some images off of
Alexia's computer screen. We show him some possibilities, and he decides that
the amulets will have great appeal, invoking the spiritual world that was so out
of favor for decades of Soviet rule. We ask if televising them can be seen as a
violation of Native wishes; these objects were once hidden according to traditional practices. Ira does not think that this is an issue. Local practice is local
practice; "sacred" in this context is part of the story people want to tell. In
North America, and increasingly elsewhere, this sort of public display of sacred images would be a delicate issue and most likely simply avoided; Native
peoples are increasingly concerned with how ritually significant objects are displayed and discussed. The photographers ask us if people in America are really interested in these ethnographic objects. In his opinion, Russian museums
have a problem drawing audiences.

We are running behind schedule and race to our next appointment, a tea at
the House of Culture with the folk dance troupe Attasikun. With Ira, we have
already purchased a huge amount of goodies—including "Chocko-pie," a
Korean-made cookie as popular in the Russian Far East as in Korea—and the
tea itself. Ira delivered the big bundle to the House of Culture earlier in the
day, and when we arrive, the samovar is ready and the sweets are arranged in
an inviting heap on the table.

The director of the House of Culture is a motherly redhead named Nina
who has been involved in culture work in Anadyr for twenty-five years. Also at
the tea is Alexander, a folklorist and choreographer; he is the lead dancer and
intellectual ballast of Attasikun. A tall, mustachioed, and attractive middle-
aged Chukchi, he has been training dancers for fifteen years. He tells us that
in many instances, Bogoras was mistaken in his portrayal of Chukchi culture
and gives us copies of one of his own publications, inscribed in English "to my
good friends."

Vladislav, a thin, intense young man, looks the very image of a choreographer, which he is. Vera, one of the younger dancers, works for the social welfare department dealing primarily with old people's needs when she is not
dancing. Antonia dances with a group in another community and has just
dropped by for tea. She also works for the Anadyr radio station, translating fea-

tures and news into the Yupik language. A Yupik woman, Svetlana Dasherkh, sits quietly with her three well-behaved children, Borya, Liza, and Alyosha. Alexander tells us that she teaches art and dance at the College of Folk Arts (kollezh natsionalnykh isskustv), which we will visit tomorrow. As we see before the afternoon is over, Svetlana is an accomplished dancer in her own right. Alyosha, dressed in a fanciful leather tunic made by his mother, has been dancing since he was in diapers and now, at age eight, is already considered a lead dancer.

The dancers speak of international tours, of performances in Singapore and Paris. Even the children have performed all over Russia and in the Netherlands, Belgium, Greenland, North and South Carolina, and Alaska. The adults have performed to acclaim in India where, Alexander feels, the audience "understood" their dances and prolonged their scheduled twenty minutes to an hour and a half. Recently they have been invited to perform in Australia and New Zealand, but in these difficult times, they do not expect to be able to go. At world performance festivals, they have shared the stage with Maori and Senegalese. One of the women says that they feel a great sense of affinity for the Australian aboriginal groups, who also have a dance incorporating the movements made while tanning hide.

Alexander, resplendent in a white leather dance tunic, begins what must be a set patter. In 1956 or 1957, during the Cold War, the Soviet state made an effort to preserve "some of the traditional culture that is in our museum." By then, the tradition was no longer a part of everyday life, but it would be self-consciously preserved through state policy. Alexander tells how they were given an extremely dark view of Alaska, as a place where Native culture had been undermined.

Nina parades around the room with various fur-trimmed costumes, trying to claim our attention. She forces Laurel to take a bite of gooey Chocko-pie. Alexander has not broken stride in his disquisition. He has traveled all over the world with the professional Chukotka dance troupe Ergyron. He tells us that the "cultural level" they have attained within the Russian Federation is high. He claims that he can distinguish "false" culture from genuinely "original," performing arts with "deep spiritual roots" from those that are "performed in restaurants." Where there is still some connection between Native arts and daily life, they can be revitalized, but if they were "made up" in the first place, then they cannot.

Laurel is intrigued by this conversation. Like most contemporary anthropologists, she accepts that "authenticity" is a will-o'-the-wisp because any lived culture is necessarily a changing culture, and all tradition is ultimately "made up." And yet, having experienced both drunken village festivals and Kodak-sponsored hula shows, she would like to find some intellectually honest means of distinguishing self-conscious cultural performances from culture experienced and passed on through the act of performance.

Alexander describes how until 1948 Chukotka people had enjoyed close connections with Alaska, ties that have been resumed in recent years. Many dances performed by the professional Chukotka folk troupe are now performed by Alaskan Native troupes because they are considered more "traditional." Alexander characterizes Alaskan Native performances for tourists as "chewing gum" (*zhvachka*). He says that you can't dance traditionally and then go sit in a Mercedes. But in another context, the dancers indicate that the flow of Yupik "tradition" has not been in one direction. They heard chants in Yupik from the Alaskan side over the illicit shortwave radio during the Cold War and made up their own dances from them. Now they have also incorporated some dances from the Alaskan side into their repertoire. Still, in Alexander's view, Chukotka natives have managed to keep more of their tradition owing to their relative isolation. The Ergyron dance troupe with which Alexander danced consists of cosmopolitan professional performers whose schooling aimed at assimilating them into a Russian-speaking state. Alexander worries that as speakers of the Native languages disappear, the cultural meaning behind their dances will also vanish. He hopes that if the residential schools disappear, children can again grow up in Native communities and the ruptures of their parents' generation can be repaired.

Laurel wonders if it matters that Ergyron is a professionally trained troupe that choreographs its work for the stage. She saw a performance many years before in New York at the Asia Society where an old Koryak woman performing among younger dancers on the stage danced as though oblivious of her surroundings. The younger women dancing beside her were very skilled and graceful, but their professionally polished performance contrasted with the almost otherworldly movements of the old lady. Laurel describes this performance to Alexander and Vladislav and asks, if once a body is no longer trained to move in accordance with the rhythms of a way of life, can such motion possibly be recaptured through formal dance training?

There are shouts of "Pravda!" from both Alexander and Vladislav. Dancing must be learned from life. Vladislav carries a video camera around to Native villages to record the dances of old women so that he can incorporate their dances into his teaching. But at the same time, Alexander is a living contradiction. He defines himself as a professional dancer, a Chukchi who has also mastered Yupik dances. As a professional, he can take anything on, "even an Irish jig," he tells us. He teaches comparative dance in the College of Folk Arts, where he highlights the difference between Native and European movement; the latter is highly disciplined, orderly, and very far removed from any meaningful ritual source.

By now, the heap of sweets is nearly demolished and the room is almost empty. The other dancers have gone into the study to prepare for the rehearsal. They practice twice a week. Today they are working on Yupik dances and begin with a dance from the relocated village of Naukan, a community

Figure 19. Koryak dancers receiving a whale, c. 1900. The woman's slightly raised arms suggest the fluid spontaneity of the old woman's performance that Laurel saw in New York. (AMNH Library 1422)

that is said to have produced the best and most respected dancers. The children perform with grace, mimicking the activities of village life with fluid dance movements. Three boys dance a reindeer sacrifice; two girls dance tanning hide. Nina points to one of the girls and tells us that she is also mastering piano. The eldest girl does throat singing, producing sounds that might resemble a locomotive mating with a whistling tea kettle. Alexander tells us that village women used to compete this way as a measure of their endurance. At the end of this rendition, the performer becomes a seabird and flies away. Two boys dance a seal hunt, and two girls execute a dance performed during the whale festival. Some of the adult women perform, one of them wearing very fashionable high-heeled boots. Alexander executes a raven dance, but the drumming does not satisfy him and he pauses to correct the musician until she gets it right. Next, he dances collecting seabird eggs.

After the rehearsal, a thin-faced man appears, seemingly from nowhere, and attempts to sell us some crude carvings. More tea is served, and we continue our discussion with Alexander and Vladislav on the subject of tradition, movement, and performance. This goes on for far longer than any of us intended and, realizing the hour, we eventually extricate ourselves and race to Pizza. We have missed our dinner appointment with Nikolay, who waited for us but has already left.

When Ira calls the next morning, she tells us that she must take her son to the doctor. He has become violently ill from some Chinese fruit juice that he was given in daycare. We spend more time in Istomin's studio, where we each purchase a print and some bookplates. The happy artist informs us, "Now I can take my vacation."

At the museum, Galina has been concerned about the reports of forest fires near Khabarovsk, nearly two thousand miles to the southwest and our next destination. Now she reports that the forest fire problem has been resolved but another disaster has hit that vicinity owing to too much rain in northeast China. Several villages on the Russian side of the Amur River have been flooded.

Ira takes us to the College of Folk Arts and then rushes off to fill a prescription for her child. The college is part of the local School for the Arts and resembles two apartment blocks. We are taken to a room where people are having tea and chocolate. Alexia apologizes for our disturbing their Friday celebration, a common practice in Russian work settings, especially in smaller towns. A woman says that this isn't a Friday party: "We do this every day. The ruble goes up, the ruble goes down, we celebrate anyway." We are introduced to the director of the School for the Arts, a quiet man who soon absents himself; the director of the College of Folk Arts, a robust, silver-haired female mathematician who does most of the talking; and Svetlana, who danced for us yesterday.

We are told that the School for the Arts initially consisted of a music division, with offerings in piano, accordion, and violin, and an art division, with specialties in decorative arts, painting, and drawing. The 1994 addition of the College of Folk Arts created the opportunity for students to also study the choreography, music, and artistic traditions of various ethnic groups in the area, including Russian and Ukrainian, Chukchi and Yupik. The art and music programs with European content are principally attended by 150 children from Anadyr, while the College of Folk Arts mostly serves about forty students from Chukotka villages.

The Native children trained in the College of Folk Arts program begin in the fifth grade and prepare to return to their communities as culture workers after graduation. The school used to have the resources to visit villages and screen prospective applicants, but now they must rely on videos and recommendations. At the school, students are encouraged to develop their talent in the area of their greatest proficiency, but they are also given a broad background so that they can teach outside their field. A dancer, for example, will also be trained in choreography and aspects of stage directing. The mathematician tells us that she works with the choreography instructor to ensure that their curriculum is mutually reinforcing.

Village administrators submit requests for their cultural needs and the college trains students for the specified jobs from the ninth grade. This year they have received ten requests for museum workers but are vague about the course of study, saying that the prospective program will have to be approved by the Department of Education in Moscow. The school is financed by the Chukotka District. The standardized folklore and ethnology curriculum comes from the District Department of Culture's Institute for Teacher Development. The instructors would like to do their own research and bring the folklore of local communities into their teaching, but they lack the resources for fieldtrips. Folklore classes are conducted in Chukchi, and Chukchi language is taught two hours a week; two hours are also set aside for English and three for Russian. The mathematician tells us that they would like to include Yupik and Even in the curriculum; it would make sense to conduct classes in (Yupik) ivory carving in Yupik. Svetlana recalls a now defunct section of the regional newspaper, *Murgin Nutenut*, that until the early 1990s published folklore and linguistic material in Yupik and Chukchi.

The mathematician explains that they used to train students as performers, but in the College of Folk Arts they see themselves as training House of Culture staff, teachers, and museum workers. The program is a response, in part, to the departure of European Russians who would have filled most of these slots in the past. It is perhaps most remarkable that even in crisis times, the work of culture is considered an essential part of the social fabric, not an expendable frill. The mathematician relates how some Native children used to study in St. Petersburg, particularly at the Herzen Institute, which has a Northern Studies Department. Many children found the environment to be so alien, however, that they could not complete their course of study. Now, moreover, there are severe financial constraints on sending Chukotkans far away for training. It is difficult enough to keep the local school in repair. As the director explains, it was not worth sending people to St. Petersburg for training where their talents would not blossom. She sees the college as a place for *zvezdochki* (little stars) to shine and not be overwhelmed by the glitz or chaos of the huge city.

We meet the decorative arts teacher, Svetlana Alexandrovna Gomozova, a beautiful young woman with flowing black hair who tells us that her true Chukchi name is Rouline. We see some examples of student work while a little girl stitches hide in the pool of sunshine by a big window. The young children work with softer hides and then progress to stiffer material. In another room, there are some very nice finished boots and slippers made by older students. Alexia has seen this sort of school in other places, but the training program here seems to be better organized and the students are doing beautiful work. Rouline, who talks about her work with great sophistication, says that she grew up in a Chukchi reindeer camp and learned all the processes of leatherwork there, beginning with tanning hide. She is also a language teacher, having been trained in St. Petersburg and Magadan.

The mathematician explains that almost everyone on the faculty has done a correspondence course in ethnology, museum studies, or folklore at the Herzen

Institute in St. Petersburg, in addition to their specialty. For example, a Chukchi language instructor must study the principles of linguistics. As we leave, this gracious woman invites us to drop by anytime. We needn't call in advance—indeed we can't. The school's telephone has been disconnected.

One of the museum staff has come by to lead us to Madame Otke's house for lunch. As we don't want to arrive empty-handed, he helps us first to locate a bottle of vodka in one of the shops. He says that we are almost fully assimilated Northerners now, walking around with a vodka bottle in our pockets. This Russian man tells us he has a Chukchi wife, but he adds that she doesn't speak a word of the Chukchi language; it was her worst subject when she was a student.

Madame Otke greets us with great warmth and introduces us to her daughter, who is a second-year law student in Moscow. We present our bottle but soon realize that she has a good supply of better quality vodka in the refrigerator. She showers us with hospitality, feeds us borscht and fish-filled pelmeni washed down with sweet wine. She shows us family photographs and gives us gifts, earrings for Alexia and an agate brooch for Laurel. She regales us with stories of her youthful experiences as a Spanish-language interpreter while a student at Moscow State University. She laments the present moment, as skilled staff leave the museum and positions are filled by local people who, she says, lack the same level of competence. She claims that after university she could have had a position in Vladivostok, but her father had insisted his educated children come back to Anadyr.

She invites us to spend the next day with her on the tundra where she hopes to bring in a supply of fish for the winter. We demur, pleading fatigue. We are both feeling very weary. Back at the museum, we are waylaid into another interview with "a local writer" who turns out to be a broadcast journalist. We are asked once more for the public record, "What is the American Museum of Natural History prepared to do for Chukotka?" Again we say that we are here to share a database because this resource is what we have to offer. Madame Otke showers us with museum publications, Lenin badges, and postcards, hoping perhaps to sway us into joining her tomorrow. We are anxious to be out the door. Igor Grigorovich insists that we stop by his room, and we do so out of courtesy. He begins a long, slow monologue about the geologist who is the subject of his monograph. Madame Otke interrupts. Wouldn't we like her daughter to give us a city tour the next afternoon? We realize how much we had been looking forward to a free day. We bite our tongues and put her off as politely as possible, give Igor Grigorovich ten more minutes, and bolt for the door.

We have one remaining errand. Realizing that we are not likely to catch a local flight to Markovo, we take the copy of the *Drawing Shadows to Stone* catalog that we intended for the Markovo museum and deliver it to the director of the Anadyr library. She is surprised to see us, and when we tell her the purpose of our visit, her eyes moisten. She hugs us. We had no idea this small gesture would provoke such a response. The volume will be part of the Chukotka collection in a library named for one of the men whose work inspired a retrospective exhibition in New York and also brought us to Chukotka. We collect our prints from Istomin, who has wrapped them in a tidy parcel, and wish him luck on his fishing expedition tomorrow. It seems that half of the town is going fishing tomorrow to provision themselves for the winter. Now we are free to warm our feet by the space heater and read.

Saturday is somewhat warmer but still cold. With a luxuriously slow start, we get ourselves to the banya, larger and newer than the one in Providenia, an impression enhanced by blue tiles, white paint, and large sunny windows. There is even a pool large enough to swim in. A mother and her daughters share the tank with us. All in the buff in sunny space, we seem to be swimming inside a Barbizon painting. It is market day, and on our way home we buy dill and radishes from a market vendor who asks us if we are nuns. We have some more free time for reading, and then Oleg arrives.

Oleg is the son of Vladimir Mikhailovich Etylin, the Chukchi activist who founded the National Union of Reindeer Herders in 1995 and was once the chairman of the Chukotka Soviet. When we met Vladimir Etylin at a conference in New York the previous November, he encouraged us to visit Chukotka. Etylin tried to help us secure our visa back in the spring but is away on business during our visit to Anadyr. In his horn-rimmed glasses and bulky green sweater, Oleg could pass for an American engineering student. In fact, Oleg has trained as a veterinarian but is also working on a dictionary of Chukchi dialects. He regrets that our schedule will not permit a visit to the northern district near Bilibino, an area with several small communities of reindeer-herding Chukchi. He laments that the so-called maritime Chukchi, hunters of sea mammals, have received a disproportionate share of scholarly attention. He has a great deal to say about the problems of reindeer herders in the new economy. In his view, the state gives them no resources and little freedom. He believes that the market in reindeer meat should be protected and that managers of reindeer farms should recognize that the children of reindeer herders need to spend summers helping their fathers in the herding camps if they are to carry on this occupation.[3] Their transport should not be seen as an unnecessary expense.

In his view, the reindeer are killed indiscriminately to meet market demand. In the past, only the weak reindeer, the ones who were not likely to survive the winter, were butchered. Now the sex ratio is out of balance and not all of the fertile females are impregnated, diminishing prospects for replenishing the herds. With his father, he would like to see the herders organize to hold a fixed price for reindeer meat. He speaks of an up-and-down market in antlers, used throughout East Asia to make medicines to boost male potency. He says that trade with South Korea fell off after the financial crisis the previous fall. Laurel can't help wondering if the availability of Viagra also had something to do with it. Oleg could go on for several hours more, but we need to meet Nikolay at Pizza.

This time Nikolay and his graduate student, Marina, are waiting. They are going to spend six weeks in Markovo studying Bogoras's "Russianized Natives"—a creole group that mingled with Russians from 350 years ago. "The problem," Nikolay tells us, "is that these people sing." They have a characteristic style of singing that has been taped, transcribed, recorded, and marketed on CDs. This, they assume, is what researchers want them to do. You show up, they sing a song, and they feel that they have fulfilled your research expectations.

Tonight, a large and dressy office birthday party fills the restaurant with the music of loud electric guitars. The celebrants are dancing and seem to be having a good time. Nikolay tilts his head to listen to the words of a song about a secretary. "The lyrics are not very P.C. I shall not translate," he informs us dryly with a smile. The noisy party is not conducive to conversation but even so, we manage to share news of mutual friends, of Shimon in St. Petersburg, Bill and Igor in Washington, David in New York, and Piers in Cambridge. Nikolay describes his gleanings in local history from the library's archive. The early record showed citizens talking about "things that were really important. Should they paint a room? Should they fix a roof? In the late 1930s it's totally transformed, all about implementing this policy or that policy." It is a pleasant evening.

Sunday is a bright, sunny day with the Anadyr Estuary almost a Mediterranean blue. The locals call this a "warm" day, although in the late morning when we go to the museum, the unheated interior of the museum is like an icebox. We still hope to have a serious conversation with Madame Otke regarding "prospects for future collaboration." Madame Otke insists first on giving us a full tour of the exhibit of ethnology and local history. She is armed with a pointer and her best pedagogical manner: "Chukotka is 730,000 square miles with 88,000 people, according to the last census in 1989. . . . The Native population includes Koryak, Chukchi, Yupik, Even, and Kereks—a subgroup of the Koryaks that Bogoras studied. The Yukaghir, who were once numerous in the region, were superceded by the Chukchi in the seventeenth century. . . . Catherine the Great knew of the Chukchi as a 'warlike people'." A mild Chukchi chauvinism runs through her narrative. She speaks of how the Chukchi and Yupik held out against Christian conversion, or rather, they accepted the missionaries' tea and tobacco and then, clever devils, came back for another round of redemption and trade goods. She crawls inside the exhibit of a Chukchi reindeer camp and lets us photograph her in the doorway of the yaranga, telling us that she wouldn't do this for just anyone.

Madame Otke describes the Chukchi's historical movement from "patriarchal" to "bourgeois" society. Laurel is still under the illusion that we have come to the museum for a collegial conversation rather than a guided tour,

Figure 20. Natalya Pavlovna Otke, director of the Anadyr museum, poses inside the yaranga in the exhibition hall of her museum. The gesture was spontaneous but she told us that she would not assume this pose "for just anyone." (Photo by Laurel Kendall)

but when all effort to draw Madame Otke into a dialogue fails, she recognizes that Madame Otke is giving us the same highly ritualized performance that she has seen in China and Vietnam. Instructors, more than labels, are expected to carry the exhibit or, in Madame Otke's words, "give the objects a living context."

Madame Otke takes this mission seriously and will describe, as one of the formative experiences of her museological education, a tour of the Lenin Museum with an explainer who presented the revolutionary hero as "someone who had actually once been alive and human." Every member of her staff, whatever their specialty, must be able to lecture in every exhibit hall. Madame Otke insists on it and monitors her staff until they can produce a smooth, seamless narrative flow. Subsequent experience of Russian museums will give us a belated appreciation for Madame Otke's animated lecture style, all things being relative.

The hall is an aesthetic disappointment, hastily clumped together, with air bubbles under the photo murals and carelessly arranged objects. This contrasts with the slick exhibits we have seen in Providenia and Magadan. And yet Madame Otke is proud of her work in upgrading the museum's hodgepodge of curiosities into systematic and comprehensive ethnographic collections on the model that she observed in major Soviet museums during her training. She points out an oil lamp hewn from stone with blue beads stuck into its base. This decoration is rare and "maybe shamanistic"—the all-purpose phrase that people, including Native curators, use to characterize unusual objects.

But Madame Otke's curatorial training has not totally negated her indigenous relationship to the powers and dangers imputed to some objects in her exhibition cases. When she began to work in the museum, her mother worried about her daily contact with evil spirits and urged her to wash her hands well on returning home from work. When a colleague thought she was pregnant and was cursing her husband, Madame Otke told her to talk to a talismanic doll. "The next day, she wasn't pregnant anymore."

We are all enjoying this conversation, and Madame Otke tells us more. Her father died when she was seven years old and her youngest sister was an infant. Years later, after the birth of her own daughter, she was working at home late at night on a newspaper article about her father. A copy of his autobiography was on her desk, and in the dead of night, she saw his image at the door. "Oh my poor daughter, you have to work late at night and take care of your child without a husband to help you. I've come to see you and take a look at my granddaughter." She heard the sound of footsteps moving toward where her daughter was sleeping and then back again to the door of her room. Her father told her that she was a wonderful daughter to have produced such a lovely child. This encounter lasted maybe half an hour. Although it was late at night, she called her mother immediately. Her mother told her not to bring her father's works home with her and that spirits must have followed her home from the museum. She told her again that she must wash her hands carefully.

The most memorable object on display is "the Shaman's airplane," a wooden model made of odd bits of wood, nuts and bolts, and floppy plywood wings. The tale is that the shaman was vexed by Native children being sent away to residential school and people going to hospitals rather than seeking his help. He told the people that he would use this plane to call the Americans to come and bomb them, and he hung it in front of his yaranga where he could make the propeller whirr and cause something to clack inside like the sound of a machine gun. A brave young Komsomol member exposed the shaman's deceit in 1932 or 1933. Much later, in 1969, he gave the plane to the museum. How many such artifacts of the struggle between deceitful shamans and brave young Communists might one find in other Siberian museums? Is the shaman today regarded as more of a hero for his having attempted to defend Native cultures against assimilation? Our guide does not express an opinion.

According to Madame Otke, the museum's most valuable holding is a drawing by the American illustrator and author Rockwell Kent. As a committed Communist, Kent made several trips to the Soviet Union in the late 1920s and early 1930s and is much loved in Russia for his depictions of life in the North, particularly for his lively descriptions and vivid prints of the years he spent in

Greenland in the 1930s. Madame Otke considers Kent's drawing too valuable to display in the museum. She tells us how Kent received a carved Yupik ivory figure from the Soviet government for his eightieth birthday and wrote to the craftswoman, saying it conveyed "the wonder of your land." In gratitude, he sent six of his works to the museum. Madame Otke commends Kent's portrayal of Northern people, even his replication of a characteristic waddling walk. She tells the local artists that they don't get it right.

We take a tea break to "warm up," although the tea room is also freezing. Over tea, Madame Otke speaks of the distinguished professors under whom she studied and of her academic triumphs. She offers the speculation that the Jesup Expedition spent so much time in Nunligran because that's where all the beautiful women are, then launches into an anecdote about Bogoras. When he visited one Native community, he was offered temporary wives. When his hosts asked him to return the favor, he and his wife departed in the dead of night. She has many anecdotes on the theme of cross-ethnic sex. One of them is about Gravetsky, a nineteenth-century governor in the region who left a multitude of redhaired, green-eyed children in his wake. A more recent visitor offered to buy the museum's ivories and, as Madame Otke tells us with amusement, the visitor said he wanted to buy her as well. We are not sure what to make of these stories, but it is interesting to see the European as a sexualized "other" through Chukchi eyes.

In a more serious vein, she speaks again of how early Soviet policies, particularly those articulated in the 1920s by the Committee of the North under the leadership of Waldemar Bogoras, held that Native people should have autonomy and that reindeer herders were already "specialists." Even without years of formal education, they could represent the people, just as Madame Otke's father had done. She echoes what her sister told us on the first day about how in the 1930s the policies changed and the new civil servants were ignorant and intolerant of local people and conditions. She says that people these days are too quick to criticize the Soviet period. In her view, Native cultures fared better under the Soviets than on the Alaskan side under U.S. control. The "Eskimo" (*eskimosy*)—as the Yupik are referred to in Russia—she encountered in Bethel have borrowed gratuitously from other continental Native American traditions, including what she sees as utterly inappropriate ecstatic dancing.

Madame Otke values the ability to travel that has been part of her role as a local intellectual. Like the museum staff in Magadan and others we encounter elsewhere, she speaks of the loss of professional mobility owing to pinched economic circumstances. She can no longer join colleagues for conferences and workshops at the major museums; she does not know if such events are still held. The curtailment of air travel and soaring cost of fuel also mean that the museum can no longer send traveling exhibits to outlying villages. In the foreseeable future there will be no repeat of their successful 1990 exhibit featuring life in Chukotka during World War II, an occasion when people found their own relatives in period photographs and were inspired to add their own recollections. With ties established through traveling exhibits, people were sometimes inspired to bring their heirlooms into the museum.

Now we seize the chance to turn the conversation toward the expressed business of our trip. "Natalya Pavlovna, what sort of collaborative projects would be useful to you and your staff?" "Anything would be fine." She brushes off the question and goes on to her next topic, a tirade against the audio tours she encountered in museums in Alaska and considers a poor substitute for a pedagogue with a pointer.

We spend the rest of the afternoon going through the remainder of the database on our CD. The exercise is peppered with questions and comments from Madame Otke and we cannot help but admire her staying power. She is surprised that we would share images in this way. She tells us that in the Russian museum system, no outsider can work with or publish material until the museum has published it first. We say that the collection is for everyone, in Anadyr as well as New York.

She tells us we should feed the spirits in our collection. In their museum, they fill shot glasses of vodka and sometimes add bread and salt, in the manner that Russians honor the dead. As the level of vodka in the glass goes down, it seems the spirits are drinking. She laughs with full-blown bicultural ambivalence. Untreated, the spirits could become angry and cause trouble. She spills out vodka to feed the spirits when we are eating in the lunch room. Laurel jokes that at the American Museum of Natural History we have spirits to tend from all over the world and we cannot possibly minister to all of their diverse tastes. Madame Otke suggests we do something about it or we will have very bad luck. Giggling, she tells us that when the Whites took Anadyr in the Civil War in 1923, they summarily executed a camp of thirteen Reds and buried them in a common grave. In 1969, flooding brought up the bodies and a memorial was built. The clothing, preserved in the permafrost, was given to the museum. She used to hear mysterious coughing until she offered vodka to the murdered soldiers.

We meet Nikolay and Marina for dinner at Pizza. The restaurant manager has assured Nikolay that there will be no party tonight, that it will be quiet enough for conversation. In fact, there is a party, albeit a small one, and reindeer is on the menu in place of the pelmeni. Laurel finds the meat surprisingly tender, but Alexia, who has spent time in reindeer camps and is a connoisseur, finds it slightly overcooked. As the party picks up, a Russian man, face flushed with drink, approaches our table looking for a dancing partner. Laurel seizes the opportunity and is led to the floor. This inspires Nikolay to dance with Marina and Alexia, and we all have a sense of a party on our last evening in Anadyr.

We arrive at the museum on Monday morning to find Madame Otke in high spirits. She is singing "Happy Birthday to You" in English, perhaps because she knows the words, but breaks off to deal with a local crisis by telephone. Among her circle of acquaintances, a baby is very ill with jaundice. She makes several telephone calls in an attempt to find the proper medication. The assistant collections manager is pulling objects from a 1995 dig out of the cardboard carton where they are stowed in smaller cardboard boxes or wrapped in newspaper. Madame Otke wants us to see an ancient two-faced figurine of which she is very proud. We spend some time in the storerooms, with Madame Otke pointing out her treasures, among them a shaman's drum which she bought from relatives for three rubles. She shows us some wonderful old volumes in the small and carefully guarded rare book room. She is thoroughly complicit in our photographing her, holding aloft a volume of Bogoras's classic Jesup Expedition monograph on the Chukchi. On our way out of storage, she makes an ironic gesture in the direction of some head casts made from skulls extracted in a local dig: "You could say these are my ancestors." They have the distinction of having been cast in the same workshop that did Ivan the Terrible's skull.

We join the staff for tea. As on the first day, Galina is cutting up a chocolate-covered wafer cake. Lyudmila, just back from a Swiss-sponsored dig of a Chukchi site, looks like the young Vanessa Redgrave playing a weathered and weary archaeologist. We saw her on Friday when she was just back. The dig was not easy: the Swiss had a nice warm tent while the Russians were in a cold trailer, and there wasn't enough food. She said they hit permafrost too soon so the dig was disappointing. Lyudmila describes her amusement at the Swiss excavation style. The Swiss cut small pits and analyzed everything—the soil, the faunal remains—while the Russians cut big pits and looked for objects. We saw her on Friday, still in her gear, army fatigues worn over several layers of clothing and thick boots. Today, Lyudmila is transformed, rested, carefully made-up. We admire our museum colleagues here who carefully groom themselves to pass the day in frigid buildings. We wish that our practical packing had allowed us some smarter clothing as a gesture of respect; we look like we're the ones who have just returned from an archaeological dig. When we express this to Ira, she tactfully observes, "You're on a sort of expedition."

Lyudmila is telling us how she liked having no television and no newspapers. When she came back from her brief field season, the government had new people in it. (In the last few days, Yeltsin has replaced his prime minister with his former prime minister and dismissed his cabinet. In little more than a week, there will be yet another prime minister.) This inspires Sergey to perform some wicked Yeltsin imitations, punctuated by the observation that "the man must be on drugs." A spate of Yeltsin jokes and other political irreverence follows. "They asked in Red Square for blood donations for Yeltsin and, of course, everyone agreed to give. They cast down a feather—they would take blood from whomever it landed on and Red Square was full of the sound of people puffing it away." "It used to be that you would be arrested for making a political complaint. Now they just think you're a fool because it's all been said." "To place a call to the next village you dial Washington, D.C., and they put it through." "The American says, 'I can stand in front of the White House and say Bill Clinton is an idiot and nothing will happen to me.' The Russian says, 'Oh yeah, well I can stand in front of the [Russian] White House and say Bill Clinton is an idiot and nothing will happen to me, either.'" People are getting carried away. Madame Otke raps on the table and says that this is all very naughty.

When we distribute American Museum of Natural History postcards as farewell tokens of goodwill to the staff, they ask us to sign them. Madame Otke again gifts us, this time with a large box of chocolate and bottles of very flowery cologne, which, she says, are from her daughter. We pull out three AMNH pins in a pathetic attempt at reciprocity. Sergey and Ira come back to the apartment with us and help us take our bags downstairs. The other Sergey, the ferocious driver, arrives on schedule with his large black van. We make several stops on the way to the airport and the taxi fills up, mostly with students on their way back to school, but there is a young man in a stylish jacket and silk shirt who carries a bunch of roses for his returning wife. Some of the students have adopted a tough look with shaved heads and leather jackets. One is accompanied by a gaggle of female admirers who ride as far as the ferry.

We get across the Anadyr Estuary but are still several miles from the airport when the taxi breaks down. The poor quality gas has clogged the carburetor. The driver keeps his sense of humor, "I'll carry you to the airport on my back if need be." When the students get abusive, he tells them not to swear in front of the ladies. We contemplate the prospect of another full week in Anadyr should we miss our flight. After Providenia, we know that anything is possible. But in forty minutes Sergey has the engine purring again. We arrive in good time, get through the exit formalities without difficulty, and sit on the runway for an hour before takeoff. The woman across the aisle is traveling with a large fluffy white cat that luxuriates on an empty seat throughout the flight to Khabarovsk.

Chapter 5

Khabarovsk
Embroidering the Border

Post Alexandrovsk, March 4, 1899
Concerning the Russo-Chinese Bank there is absolutely no reliance on them, and I tell you quite frankly that I don't want to deal with such fools. Just listen to what happened to me. I recently had to wait three weeks in . . . South Sakhalin for 100 rubles still needed for traveling. Within one week I sent two English telegrams to this company, with the second I had paid for 10 words return answer, but did not get any reply at all. Getting desperate, I telegraphed a gentleman I knew at the firm Kunst and Albers in Vladivostok to look into the matter. This gentleman informed me that the bank had already dealt with it—sent the money to a certain Alandesberg in Alexandrovsk (!) This dignified gentleman is a former officer of the guards, double murderer, and now owner of some shop here. So I telegraphed him and he acted in the same way as the bank, namely that to inform me is not required, that he intended the government fund to pay me the sum by telegram. Then he answered: "Have sent money in letter by mail." So I had to wait another week thanks to that clever company. Now here again I have the same comedy: I telegraphed to Nikolayevsk to where I would like the credit transferred; I just received the answer that they cannot understand the telegram, could I give them further explanation. Could you please inform Mr. Jesup of these peculiar happenings and see that he gets a mentally sound firm to attend to our business?

—*Laufer to Boas*

Berthold Laufer was a singular individual. He would be eulogized as the premier Sinologist of his generation, the author of respected monographs on Chinese jades, bronzes, and ceramics, studies and papers on such eccentric topics as hermaphrodites in Chinese history, the cricket cage, and the pigeon whistle. A fellow Sinologist described his astonishing range and sometimes novel interests as "ethnographic,"[1] for want of a better word, but few anthropologists today have heard of him, much less associate him with Boas's Jesup North Pacific Expedition.

Laufer was an unlikely anthropologist. He had been trained in philology at the University of Leipzig and by the age of twenty-three, when Boas recruited him for the expedition, he had already studied Persian, Sanskrit, Pali, Malay,

Figure 21. This studio portrait of a Nanai family, attributed to Emile Ninaud,
was acquired by Berthold Laufer. Nanai garments are inspired by Chinese robes, but
the decorative motifs on their embroidered and appliquéd bands are unique as are
the designs on the birch bark hat on the man seated on the far right. The painted
backdrop evokes the region's lush landscape, an image also captured in the dioramas
of the present-day Khabarovsk museum. (AMNH Library 41614)

Chinese, Japanese, Manchu, Mongolian, Dravidian, and Tibetan from some
of the greatest scholars of the day. By the end of his career, he would have the
distinction of speaking "an embarrassing number of languages."[2] Laufer's linguistic abilities brought him to Boas's attention, but Laufer seems a surprising
choice for Siberian fieldwork, a budding savant whose explorations into Asian
cultures had theretofore been conducted in the rarefied air of a German university. One misses the logic of Boas's assertion that "Dr. Laufer had devoted
himself to the study of the Tibetan language and of the history of Asiatic cultures, and was well prepared to take up the problems offered by the Amur
tribes."[3]

In contrast with Bogoras and Jochelson, who were returning to a part of the
world they knew well, albeit from the sad circumstance of political exile, this
was Laufer's first visit to Asia. And unlike the Russian ethnographers, whose
wives accompanied them to the Russian Far East, Laufer would work alone.
Gerald Fowke, the American archaeologist who was to accompany him, left

the field after a few months complaining of insects, running sores, dirty Native dwellings, and a general incompatibility with Laufer. Even so, Laufer flourished in the field, at least initially. He arrived on Sakhalin Island in July 1898 via Vladivostok and Khabarovsk and spent the next eight months visiting Nivkh, Even, Ainu, and Ulchi villages, delayed only by a severe bout of influenza, a near encounter with highwaymen, and a near drowning when his dogsled broke through thin ice. He made wax cylinder recordings to aid his linguistic work, was an avid collector of beautifully decorated wood and birch bark boxes, and was particularly proud to have encountered "many shamanistic and other myserious practices to the surprise of the local Russians who, after having lived there for many years have never seen these things."[4] In March 1899, he returned to Khabarovsk to begin a new phase of fieldwork.

From Post Alexandrovsk Laufer wrote to Boas:

Concerning estimation of cost for my work on the Amur, I think I need approximately 3000 rubles till fall. Your [estimate] up to now covers, I should say, traveling expenses but not a big ethnographic collection. I ask you urgently to put aside a special sum for that, because all objects, the smallest as well as the biggest are awfully expensive. For some time the Natives have known the real value of their possessions and what they can get for it. The demand for their things, from Russian amateurs and dealers alike, is very high and so the prices are going up. . . . There is absolutely nothing you could get for free from them, they even want payment for trivial communications in money, tobacco, tea, spirits, etc.[5]

By April 19, 1899, Laufer had reached Khabarovsk and settled in.

I have now taken here a lodging built of rough planks resembling a coffin and have begun to engage myself in a linguistic and anthropological study of the Nanai, of whom I have fortunately met a good many excellent representatives in this place; several individuals speak Russian very well and know about a store of traditions, so that I may speedily succeed in the pursuit of my work. The terrible hurricanes of this season [and] a deficiency of roads now prevent [me] from traveling; it is necessary to wait, till ice is broken and navigation begins. Then I have in view to visit the Golde [Nanai] and Gilyak [Nivkh] tribes living between Khabarovsk and Nikolayevsk, which will be the work to be done in the summer.[6]

Coming into Khabarovsk, we have an airplane's-eye view of the Amur in flood. When Alexia looks out, she sees a double sun, eerily reminiscent of the scene in *Star Wars* when Luke Skywalker and company arrive at the planet Tatooine. The intense reflection of the setting sun on the broad expanse of river provides the illusion but after Anadyr we may as well be landing on another planet.

On the ground, we collect our bags and walk out of the air terminal into the balmy summer evening. There is no customs check for our domestic flight. How far from the far North we are, nearly two thousand miles south of Anadyr. Laurel finds herself staring at a row of trees in full leaf outlined against the sunset. It seems like a very long time since she has seen a tree. Men are in shirtsleeves and women in printed summer dresses. The rush of mild air would be delicious were it not for our layers of Arctic thermal clothing, which now generate an almost nauseating heat.

The Central Hotel rambles beside a large Lenin Square. This square has gone through several names, beginning with Nikolaev Square (after Nicholas II, the last Russian tsar), then Republic Square in 1917, then Freedom Square in 1918, and finally Lenin Square since the 1920s. Today it is still Lenin Square, with a statue of the leader; the proclamation affixed to the pedestal reads, "Communism is a higher form of socialism in which people strive not just for their own improvement, but for the greater good of society." The Central Hotel has no elevator. We haul our luggage up the spacious staircase to the third floor, to find another remnant of Soviet times, the floor concierge. She will claim our key whenever we go out, providing us with an official chit we must use to reclaim it. Alexia mutters about not having had to bother with the chits for years. We have arrived during one of the annual maintenance periods for the water system in that part of the city where the hotel is located, so there is no hot water in our room. We've already experienced this further north, and it does not seem so daunting here in the late summer weather. Alexia looks for an electric kettle or thermos of steaming water and eventually borrows an electric kettle from the concierge. These deficiencies aside, the window offers a nice breeze and a view of the square. The synthetic crimson bedspread and curtains are embroidered with cranes and pine trees, a reminder that China is across the Amur River. Russian traders make routine day trips from Khabarovsk to a market just over the Manchurian border. No visa is required for these short forays.

The next day begins with a visit to the hotel's "ironing room," where guests can press their own clothing in a white, starched, institutional setting. Scrubbed, pressed, and dressed in our lightest clothing, we are out running errands. For a frontier town, Khabarovsk boasts a mélange of remarkable architecture, of pillared neoclassical façades, wooden gingerbread trim, and two-storied stone structures that suggest a meeting of neo-Gothic and Swiss chalet.

As we walk toward the museum along Muravyov-Amurskogo Boulevard, one of the central streets in the "old town" of the city, Alexia is struck by block after block of restored buildings, a marked contrast with other cities she has recently visited. Vladivostok, Krasnoyarsk, and even St. Petersburg are filled with crumbling Soviet and pre-Soviet structures. Moscow, of course, got a face-lift in the relatively prosperous years between 1994 and 1998, and Alexia is heartened to see that this happened in some other city centers as well. Then again, unlike Vladivostok, Krasnoyarsk, and other cities that were closed to foreigners until 1990, Khabarovsk was never off-limits. This openness, and the early concomitant opportunities for joint ventures, meant that there were financial resources and perhaps more incentives to maintain the city infrastructure. The apparent plethora of joint ventures is evident in the brightly illustrated billboards we encounter advertising Korean and Japanese companies and office products such as Xerox photocopiers.

From its mid-nineteenth-century founding, Khabarovsk has been a meeting place of cultures and artistic styles. At the end of the nineteenth century, when its river port was completed, Khabarovsk was an established trade center doing a brisk traffic in furs. In 1880, Khabarovsk became the capital of the region, and by 1884 it had a population of 5,000. By 1899, when Laufer was inhabiting his coffin-like lodging, this number had tripled, largely due to the construction of the Trans-Siberian Railroad and a new north-south rail link with the major port of Vladivostok on the Sea of Japan; this rail connection made it possible for immigrants from European Russia and elsewhere to flood the region. Khabarovsk remains a commercial center, but instead of furs, today the trade is in timber, minerals, and communications for the entire Russian Far East.

Our first day in Khabarovsk coincides with the first day of school. The streets are full of students in their best clothes. The girls have frilly white blouses and very short skirts. One pair of high-school-age Lolitas wear stylish long, fitted jackets over skirts that are short enough to give the illusion that they are not wearing skirts at all.

At the currency exchange, the rate is now down to 9.3 rubles to the dollar and we are approached by several people hopeful of trading for hard currency. Our next round of airplane tickets must be purchased from the special office that services foreigners, even though, as of today, September 1, 1998, the inflated foreigner rate for air travel is abolished. The ticketing agency could be anywhere in the world, with big glass windows and banks of computer terminals. We walk out with Kamchatka Air tickets for Petropavlovsk, the day after tomorrow, and Palana, two days later. It seems so simple. Of course, nothing is ever as simple as it seems.

Our lunch consists of steamed fern fronds and mushroom soup in the café on the ground floor of the Sapporo Hotel. The Sapporo is a phantasmagoric brick complex, a mix of neo-Gothic and Byzantine with the look of a loving restoration. In fact, this is a new hotel, built on a vacant lot to harmonize with the equally fantastic building next door, a library that has been lovingly restored. The Sapporo boasts an expensive Japanese restaurant on one of the upper floors. The bathroom fittings are definite imports; you have to be able to read the Chinese ideographs, as a Japanese user would, to know that the toilets can be flushed with a minimum of water for the "lesser comfort" (push lever to the left), more for the "greater comfort" (push lever to the right). This corner of downtown has a historic link to Japan, beyond this present-day tourist hotel. The guidebooks tell us that in 1912, a Mr. Takeuchi lived in the building directly across the street, at the corner of Komsomolskaya Street and Muravyov-Amurskogo Boulevard. Takeuchi was the official representative of the Japanese community in early twentieth-century Khabarovsk.

It is a short walk from the Sapporo Hotel to the Khabarovsk Regional History Museum. On the way, we pass a group of stylish high school girls posing for each other's cameras, striking voguish postures in front of the Civil War monument. Ingrid Summers, an anthropology graduate student from Columbia University who has been doing fieldwork in Khabarovsk for the past year, joins us outside the museum. A familiar face from New York, looking cool and fashionable in a blue linen summer dress, does not seem so out of place in this cosmopolitan city.

The Khabarovsk Regional History Museum, infelicitously translated as the "Khabarovsk Lore Museum" in one brochure, is an imposing turn-of-the century brick structure, beautifully cared for and surrounded by large trees. There is nothing drab about the Khabarovsk museum; the exhibition rooms have sparkling glass cases, polished wood, and fresh paint. It is far and away the largest, best endowed, and best maintained museum that we will see, the premier institution in the regional hierarchy of museums that we have been visiting. The museum has a particularly distinguished and well-financed history.

Once inside, we are met by Tatyana V. Melnikova, the chair of the Ethnology Division and an expert on Amur River cultures. She has a perky, pixie haircut and wears a paisley print dress. She does not look at all schoolmarmish, but she carries a wooden pointer identical to the one that Madame Otke brandished in her own museum in Anadyr. This is an ominous sign. These pointers must be standard issue, an essential piece of curatorial equipment. We learn later that the Russian Ministry of Culture mandated the use of pointers in museum tours by an official decree in the mid-1970s. Effective pointer wielding was part of the training given to future museum workers in the Soviet system. Traces of this tradition of earnest museum pedagogy can be found in other museums of the socialist world. Laurel recalls a dainty young woman dressed in a silk *ao dai* who flourished her pointer like a dance accessory as she discoursed upon the myriad courtship practices of Vietnam's minority nationalities.

Although curators at the American Museum of Natural History are expected to "present their science to the general public," this is generally construed as giving an occasional public lecture, briefing docents, writing for the popular press every now and then, and carefully weighing each word that goes into an exhibition label. Russian curators seem to be always "on call" to visitors, but with the exception of this museum, from what we have seen so far, the visitors are few. What would Tatyana think of our current fashion for putting virtual curators into exhibition halls via video monitors. Would she see this as a relief or would she, like Madame Otke, miss the empowerment of the pointer?

Tatyana leads us on a forced march through the wildlife and ethnology halls, delivering a set script, attempting to stuff us with every possible fact and detail. We miss the young man who so ably and entertainingly led us through the gold mining exhibit in Magadan. The notion of entertainment divides the old, didactic, and once adequately subsidized socialist museum from circumstances more familiar to us, where museums are one among many possible leisure activities and the paying public must be tantalized to enter the door.

The Khabarovsk museum is making this transition. The dioramas have a romantic appeal with sugary sprinklings of snow on the simulated pine trees. The exhibition technique is world class, and the artifacts are stunning. There is nothing drab or threadbare about this museum. Today, on a weekday afternoon, the halls are filled with families intently gazing at taxidermized birds and wildlife, drawn in by a special program in honor of the first day of school.

Tatyana begins our tour at the geography map and describes "the unique Eurasian position of Khabarovsk." The last ice age did not reach this far south; otherwise extinct flora and fauna survived. We encounter giant wood-boring beetles the size of small mice and some of the 108 types of fish found in the Amur River—"only the Amazon has more varieties of fish." We pass by stuffed seals basking on the banks of a simulated Sea of Okhotsk. We meet a wolverine and hear, yet again, how wolverine fur does not hold moisture and is therefore good for collar fur because it does not ice up from breath vapor. All the curators in Siberia seem to have learned this tidbit in some standard museology curriculum.

There is a regal-looking stuffed tiger. Tatyana has ample things to say about the tiger. The Nanai, indigenous inhabitants of the Amur region, respected the tiger. When they encountered tiger tracks in the forest, they would back away from that spot, showing deference to the tiger. Nanai hunters would kill the tiger only in self-defense. They would never use its hide or flesh and shunned the use of tiger bone, a potent medicine whose popularity among affluent Chinese now threatens the Siberian tiger with extinction.

Tatyana gestures to the lush diorama and tells us that the Amur region retains this Eden-like splendor away from the railroad tracks in areas that have not been ravaged by forest fires. As we heard from Galina in the Anadyr museum, the forest fires were particularly bad this summer until stanched by the heavy rains that brought the recent floods. In a low-voiced aside, Ingrid tells Laurel that Moscow was slow to respond to the forest fires: "They sent aid to Greece instead." According to many locals, firefighting aid and equipment went to Greece to bolster Russia's international image while the Amur burned.

A photo mural commemorates Vladimir Arsenev, a renowned naturalist who was the museum's first director. A polymath with an avid interest in the region, Arsenev began his career as a surveyor. He indulged in ethnology, collecting legends among Amur River peoples and describing 228 archaeological sites in what is now the Maritime Territory (*Primorski krai*). He is perhaps best known for his novel, *Dersu Uzala*, the story of an early twentieth-century encounter between a Russian surveyor and a Nanai hunter when the newly created Trans-Siberian Railroad brought scores of Europeans to the region. A film version of *Dersu Uzala*, directed by Akira Kurosawa, gained international renown in the 1970s, long after Arsenev's death.

Under the gaze of this significant ancestor, Tatyana lectures us on the history of the museum, which opened in 1894 inside a local pharmacy but by 1896 had expanded to this grand old building. Laufer visited in 1898 to study the collections before beginning his fieldwork. Like so many museums established in colonial moments, this one began in an effort to record the natural history of the region and soon embraced ethnology. The museum memorializes a prominent Russian political and military figure from that period, Nikolay Grodekov, then governor-general of the vast Maritime Territory which at that time stretched over one thousand miles from the Amur River to Lake Baikal.

The ethnology exhibits are gorgeous, resplendent with examples of Amur River embroidery and appliqué work, all artfully displayed. Tatyana herself chose the objects and photographs, both to show the traditional cultures of Northern peoples and to produce an aesthetic effect. She worked hand in hand with a professional museum designer, specially commissioned for this task when the entire building was refurbished in 1994. The exhibits in the first ethnology hall represent all of the peoples of the Russian Far East, a tradition dating from the time when Khabarovsk held sway as the regional capital and objects were brought to the museum from distant places. Here we encounter life-sized photographic mock-ups of the manikins from the Smithsonian's *Crossroads of Continents* exhibit. The mock-ups were made to accompany a spin-off exhibit from the Smithsonian, *Crossroads Siberia*, which toured the Russian Far East in 1991. The Khabarovsk museum managed the tour on the Russian side and, when it was over, put these leftover mock-ups to good use in its own halls. Some of these mock-ups exhibit garments from the American Museum of Natural History's Siberian collection. Khabarovsk is, indeed, a crossroad.

We marvel over a wedding apron from the Ulchi of the Amur River region. This remarkable tapestry incorporates pieces of Chinese brocade, silk appliquée, and reindeer beard embroidery, and the garment is stitched together with thread from a reindeer's esophagus. In exchange for furs, silk and jade flowed to the Amur River peoples, who developed their own elegant combinations of style. A Negidal shaman's robe is betasseled to simulate feathers for the shaman's soul flight in the guise of a bird. The costume was part of a large collection made by a local school in the decade after the Revolution. Laurel wonders if the children were asked to bring in relics of discredited traditions. Alexia explains that while families were not physically forced to surrender such heirlooms, they were encouraged to do so with promises of financial and political benefits.

Against a forest diorama a manikin is fitted out in the fancy clothing that Negidal men wore for the ritually significant first day of hunting, an elaborately appliquéd jacket cut in a Chinese style and a decorated cap festooned with a red

Figure 22. One of the many hand-drawn illustrations used to illustrate Laufer's study of the textile motifs of Amur River peoples. (*Memoirs,* AMNH, vol. VII, plate XII)

squirrel tail. The complete ensemble included elaborately worked bands to bind up the costume's wide Manchu-style sleeves during practical work and to keep the snow out. Earmuffs were essential because the elegant cap offered scant protection from the piercing cold. Was it the hunters' vanity that required a beautiful costume so unsuited to the climate and the task at hand?

Tatyana describes the carefully worked yoke and borders of the hunter's jacket as protecting the margins where "evil spirits" (*zlye dukhi*) might enter the body. As we wander through the halls we will hear more about evil spirits, as we did in Anadyr. This is an English translation of a Russian translation of many Native words and concepts. Native understandings would have been more complex, and perhaps the spirits were not always evil so much as capricious or easily offended. A translation of a translation is a poor lens through which to view the spirit worlds of other peoples; too often it is all we have left.

Tatyana tells us more than we want to know about hunting and fishing, about the variety of boats used on the Amur River, about methods for manufacturing wooden boats and for preparing and working birch bark, about weaving with willow reeds and nettle bark. Our eyes begin to glaze over and we want very much to sit down.

Laurel finds herself summoning the ghost of the French philosopher Michel Foucault, who wrote that categorization is an act of domination. How many recent critiques of museums have borrowed from that insight? Does Laurel now find herself in a particular room in hell where ethnographers are made to suffer for their sins? Academic fashions aside, Laurel cannot quite believe that the record, in and of itself, is a bad thing, or that Tatyana's knowledge and intentions are less than admirable. She is glad that these things are known and recorded. In her own work, Laurel has encountered Native people for whom museum collections and old ethnographies are the only surviving fragments of a meaningful past. She cannot write the entire enterprise off as a nineteenth-century mistake. But she would prefer to read the details from a reference work while seated in a comfortable chair.

Tatyana's relentless performance fills space and time but ultimately says nothing. Does the sum of weapons, tools, and embroideries make a Nanai or a Negidal? How did they fare in the time between the ethnographic "then" and this time? There is no room in this presentation for history as a never-ending process. But this is a common failing of many ethnographic exhibits. The Hall of Asian Peoples in our own institution in New York describes its exhibits as depicting "traditional life before 1900," as if time stood still until injected with a dose of modernity from the West.

We endure an elaborate description of how fish skins are prepared before being stitched into the beautifully decorated tunics that resemble Chinese robes. Laurel asks a curatorial question: "How is the fish skin treated in the museum? Those in our collection become brittle over time, like potato chips." Tatyana smiles wryly. The problem is recognized. The skins would have originally been treated by Native women. The Native women advise the museum staff to massage the garments periodically with their hands, but this is not a museum practice. One of the fish skin robes on display, a robe that could be nearly one hundred years old, came into the collection in 1993. It was in wonderful condition when they received it, having been regularly massaged. Tatyana clearly loves to talk about the real people, known people, behind some of the objects in the cases, but we must first derail her set presentation with our questions.

"Do curators routinely consult Native people for advice about their collections?" Whenever Native people visit the museum, Tatyana asks them for information and, of course, she asks about material in the museum's collection when she does fieldwork. She was away just this past weekend. "In other museums, colleagues have told us they no longer have money for expeditions." She offers half a smile. That is true here as well, but Tatyana takes advantage of outsiders' projects, an opportunity that turns up maybe once a year. Her trip over the weekend was with representatives of *National Geographic*.

An entire wall case devoted to "spiritual culture" contains many carved votive figures. The spirits of the forest and the river require offerings of water, berries, and fat, but these can be quite small because offerings expand upon contact with the spirit world. Laurel jokes that in Korea it is just the opposite, that even though food may be piled high for shaman rituals, when the spirits arrive they see only paltry and insufficient tribute. In Siberian villages, the carved votive figures are periodically "fed," smeared on the mouth with fat. "Is this still done for the figures in the case?" Not that, but every year an old Nanai woman comes and offers vodka to the spirits. "And there's the cup," says Ingrid, pointing to the little white porcelain Japanese sake cup beside one of the carved figures in the adjoining case.

We talk about shamans today. Tatyana has heard of two women who have the gift but are resisting the calling because it is painful to live between this world and the spirit world. If they accept the calling, it must be validated by an established shaman. We enter a complicated discussion. Can there be shamans after the last shaman dies? Have the surviving shamans passed on their knowledge to students? Tatyana emphatically denies that anyone can "study" to be a shaman. Shamans are chosen by spirits. Established shamans have a role in legitimating their calling but not in teaching it. Laurel, familiar with shamanic culture in Korea (where deep mastery of technique is essential), will not give up. "Of course shamans are chosen by the spirits; no one can choose it as an act of will, but once they are chosen, how do they learn what to do?" "Well, yes, younger people do work with and around more experienced shamans, but . . ." Alexia thinks that ethnographically engaged intellectuals deny the learned part of a shaman's practice because, in the post-Soviet world, they want the possibility of magic. It was denied them for so long, and so vociferously. For our guide, learning seems to imply charlatanry, a "Soviet" view of shamans and their work. Laurel yields the point in favor of a reenchanted world.

We are relieved to reach the end of the ethnographic hall. Ingrid slips away to another appointment, and we are ushered into the director's office. Nikolay Ivanovich Ruban, dapper with a well-trimmed beard and twinkling eyes, inhabits an office that could be found in a major American museum, a bright, white space with an abundance of plants, full of electronic equipment, and with a large table for meetings. He asks us what we are up to. For once, it seems almost silly to talk about sharing our database given the quality of their spectacular Amur River collections. The Khabarovsk museum is also part of the electronic world. They have a Web site with a general description of the museum and they are creating their own CDs of their collections.

Ruban wants to do business. Are we in the market for exhibits? Are we or our colleagues interested in joint expeditions? We know from Tatyana that this is the only way Russian museum scholars now get to the field. The Khabarovsk staff are doing several archaeology expeditions with the Japanese. Archaeology expeditions are Ruban's passion; he could go on at great length about their current projects. If our archaeologists do not speak Russian, that is not a problem. A member of his staff learned Japanese in order to work with that team. The archaeology museum, now under construction, was Ruban's inspiration, and he pushed for it. Would we like to see it tomorrow? After three hours with Tatyana and her pointer, it is a struggle to give the gracious response that professional politeness requires.

From Ruban we learn that the Khabarovsk museum reports directly to the Ministry of Culture in Moscow. As a district museum within a distinct hierarchy, the Khabarovsk museum was once under the provincial museum in Vladivostok. Funds for museums are disbursed through Departments of Culture along an administrative chain of command from Moscow to the province (*oblast*), from the province to the region (*okrug*), from the region to the district (*raion*), and from the district to the city or town (*gorod/poselok*). In recent years, the Khabarovsk museum successfully positioned itself higher up on the feeding chain and thereby ensured it would secure a larger share of the dwindling funds allocated for cultural work. From what we gather in later discussions with colleagues, the Vladivostok and Khabarovsk museums continue to vie for the claim to being the preeminent museum of the Russian Far East. Ruban describes his museum as a methodological center for the Far East. This rather grandiose title was earned in the early 1990s when the Khabarovsk museum held several workshops on museology and occasionally sponsored conferences, activities that are no longer possible for economic reasons.

As elsewhere, the Khabarovsk museum is experiencing financial difficulties, but given what we have seen, their deprivation is relative. They are in far better shape and running a vastly more ambitious operation than any museum we have seen so far. They receive only 15 percent of their budget from the government, and in order to maintain the building, pay curators, and otherwise sustain operations, they must rely on their own ability to bring visitors through the door. Indeed, this is the first museum we have visited in the Russian Far East that actually seems to bring in significant numbers of leisure-time visitors. Ruban says that the admission fees would not cover the cost of their heat and light, but because the museum is a state-run enterprise, they can run these critical services on credit up to a certain ceiling (much as unpaid civil servants are extended credit in the state-run stores). No matter how bad things are in the current moment, Ruban is determined that the archaeology museum will open on schedule in October.

Ruban runs through the organization of the museum, the list of departments and divisions, the exhibition halls. With a staff of 120, of whom 40 are curators, this museum boasts the same ambitious mingling of science, history, and culture that we have encountered elsewhere, but on a larger, indeed imperial, scale. Tatyana heads the Ethnology Division, with its specialization on the peoples of the Amur region and a broadly mandated interest in all of the peoples of the Russian Far East. The newest member of her department was hired to research the region's cultural and historical relations with China,

Korea, and Japan. Here, as elsewhere, ethnographic horizons expand and contract with geopolitical and economic landscapes.

We ask how the new ethnology hall, opened in 1994, differs from what went before. Tatyana and Ruban laugh, but we expected this. The conceptualization is utterly different. The space has been expanded. Administrative offices and a procrustean presentation of regional history have been supplanted by exhibits "of greater interest to the public." The curatorial perspective has also changed. "We used to present the history of the Revolution [1917] and of the Civil War [lasting until 1920] in the Russian Far East as a heroic story. Now there are no heroes, only victims." This is a replay of our conversation in Magadan, but here the rewriting of older stories is described with institutional self-confidence rather than angst. Later Ingrid will tell us that the current portrayal is a "grim and ghastly mural," a realistic rendering of the bloody battles fought in the area while Russian loyalist forces, the Whites (*belye*), held out against the Soviet forces, the Reds (*krasnye*).

Somehow the Khabarovsk museum had the wherewithal to mount new and appealing exhibits, and this afternoon their halls were filled with spectators. The museum is mastering the market. We will learn from others that Ruban came from the sphere of "trade" (*torgovlya*), a put-down since "trade" in the Soviet era connoted access to luxury goods in the course of supplying well-placed people. Ruban certainly displays an ease with the workings of museums in the new context of market capitalism.

We depart into the cool early evening, our heads reeling from their stuffing with ethnographic detail and the exercise of trying to second-guess Ruban's second-guessing of us. The late afternoon sun is still shining brightly on the Civil War memorial in Central Square at the head of Muravyov-Amurskogo Boulevard (which becomes Karl Marx Boulevard when it reaches our hotel). Parked in the square is a beige bus prominently labeled "Sheraton Walker Hill Hotel," a vehicle that in another life made a circuit from Kimpo Airport to a hotel complex on the outskirts of Seoul. Who there would have imagined its recycling, in pristine form, on the streets of Khabarovsk? In the early 1970s, before it got its face-lift as a Sheraton, the Walker Hill Hotel was a dingy R and R watering hole with a government-run school for prospective hotel employees on the premises. The school was Laurel's first Peace Corps assignment, and an uncomfortable one it was. In the dead of winter, Laurel hovered beside the solitary kerosene heater, teaching English conversation to a class of fifty prospective hotel employees, flapping her hands like puppets to simulate a dialogue. "How do you get to Citizen's Hall?" "Are you driving or going on foot?" Former students would shout these lines back at her, complete with hand gestures, whenever she encountered them during their subsequent careers in Seoul hotels.

Ruban drives past in his shiny white car, breaking Laurel's reverie, and offers to drop us off at our hotel, but we have other plans. Large red lanterns strung across the façade of an imposing restaurant on the opposite side of the square beckon with the promise of Chinese food. The Hong Kong restaurant is a cavernous white room dominated by a karaoke screen, but there are few guests and the screen is mercifully mute most of the time. We have a very oily but otherwise good Chinese meal: fried tofu, eggplant, and steamed rice, washed down with a good, cheap Russian champagne.

The next morning Alexia goes running in the nearby park, ecstatic to resume this habitual exercise she had suspended during the several weeks of chilly weather and smaller towns of Providenia, Magadan, and Anadyr. The paths around the pond in Dinamo Park are strewn with broken concrete, remains of campfires, a few empty vodka bottles, and cigarette stubs. Some well-heeled women in skirts and blazers make their way to work along one of the wider paths. Just one man, probably in his seventies, is out exercising in shorts and a t-shirt. No one pays attention to him, but a few glances are thrown Alexia's way. Only children and men are generally seen exercising outdoors in Russia. During the months she spent in a town in central Siberia, when the deep cold subsided in April she went running as early as six A.M. in order to avoid becoming a public spectacle. At that hour, the few all-night revelers staggering home would rarely take note of a woman jogger. Here in Khabarovsk early morning exercise is certainly more appealing in the warm air, but the dirt roads of the central Siberian town were easier to navigate than the torn-up pavement of this urban park.

Back at the hotel, the floor concierge delivers our laundry in the very unconciergelike costume of a smock and kerchief. We realize that our erstwhile well-groomed duenna doubles as the laundress, and hand her the nominal fee. She looks weepy and says that times are hard. We assume this is a pitch. Laurel wonders if this isn't what visitors want, a little intimate brush with Russian hardship? She has seen tourists in Cambodia asking their guides about Pol Pot times, ghoulishly collecting accounts of family members who were killed or starved to death, a little personal encounter with history from the safety of an air-conditioned tour bus. As it turns out, our concierge has much to weep about today.

We are at the museum by ten, in time for a final meeting with Ruban, a formality, an exchange of greetings, and an affirmation of our mutual good intentions. We are once again in Tatyana's care, but much relieved that today her pointer has been replaced by a notebook and pen. When she says that after the morning's program she would like to introduce us to each and every remaining exhibit in the museum, we hope that our recoil is not obvious. She is genuinely kind, but how could we dream of taking more of her precious time? Alexia asks Tatyana if she has been affected by the flooding of the Amur. Oh no, she tells us. Khabarovsk people are affected only if they have dachas by the river; the river floods on an annual basis, but this year it is not so bad. Not having a dacha, Tatyana has been spared the misfortune of floods.

We are walking through the shady streets of the oldest section of Khabarovsk, a pioneer settlement of wooden structures with frilly trim, a style once typical of Siberian towns before concrete structures dominated the Soviet landscape. This is the Khabarovsk that Laufer would have known. He returned here from Sakhalin Island in March 1899 in a state of exhaustion. When he wrote to Boas, asking for a salary increase to replace his tattered clothing, he described himself as a "learned man who puts his health and life at stake" and questioned why he should be satisfied by his ideas and ideals alone, without sufficient reumuneration.[7] Nevertheless, when the rivers became navigable at the end of May, he spent the next four months visiting Nanai and Nivkh villages along the Amur and Amgun rivers, reporting to Boas, "The trip during summer on the lower Amur was really more trying than the winter campaign on the island of Sakhalin. Nobody who has not been there can have an idea of the dreadful horrors one has to undergo on account of the insect-pests combined with heat and sixteen months' lonely life in wilderness, which resulted in an extraordinary state of nervousness I never experienced before. I therefore intend to use my sojourn here [in Yokohama] likewise to recover my health."[8] But little more than a year later, he would be back in the field, undertaking another ambitious project for Boas in China.

The creation of Khabarovsk, as an administrative town and trade center on the Amur, was meant to anchor the Russian hold on lands newly acquired from China in 1858 with the Treaty of Aigun (Ai-Kung). The establishment of the city also closely followed the brief British and French incursion into the Russian Far East during the Crimean War in 1854. This neighborhood is a historic district and many of the buildings have been carefully restored, a project begun some ten years earlier. Tatyana, minus pointer, still manages to instruct us on the area's origins as a Nanai settlement. She gestures to a nearby monument commemorating the settlement of Khabarovsk by order of Count Nikolay Muravyov, the governor-general of Eastern Siberia at the time. The monument was built directly on top of a Nanai sacred site, an imperial boot in the face forever.

As early as 1651, Native people in the area had been attacked by forces in the employ of the Russian tsar who raided along the Amur River, burning villages and killing the inhabitants. Yerofey Khabarov, for whom the Russian outpost was subsequently named, headed the Russian expedition. Khabarov was one of many early Russian colonists making their way to Siberia from the old Russian city of Veliki Ustyug, northwest of Moscow, and like others, Khabarov cast himself as a conqueror "discovering" new lands. Although he was reprimanded by the tsar for his excesses, he lost little face, and in addition to having a city named after him he made his fortune in the fur trade.

We move from the monument on the sacred site to material culture in CD format on a computer screen. The computer room is on the ground floor of a restored two-story wooden building that was once a private home. This is the site of the archaeology museum scheduled to open the next month. The CD demonstration goes off without a hitch thanks to their state-of-the-art system, a unique experience in our travels. Tatyana is delighted with the images, gives us more information, and asks the museum's computer wizard to make a print out of a photograph of one of the Nanai talismans that Laufer collected. Her choice is a small wooden figure in human shape, rosy cheeked and wrapped in a cloth cape and hood, possibly a shaman's spirit helper.

Our performance over, Tatyana takes us upstairs where the archaeology museum is very much under construction. Boards and cans of paint share floor space with partially completed dioramas. The semblance of chaos reminds us of home. We can safely bet that these fully imagined but now only half-realized rooms will be ready on schedule and that the curator and the designer will have a few additional gray hairs before they lift the celebratory glass.

Yuri Mikhailovich Vasilev, a silver-haired archaeologist on loan from the Vladivostok museum, is directing the installation. He worked on the old archaeology exhibit twenty-seven years before and knows the material well. He has the confident authority of an expert whose experience has earned him the stature to tell the story his way, to get it right this time. He describes himself as a specialist in the archaeology of the "medieval period," the tenth to thirteenth century in the Russian Far East. The exhibit begins with a panel profiling early archaeologists who worked in the region. As in so many places, the first were amateurs: administrators, surveyors, and missionaries made "discoveries" in their travels, gathered, artifacts, and wrote up their descriptions of the sites. Arsenev, the surveyor-turned-museum-director, is among this pantheon of heroes.

Yuri Mikhailovich begins his archaeological story with a presentation of Paleolithic sites worldwide. The exhibit includes profiles of distinguished paleontologists, including Robert Broom, Louis Leakey, and Raymond Dart, whose work in Africa began to flesh out the story of our earliest human ancestors. There are no Paleolithic sites in the Russian Far East; the earliest sites date to only 10-15,000 years ago. This introductory section is for the benefit of schoolchildren who will visit the museum, to give them the big picture of human history. In another time, Yuri Mikhailovich would have had to bracket this presentation with Marx and Engels's observations on primitive society, but he tells us that this is no longer necessary.

There are rich Neolithic sites around Khabarovsk, and Yuri Mikhailovich sketches the possibility of a common Neolithic culture across a broad region that includes locations in China and Mongolia where, from nearly 6,000 to nearly 4,000 years ago, people lived in villages, cultivated millet, domesticated dogs and pigs, and produced pottery. Yuri Mikhailovich laments that from 1935 until the 1990s, the Russians and Chinese had done no significant systematic comparative work.

The archaeology museum's Neolithic exhibit includes a hut by the same designing hand that reproduced Native structures in romantic forest snowscapes

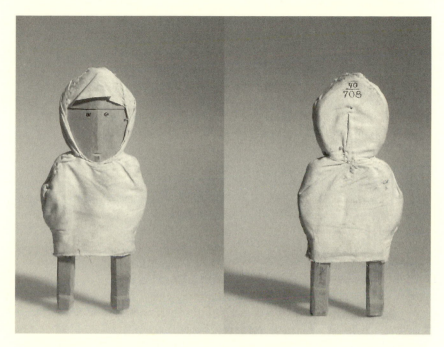

Figure 23. This is the image that Tatyana saw on the computer screen. She identified the hooded figure as a Nanai shaman's spirit helper. (AMNH 70/708, courtesy of the Division of Anthropology, AMNH)

in the larger museum. Yuri Mikhailovich hastens to explain that the hut is pure artistic extrapolation from the dwellings used by hunting peoples in this same region in historic times. "And there is no evidence for this, either," he says, gesturing theatrically at a picture of a mammoth hunt in tones of pink and pastel. Mammoths could have been hunted in the region—it is a reasonable speculation that they might have been—but no kill site has been discovered. He both disdains and defends the inclusion of the mammoth hunt, acknowledging the need for a little drama to attract the museum visitor. Laurel smiles at this familiar dilemma.

The next room has a great many Neolithic pots and shards from local excavations, including some impressively large coil pieces and an extensive assortment of grain pestles of worked stone, evidence of early grain cultivation. Laurel recognizes a piece of incised terracotta, a sizable remnant of a broken pot, like finding a familiar face among the crowd in a foreign city. Not being an expert, she poses her question carefully: "Do the Japanese archaeologists see a resemblance between this piece and their own Jomon artifacts?" It is, in fact, a Jomon piece, a gift from the Japanese archaeologists who have been digging for their own cultural roots in the Russian Far East.

The designer has left his mark in this gallery, too, simulating a fishing hut dug into a river embankment. Fish were a primary food source in the local Neolithic. Yuri Mikhailovich speaks passionately about the deterioration of the Amur River environment. "Even fifty years ago, the fish were so thick that you could catch them with your bare hands. If you stuck in a harpoon during the salmon run, you could impale one without even aiming."

He takes us into the petroglyph hall, a small, empty room whose walls are only half painted wine red. In the curator's vision, the hall is already complete, a celebration of Okladnikov's pioneering work on interpreting the Neolithic petroglyphs found in the region. Some of these sites, dating from more than 5,000 years ago, are located just forty kilometers downriver from Khabarovsk, near the Nanai village of Sikachi-Alyan. These petroglyphs, like those found in southern France and the American Southwest, provide invaluable glimpses into the social life and cosmology of Neolithic cultures. According to Okladnikov, many of these designs can be found in the textile motifs of Nanai clothing.

In the Bronze Age room, some of the more sophisticated ceramics (second to first century B.C.) resemble Korean Three Kingdoms (third to seventh century) pieces. Yuri Mikhailovich notes some joint expeditions with South Korean teams, an on-again, off-again collaboration that is on-again this year. In recent years, he and his colleagues have also participated in joint projects with China, North Korea, and Japan. An international scholarly crossroads is being constructed upon the remnants of an ancient highway. Yuri Mikhailovich has made several trips to China and is aware of widespread unemployment there and other problems that are "not widely discussed." Even so, he regrets that Russia has not followed China in adopting a gradual approach to economic transformation.

The final room is devoted to the medieval era, Yuri Mikhailovich's period, the time of the Nüxhen (Jurchen), who conquered much of north China in the twelfth century only to relinquish their prize to the even more formidable Mongols. Yuri Mikhailovich describes the Nüxhen as descended from the same ancestral stock as the Nanai, Udege, and other Amur River peoples. Laurel muses that while the Jurchen/Nüxhen are barbarian invaders in Chinese history books, here they are the home team.

We ask our now standard question: How does this new archaeology museum differ from the exhibits he worked on twenty-seven years ago? Yuri Mikhailovich explains that it is not just a matter of changing politics or the freedom to include any scholar he considers appropriate to the scientific story he is trying to tell. There has been a great deal more archaeological work in the intervening decades. Also, the computer has streamlined the researcher's painstaking work of sifting data from archaeological sites and the curator's task of tracking objects for an exhibition. But then, as now, the major element in the success of an exhibit is whether the curator and the designer can work well together. "Amen to that," says Laurel. And of course, his biggest problem is money. "Amen again."

We mention how impressed we are with the curators in the Russian Far East who plan futures with no resources or support. He warms to the topic of doing one's work well: "Every gem should have an appropriate setting, and so should every object on display, so that its meaning and beauty are revealed." In Japan, he has seen a government's commitment to the presentation of history in public museums. The Russian government does not value history, and without knowledge of history the nation is weaker, he says. But "history," as we have seen, is a problematic notion.

Laurel points out that Japanese museums usually present their history as if it were the story of a single homogeneous people, an approach that distorts the Japanese past and present. The Russian situation is so much more diverse. "Like the United States," he says. "Yes," Laurel says, "and we're losing government support for our museums right and left." He gives her the look of disbelief that Russian museum people deliver whenever this curator in a large and relatively well-endowed American institution finds herself naively suggesting that funding is a common global problem of the museum world. We tell him of the *Enola Gay* incident, how curators at the Smithsonian Institution, critically dependent upon government support, thoroughly revised the content of an exhibit dealing with the bombing of Hiroshima under protest from World War II veterans' groups. This old hand at Soviet museums observes that it is very bad when governments dictate a historical line.

Outside, in the September sunshine and on our own again, our official work is done and all of Khabarovsk is at our feet. An art museum stands next to the history museum. A sign in Japanese advertises "local products," indicating that the shop sells items suitable for the requisite gifts that Japanese tourists are expected to distribute back home. Several Japanese signs around the town betray dreams of a tourist windfall. The prospect of Japanese roots-seekers was probably a factor in the decision to open a new archaeology museum. Ingrid has seen them from time to time, but the Japanese are not here, at least not right now. Amur River dreams of easy tourist yen are, it seems, a casualty of the slump in the Japanese economy.

In addition to "local products," the art museum promises an exhibit of "Soviet Art." We go inside, anticipating a funky encounter with Socialist realist oil paintings of labor heroes and heroic mothers and stirring poster art. We are ushered into a vast room that could be a gallery —there are some paintings on the wall. The sign on the door says, "closed for inventory," but we are told the sign does not apply to foreigners. Indifferent art of indifferent provenance hangs on the walls, pedestrian nudes and landscapes, none of it in any sense "Soviet." There are heaps of other merchandise as well. We realize that we have been ushered into the museum shop in the hope that we will spend some of our rubles. The prices have not yet been raised to match the declining value of the local currency, so we have every incentive to examine the handicrafts and jewelry. There are a couple of silk jackets, embroidered and appliquéd in the signature style of Amur River decorative arts, but compared to the garments in museum cases, the workmanship is crude. We buy small talismanic animals, a sort of bog hog intended to be cast away, taking one's own afflictions with it, as Andrey Samar, a Nanai ethnographer, explained to Alexia during a conference in Vladivostok the previous spring. The proprietor says the artist is from a Nanai community. Then we discover the amber counter, everything at amazingly low prices. We do not leave empty-handed, much to everyone's satisfaction.

The shop clerks reveal that the exhibit is actually of Soviet-era ceramics and that it is inside the museum, just up the stairs from the shop. For this, we buy two tickets at the foreigners' price of eighteen rubles apiece, about $1.50 US each at the new rate of 11.9 rubles to the dollar. Since we first changed money in Providenia three weeks ago, the value of the ruble has been cut nearly in half.

Before visiting the exhibition halls, we have to cover our shoes with the commodious slippers provided by the museum. Now it is Alexia who experiences déjà vu. Slippers used to be required in the art museums of St. Petersburg to protect the exhibit space from dirt that could be tracked inside from city streets, but she has not seen them in museums in Russia for years. Like the intensive security checks we have been subjected to in far northern airports and the room chits in our hotel, this is an anachronism from Soviet times.

Beslippered, we pad up the ornate staircase. The building is a Beaux-Arts creation of marble and stained glass, beautifully restored in 1996 and lovingly tended. It is empty, save for the babushkas whose job it is to keep the visitors in line. Guidebooks warn of the schoolmarmish ferocity of these women in Russian museums, but this group seems rather forlorn. They usher us from one room to another and do their best to corral us into seeing every last exhibit, all the while thanking us for visiting their museum. Since there are no other visitors, we have given some purpose to their day.

It was Soviet policy to provide art museums in every major town with samples of work for each major period. Some of these were appropriated from wealthy estates in the 1920s as the Soviet government nationalized private property, and Khabarovsk's holdings are no exception. The paintings on display are arranged to emphasize the evolution of the craft in Russia from the work of the Academy of Art in the late eighteenth and early nineteenth centuries to the futurism of the early twentieth century.

We walk briskly through the halls exhibiting icons from the early Russian period and the floating cherubs and stiff reproductions of the classical style dictated by the Academy of Art from the early nineteenth century. We come to a hall hung with superb examples of the late nineteenth-century "Itinerant school," so called because of the artists' desire to travel the countryside and depict daily life, social problems, and scenes from Russia's history. Originally known as the rebellious "group of fourteen," graduates of the elite Russian

Academy of Art in the late 1860s claimed the freedom to choose their own themes for painting in a time of social unrest and intense challenge to the old order. The Itinerants' work often reflects dissatisfaction with the moral order while elevating daily life and hard work. They are almost inevitably present in Russian museum collections. Here in Khabarovsk we see Ivan Shishkin's lush, detailed Russian forests with rays of light cast through branches and Vasily Vershchagin's vivid realism expressed in intimate portraits of various Turkish folk—a soldier, a woman with her child, an old woman. We are treated to a wide range of paintings by Vasily Surikov and Ilya Repin from what is often referred to as the Golden Age of Russian art, the 1870s and 1880s.

We keep asking about the Soviet era ceramics. A kindly babushka, who apologizes profusely that she is not well enough informed to explain the exhibit to us, leads us to a solitary case of figurines in the corner of a back hallway. It is 1950s kitsch, mostly cherubic children with rosy cheeks. The most interesting piece, in part because she seems so out of place, is a svelte, Garboesque woman with high cheekbones, wearing ice skates and striking a sultry pose, neck thrown back, pointed breasts thrust forward. We are ready to move on after a few minutes, and the babushka is anxious for us to see the rest of the museum. We nod, smile, and flee through a gallery of hideous Baroque European art. We are descending the staircase, making polite excuses to the babushkas who are all hanging over the stair rail, almost out the door, when one of them asks, almost quizzically, don't we want to see the gallery of Native artists? That stops us in our tracks.

This gallery turns out to be the best of all. These twentieth-century Soviet and post-Soviet pieces were self-consciously created to celebrate Native handicraft development, as documented by the photographs of artisans at work that hang in each gallery beside the objects. The workmanship is gorgeous and the objects are displayed to their full glory. Among the treasures are framed pieces of fantastic appliqué work and costumes that show a respect for traditional materials and skills and a creative flair. The more recent robes incorporate long, shimmering beads and faux pearls. One fur robe makes a smock-like silhouette with fields of beige and golden brown fur and midnight blue brocade. It has a big fur ruff around the neck. It is possible to imagine a soignée woman, circa 1920, wearing this costume as she descends from a limousine on Park Avenue.

The intricate and appealing basketwork seems to have been collected in two waves, in the 1920s and the 1970s. There is also a 1983 version of the fancy "first-day-of-hunting" suit that used to be common among the Udege, Ulchi, and other Amur River peoples. Unlike the one we saw in the regional history museum, this one incorporates rick-rack into its rich design, a modern touch. Some of the carved wooden charms and talismans date from the 1990s. This is encouraging, more oblique evidence that the beliefs that engendered the making and feeding of talismans are still intact and perhaps fortified by the museum's interest. As elsewhere, there are framed fur and hide rugs, and as a sign of the art museum's regional prominence, yet more machine-carved walrus ivory from distant Uelen in Chukotka.

There is little commentary about the objects on display, but a few framed pictures on the wall put faces to the people who made them. Image 201 is simply and frustratingly labeled "women artisans in traditional dress." One woman's garment is cut and edged in the traditional way but made from rose-printed cotton. Amur River peoples have not been bashful about incorporating new elements: Chinese brocade, Japanese and American cotton, rick-rack, faux pearls. Other photographs show a woodcarver at work, a child in traditional dress, and a young woman in an elaborate robe and jewelry. The babushka in this hall is able to give the woodcarver a name, "U," and to identify the small child and young woman as his children. Several pieces of U's work are on display in the gallery.

The art museum and the ethnographic exhibits next door replay the familiar dichotomy: Native peoples are the subjects of "ethnography" in the natural history museum, whereas works of "primitive art" appear at the art museum. The Khabarovsk Regional History Museum provides far more context than we were prepared to digest at one sitting. The art museum elevates individual robes, baskets, and carvings as works of art in their own right and, in at least a few places, acknowledges the artisans who produced individual masterworks. But, as in so many art museums, there is next to nothing about the uses or meanings of these objects in the worlds that produced them. What we see is a demonstration of stellar skill.

We exit past a temporary gallery where Native American and local Native art works are being mounted side by side for a temporary exhibition. The art recalls the gallery of Native art in the Anchorage Museum of Art and History in its sometimes romantic adaptations of traditional motifs. The silhouette of a naked woman with a talismanic bird figure in her belly seems a recurrent theme, an image pregnant with symbolism. There is a paper cut of a Nanai tree of life with the shaman as Jack-in-the-beanstalk making his ascent to the spirit world. The paper cut is several feet high; the delicate patterning of scenes along the trunk and branches is a virtuoso elaboration on the patterns that Nanai women cut from paper and birch bark, recalling the patterns that Laufer collected one hundred years ago.

Outside the museum, hoping to make some long-distance telephone calls, we look for the town's Intourist Hotel, one of those formerly reserved for foreigners across the Soviet landscape. Its broad white expanse, visible in the distance, retreats from us like a mirage until we have made a full circle of the historic district. It is one of those buildings intended to be reached only by car. We climb up an embankment and go through a parking lot and finally arrive at the main entrance. With a little more scrambling, we locate the business center on an upper floor of the hotel's dark, uninviting interior. Alexia tries, again fruitlessly, to phone Viktoria Petrasheva, our contact in Petropavlovsk, Kamchatka, the next stop on our itinerary. Laurel tries to telephone her husband and, failing that, sends him a fax. The number of the Oktyabrskaya Hotel, where we hope to make a reservation in Petropavlovsk, does not seem to work, nor does our American anthropologist friend Alex King's telephone number in Palana.

At a book kiosk Laurel buys a lined notebook for the next volume of her travel diary. Its black cover is decorated with a haunted house, flitting ghosts, and words that look like they could mean "Halloween" in a language the clerk identifies as Hungarian. Laurel imagines a parallel between our travels from museum to museum and the American child's going out for trick or treat, wondering what lurks behind the next door. Museums, in their own way, are haunted houses.

We walk by the river, which is edged by a narrow stretch of park and a promenade. Our overdue lunch consists of rounds of bread with cheese melted on top and boxes of juice from a concession in the park beside the river. A small party of deeply tanned Asian men and women, mostly men, faces ruddy from drink, are singing an unfamiliar but unmistakably Korean song. One of the men dances, gracefully extending his arms and flexing his shoulders. For Laurel, this scene recalls South Korean office outings on spring days more than a quarter century ago. Could they be South Korean tourists? They are too coarse-skinned and tanned for city people. The group in the park is not old enough for senior citizens' travel, and they are smaller, leaner, and generally more threadbare than any group of South Korean farmers who would have the means to take a senior citizens' club package tour. And who, in South Korea, is traveling abroad for pleasure in 1998, a year of austerity imposed by the market crash and the IMF's stringent conditions for reform? Foreign travel is currently construed as an unpatriotic act. Could these picnickers be local? Could they possibly be North Koreans?

Three commodious wooden barges, tied to the bank, are so elaborately decorated with gingerbread trim that they ought to be floating restaurants. In fact, they are a customs clearing point for goods from China. It is here that one of the indeterminately Korean men from the picnic approaches us, offering his camera and hoping to have his picture taken with one of the foreign women. He is surprised when Laurel addresses him in Korean, but takes it in stride. The group is originally from Heilongjiang, the Chinese province just across the river, but they have come to work as laborers in Khabarovsk. He tells us that he lives in a small room beside the market.

Alexia is aware of this population; on the hotel television, she had caught a news piece on the importation of Chinese workers from across the river to meet a shortage in agricultural labor around Khabarovsk. Of course some of these "Chinese" would be ethnically Korean In the early twentieth century Koreans settled in Manchuria and the Russian Far East in large numbers.

Most were escaping famine and economic hardship, but this population also included Korean nationalists on the run from the Japanese Colonial Authority after Japan's annexation of Korea in 1910. By that year, more than 50,000 Koreans were living in the Russian Far East; by 1935, the number was more than 200,000. In 1937, when Japan began its incursion into Manchuria, most Koreans in the Russian Far East were Soviet citizens and many were ardent Communist Party members. Even so, a paranoid Stalin decreed that all "Asiatic" peoples living in the Russian Far East were to be forcibly relocated to Soviet Central Asia. Many did not survive the journey. Since the early 1990s, some Koreans have begun to return to the area from Central Asia. Today there are more than 400,000 Koreans in the Russian Far East, and officially, another 431,140 live across the Amur River in Heilongjiang.

We walk along the main street where vendors have set out mushrooms and vegetables. We buy and munch some not very satisfactory steamed corn, and dip into some gift shops where Laurel buys amber earrings and Alexia buys a bracelet of amber set in silver. All of the amber on sale in every gift shop, indeed everywhere in Russia, is from one place, Kaliningrad, in the northwesternmost corner of the former Soviet Union. It could not be further from here.

We continue our promenade. Alexia strikes up a conversation with one of the elderly women who have set bathroom scales on the street where people can pay to be weighed. The woman is a pensioner who, like many others, has not been receiving her checks. Even if she is reimbursed for the missed payments, the money will not be pegged to inflation and will be worth only a fraction of her entitlement. The pensioner jokes that even in bad times, women will still want to know how much they weigh; it provides a small but steady income. Across from the woman with her scale hangs a sign in frilly calligraphic script that advertises a school promising to train young women in the "lost arts of charm and decorum." We learn from Ingrid that this organization prepares young Russian women for relatively highly paid employment as hostesses in Japanese hotels and restaurants.

We find the central market, but at the end of the afternoon, many of the clothing stalls have already closed. There is more action inside the covered food market. We sample some local honey from an immaculate white-tiled concession stand. Laurel is drawn to the pungent odor of scallions, garlic, and red peppers at the Korean food vendors with their piles of pickled vegetables and mushrooms. Laurel shouts a Korean greeting which is returned, and an exchange of pleasantries ensues. The repartee, by its very naturalness, confounds Laurel's experience of Korean market women. In a Seoul marketplace, unless she were already known to the vendors, there would have been gasps of incredulity and a flutter of confirmations that yes, seemingly natural sounding Korean had come out of her Euro-American mouth, and then the questions, "Where did you learn?" and "Are you a missionary?" How odd to be treated like a normal Korean-speaking human being. How strange that it should seem

Figure 24. This pensioner, posed with her daughter, uses a bathroom scale as a street side concession in Khabarovsk, assuming that, even in bad times, women will want to know what they weigh. She had not received a pension check for several months and even if she should receive her allotment, the amount would not be adjusted for inflation. (Photo by Laurel Kendall)

so strange. These women, unlike their cousins in the homeland, are a minority in a multiethnic society, spending much of their lives within the Russian language. For them, ethnicity is not inextricably tied to language.

The market women urge Laurel to buy some of their wares and despite a dinner appointment, she is tempted. This is the food of her second home, of warm, nurturing circles that took her in despite her strangeness. She tells the market women that because she is staying in a hotel, it is impossible to boil rice and make a meal. "You can get a *tosirak* in there," a helpful woman offers, pointing to the stall across the way. Laurel remembers *tosirak*, a small tin lunchbox filled with rice and pickled vegetables and possibly a scrap of fried fish, which, in Korea of the early 1970s, could be warmed on top of a pot-bellied coal stove, then the standard source of heat in offices. She imagines the contents of a huge pot of rice being ladled into take-home containers, but when she investigates the stall, it has only packaged foodstuffs. Come to think of it, Laurel has not seen a proper *tosirak* in South Korea for quite some time now, apart from children's plastic containers with "Hello Kitty" on the lids. The pot-bellied coal heaters disappeared long ago, and cold rice is easily reheated in a microwave oven. In a few days, Laurel learns that Toshirak is the name of an instant noodle product in its own disposable cup imported from South Korea and popular throughout Russia.

The rapid change in the exchange rate has caused a run on the banks. When we go to change money again, just before dinner, a sign at the bank reads "*net valuty*," no foreign currency available. When we pay the hotel bill later that night, the declining value of the ruble will be even more apparent. The charge is 243 rubles per night, but we receive a 15 percent discount since there was no hot water. At yesterday's rate this was about $30 US a night, but by today our bill totals only about $24 US a night. At the reception desk a young man asks Alexia, "Why did you come to this country? It is so hard to live here." When she tells him that we like his city, he responds, "Well, for you it may be nice, but for us it is horrible."

Ingrid meets us at the hotel and we go back to the Hong Kong restaurant, filled with customers tonight. Perhaps for this reason, the dishes are tastier, less greasy. The trade-off is a steady barrage of karaoke music; we dine against a background of reggae, "Moscow Nights," "Auld Lang Syne," and some sentimental Chinese pop songs that inspire the guests at one table to stand up and croon into the microphone, but we manage a conversation, even so. We tell Ingrid about our nearly aborted taxi ride in Anadyr, how Sergey the driver fixed his engine on the spot. Ingrid nods knowingly, "Russians can fix anything. Think of the Mir Space Station."

Over dinner, Ingrid tells us about the ten days when water was turned off in several neighborhoods of Khabarovsk. An electrical fire at one of the city water stations shut down the pumping station. Simultaneously, a chemical plant upstream along the Amur had been flooded and there was a risk that it would contaminate the drinking water supply. When the municipal govern-ment began trucking in potable water, it was interpreted as a confirmation that the water supply was indeed contaminated, instead of just shut off due to me-chanical failure. Like her neighbors, Ingrid stood in line at one of the still available pumps with her buckets, having been told that what she carried home might be all the water she would have for ten days. Word came that the tap water was back on. Could the crowd at the pump believe it? Was it safe to abandon the queue? If the water really was back on, could they trust it? Every-one thought of Chernobyl, where the full extent of the contamination was not revealed until it was too late. In the end, Ingrid waited her turn to fill the buck-ets; the stores were sold out of bottled mineral water.

The concierge is not at her post when we return. No concierge, no key. We are locked out. We sit restlessly by the empty desk, impatient to be packing up for our early morning departure. Alexia goes to find the concierge, who is in tears. Her husband, a geologist, had died the previous day. She describes her husband as having been unable to cope with hard times. She says, "Women are stronger." We nod, thinking of this woman of science (the concierge herself is a retired geologist) doing laundry in a large hotel.

At the airport the next morning, we are going through the metal detector when the airport personnel challenge us. As foreigners, we must use the special lounge in the separate foreigners' terminal—another Khabarovsk anachro-nism. Alexia says that this simply does not happen anymore in other parts of Russia; it does not happen anywhere else in the world. The airport worker snaps, "We don't criticize the way you do things over there." A young woman in uniform leads us to the foreigners' terminal. As we cross the parking lot, Laurel softly whistles "The International." Alexia doubts that the young woman would have recognized the tune, much less caught the irony.

At this large, beautifully finished, and nearly empty departure lounge, a well-dressed group of New Russian men are ushered out to the plane, "busy selling off the oil and the forests," Alexia comments. Now it is our turn to ride an empty shuttle bus out to the gangway, the same dusty, rickety bus that has just transported everyone from the main departure lounge. We are soon on our way to Petropavlovsk.

Chapter 6

Petropavlovsk
Once Almost a Boom Town

Kamenskoye, December 3, 1900
We left Kuel in the afternoon of November 4th with 20 dog sleds and arrived in
Kamenskoye the night of the 7th. . . . During the overnight stay in the yurts, into
which we had to enter through the smoke hole, we continued to take measurements and
notes and make collections. When we left Kuel it was -26 C, but the temperature
started to rise . . . since our arrival in Kamenskoye. For two days it even rained; there
was a snowstorm with winds . . . [that made it] difficult to stand; the three of us had
to stand together to make observations, as we could have gotten lost in just a few
meters from the yurt and be quickly covered with snow.

—*Jochelson to Boas*

Bogoras and Jochelson spent December 1900 together in the village of Kamenskoye at the far north of what is now the Koryak Autonomous Region in Kamchatka. Hard travel had preceded their reunion. In the summer of 1900, the Jochelsons had landed in Kushka on the northern shore of the Sea of Okhotsk, intending to study the reindeer Koryak who herded in the area. Unbeknown to the Jochelsons, this region had been decimated by a measles epidemic the previous winter. Jochelson reported to Boas, "According to the church registers, 179 persons out of a total of 500 had died at Gizhiga, down the coast, between December 25, 1899 and March 1, 1900 . . . The Reindeer Koryak, who are in the habit of wintering near this place, had moved far into the mountains with their herds, in order to escape the ravages of the prevailing epidemic."[1] Because the subjects of their fieldwork had disappeared, Jochelson and his party traveled overland through swampy high tundra to the Koryak village of Paren. They passed through a deserted landscape, short on provisions because they had counted on getting fish and meat from passing Koryak and Tungus. Jochelson, his wife, and their field assistant were lost on the tundra for three days when, after chasing a derelict pack horse, they became separated from their guides. Without food, fire, or protection from wind and frost, at night, "There was nothing left to do but lie down hungry on the tundra wrapped tightly in our blankets. We had a Winchester with us for protec-

Figure 25. The dogsled was a common means of transportation in the far North. Both Bogoras and the Jochelsons traveled extensively by dogsled in the winter of 1900–1901. The Jochelsons' party employed twenty teams, but when Bogoras traveled south from Mariinsky Post he used only three: "We could carry no heavy loads, however, and had to leave everything behind except our scientific instruments and a few objects for barter." (AMNH Library 1451)

tion against bears whose tracks we frequently came across."[2] Only when they had managed to collect from the sparse tundra shrubs sufficient wood to make a smoky fire did their guides finally locate them.

Further disappointment awaited the Jochelsons when, after sixteen days of hard travel, they reached Paren, a Koryak winter village, only to find the village deserted, the residents not yet returned from the summer encampments where they caught fish and hunted sea lions. Jochelson sent his guides to the nearest fishing village and they returned, a few hours later, with several Koryak, including three village elders who advised the Jochelsons to continue on to the permanent settlement of Kuel, across the Shelekhov Gulf from Kaminskoye where they expected to meet Bogoras.

Bogoras traveled south from Mariinsky Post with three teams of dogsleds. "We could carry no heavy loads, however, and had to leave everything behind except our scientific instruments and a few objects for barter. This obliged us to rely almost wholly on the food-supply of the country, and during the whole time we lived on dried fish, reindeer-meat, seal and walrus blubber etc."[3] Such journeying was only a backdrop to the scientific work that consumed them.

At the end of a month spent studying the Koryak language in Kamenskoye, Bogoras went further into Kamchatka where he continued to work with Koryak. He had heard from Kamchatka Cossacks at Mariinsky Post that the "northern Kamchadal" had not been thoroughly russianized and was delighted to find eight villages of Itelmen ("Kamchadal"), original inhabitants of Kamchatka, who still spoke their own language.

He left Kamchatka at the end of February. His journey back to Mariinsky Post led through nearly deserted villages of Kerek, Koryak-speaking walrus hunters living along the eastern coast of Chukotka whose livelihood had been disrupted by American whalers who had driven the walrus north; the Kereks were thus "rapidly dying out from continual starvation."[4] Leaving the coast, his path back to the Anadyr River lay through uninhabited mountains. In the absence of Native guides, his party relied on the course of frozen mountain rivers to lead them over the watershed and then down to the tributaries of the Anadyr. During this journey, he caught influenza and lost his voice for two weeks so that he could communicate only by sign language. At one point, he was so ill that the Cossack assigned to his party asked for instructions regarding the delivery of his body and his official papers, in the event of his death en route.

Kamchatka looks a little bit like Wisconsin. It is green still in the early autumn, and we travel from the airport to the town through a countryside where wooden dachas, little houses with vegetable gardens, snuggle under trees. Wildflowers bloom in clumps of tall grass. None of this would seem remarkable if we had not already spent time in bleak Providenia and Anadyr. We are still very far north, but north is a relative condition—we are only slightly north of London's latitude—and the local landscape seems perfectly luxuriant relative to the tundra of Chukotka. For the first time on the trip the natural beauty of the landscape seems to overpower and soften the ponderous Soviet concrete block construction even when it catches up with us again on the outskirts of town.

Petropavlovsk is rimmed by spectacular volcanoes, but they are completely hidden today under a heavy cloud cover. There are frequent tremors and earthquakes here. The taxi driver seems to enjoy telling his passengers about them. Passing a cluster of five-story apartment blocks, he says that this northeastern region of the city is considered a prestigious place to live because it is less susceptible to quakes; a quake measuring seven on the Richter scale in another part of the city was felt here as only a five. The driver explains that the buildings rest on a cliff of shale that acts as a shock absorber. He points to the barely distinct structures on the top of the buildings and expresses amazement that folks lugged dirt up several flights of stairs for these rooftop greenhouses.

As we turn onto the main highway, the driver points to a deserted pile of green metal cylinders with pointed ends lying in the grass. "See, we relied for years on the military," he says with an edge of nostalgia. It takes us a moment

Figure 26. This hand-drawn map from the Anthropology Archive of the American
Museum of Natural History illustrates the wide-ranging travels of Bogoras and
Jochelson. (Accession envelope 1902–20, image 34, courtesy of the Division of
Anthropology, AMNH)

to realize that these are abandoned rockets. Like much of Siberia, Kamchatka was closed to foreigners and to most Soviet citizens for nearly fifty years, up until 1990. During the Cold War, Kamchatka served as a base for military operations and early warning radar systems. A few regions of the peninsula were also used as target areas for Soviet missile testing, and the port in Petropavlovsk was a major Pacific Fleet submarine base.

The taxi driver, who came from Moscow to serve in the army, began to work in a cement plant after being demobilized. When the government construction business went dry with the end of the Soviet Union in the early 1990s, he took up taxi driving. A few years past, would Kamchatka have seemed like a land of opportunity, a Pacific gateway? The driver tells us that times were better prior to the opening of Kamchatka to foreigners; people received the special hardship pay reserved for those working in the North and had fewer worries. He tells us that these days, nothing is being built except banks. As he speaks, we come to an intersection with a single multistory, gleaming glass building owned by one of the several new banks, the landscape's solitary embodiment of "new money" in the hands of New Russians. This glass-encased bank, and a building of similar construction housing the headquarters of the major fishing concern in the center of Petropavlovsk, are the primary icons of the growing concentration of wealth in this former military outpost.

The town of Petropavlovsk is built on a hillside overlooking a scenic harbor with pine trees on the cliffs. From a distance it seems idyllic, as if it could be in Marin County, California. On closer inspection, much of the construction looks shoddy, recently built but already decaying. The passenger ships that used to make the Vladivostok run were all sold to the Chinese. In the mid-1990s the city was poised to be a boomtown, but the port is less active now than in the past.

We were concerned that we had not been able to reach the Oktyabrskaya by telephone from Khabarovsk to reserve a hotel room. The taxi driver tells us not to worry, that there is almost always a vacancy at the Oktyabrskaya. He is right. At 1,030 rubles per night ($80 US), these are the most expensive rooms of the trip, but also the most commodious. There is even hot water twice a day, although of course there is no heat despite the bone-chilling damp weather. This Oktyabrskaya is freshly renovated, a change from only a few years back when, according to one recent traveler, the hotel had $50 rooms devoid of toilet seats.

The foreign exchange service is in the basement of the local G.U.M., formerly the government department store but now given over to private concessions. The exchange window is already closed for the day but a young man in a leather jacket is lurking close by, anxious to change money at the new official rate of 12.81 rubles per U.S. dollar. He efficiently figures the exchange on his pocket calculator. The ruble is shrinking fast. We calculate our immediate needs and change the minimum.

At loose ends, we wander through the department store. Laurel, who wants to upgrade her travel wardrobe for official meetings with museum directors, finds a packable and reasonably warm little black knit skirt, made in Germany. Alexia finds a sporty black jacket made from a ribbed knit that seems to be popular from New York to Kamchatka. The jacket is manufactured in Russia, a hopeful sign that Russian light manufacturing has begun to rebound. In the early 1990s, the only clothing available in these private stalls was made from faded or garish fabrics, poorly sewn in Russia, China, or Turkey.

The shop clerk urges us to buy, reminding us that the prices are still pegged to the old rates of exchange and that this will not last. We go back to the foreign exchange window. No one is there, but one of the vendors discreetly catches our eye and the transaction is made. Shopping bags in hand, we are heading out when Alexia overhears some shopkeepers muttering about the foreigners who are smiling because they are able to buy while the ruble falls. Ashamed by her relative wealth, Alexia quietly hands a bill to the beggar woman clutching a Russian Orthodox icon who has posted herself in the doorway of the store.

The guidebook lists a Japanese restaurant. Because this city is considered a gateway to the Pacific, we have high expectations. The restaurant is difficult to find, set back from the road on the ground floor of a moldering, concrete highrise, but the cab driver assures us we are in the right place. The restaurant is so empty that we are surprised when the hostess says they would be happy to serve us. They will tell us later that people gather there only on Saturday nights for the over-thirty singles night ("Komu za 30"). We marvel that they bother to stay open the rest of the week.

The expansive dining room has a glossy counter that could pass for a sushi bar. The restaurant opened five years ago, in 1993, as a Russo-Japanese joint venture, but the Japanese pulled out three years ago, taking with them the possibility of the restaurant's serving any of the Japanese items still listed on the menu. We settle for fiddlehead ferns and a seafood salad. The main course is a goulash of rice, squash, tomatoes, eggplant, and mushrooms. We are surprised to find our salads garnished with purple-tinged radicchio, a designer vegetable in the United States. Here, it is grown locally and not considered particularly special.

When we emerge from the restaurant, there are no taxis in sight. We make our way through the maze surrounding an athletic field and a parking lot in the hope of gaining a more opportune position to flag one down. Alexia tries to get us a ride in a private car, someone who will take us back to the hotel for a fee. She has done this all over Russia, but rarely with such a slow response. Eventually, a fair-haired young Russian stops for us. He is wearing an embroidered Cossack shirt with a high collar and a fastening on one shoulder. We notice a Louis Vuitton bag in the back seat of his car, or perhaps it is only a Korean knock-off. He describes himself as a "church worker" and refuses to take money. There is a strong scent of ecclesiastical incense in the car.

Back at the hotel, evening television offers a Rolling Stones' concert, but this is not the concert the Stones performed in Moscow on August 12, a few weeks earlier. The Moscow concert was plagued with technical difficulties and consequently could not be broadcast; their Bremen concert, with Russian voiceover commentary, is being broadcast here by way of compensation. We sit in the Russian Far East and watch with rapt attention the middle-aged Mick Jagger, still flaunting it.

The next morning, Alexia tries yet again to reach Palana, and again no luck. The attempted telephone call gives us a late start for our meeting at the museum and we are unsure of the location. It is not where the guidebook said it would be, in Lenin Square, just down the hill from our hotel. We jump into a cab and anticipate a long and uncertain journey. The cab drives around the block and deposits us in front of an old stone building with a cannon in front pointed at the harbor. This is the Petropavlovsk Regional History Museum, begun in 1911.

Relative to the Khabarovsk Regional History Museum in a major regional center, this is a small museum with a full staff of twenty-five, of whom ten are "scientific," or research, staff. Compared with a local museum like Providenia's, of course, this museum is enormous, a significant subregional center, with subsidiaries in Esso (which we plan to visit) and the Commander Islands. Although the Petropavlovsk Museum has official oversight for these local museums, they are financed by district budgets via regional budgets, which in turn come from the Kamchatka provincial administration. The Petropavlovsk museum, financed through the Department of Culture in the Petropavlovsk regional administration, is one step closer to the source of finances—Moscow—and consequently receives a larger portion of the pie than its subsidiaries.

The admissions clerk scolds us for being late and collects an entrance fee from us. She also wants us to pay for a guided excursion through the exhibits. Alexia draws the line at this on the grounds that we are museum colleagues who have come on business. The arrival of Margarita Ivanovna Belova, the head of the decorative arts division, changes the mood. She is a pleasant-faced woman with short blond hair graying at the temples, plump and affable, and thoroughly devoted to her work. She holds a degree in art history from Leningrad State University and works especially with women artisans. She has a wooden pointer in hand; we exchange knowing glances and resolve to endure. The director is out of town. The vice director, who happens to be married to the director, is in a meeting with the civil authorities, asking them, among other issues, to turn on the heat in the museum. She will meet with us at eleven.

Margarita Ivanovna leads us to an exhibit of contemporary (post-1970) Koryak handicraft. She collected most of it herself from artisans with whom she has worked for years. We enter through an empty gallery where a veritable herd of reindeer heads lines the floor, waiting to be mounted on the wall for a new temporary exhibit. Wildlife and hunting are big draws in Kamchatka, pulling hard currency from across the Pacific. This is becoming one of the most significant aspects of the informal economy, with some hunters paying as much as $15,000 US for three weeks of unrestricted big game hunting, posing an even greater threat to the wildlife of Kamchatka than local poachers. The museum seems to be hoping for its own small corner of the market. The exhibit includes tourist brochures in English appealing to international hunters.

Two sets of wooden sculptures dominate the contemporary art gallery. One is a group of Koryak dancers, and the other portrays a herder family gathered around their tea kettle. The sculptures evoke a sense of dynamism, suggesting the bent knees and fluid shoulder movements characteristic of contemporary Koryak dance. Two of the three figures hold drums and one woman is shown with a wisp of a smile, perhaps inspired by the drumming. Clearly, these pieces do not serve the same function as those precise if sometimes painfully stiff recreations of physical type, dress, and bearing found in old-fashioned ethnology displays. The statues are slightly abstracted, interpretive pieces; they are not intended to convey information as much as artistically evoke well-known themes that celebrate the Koryak way of life. Inevitably they romanticize, but they do not obviously patronize. Margarita Ivanovna tells us with enthusiasm that the statues were carved by a Ukrainian couple long resident in Palana. Laurel says, "It's the work of someone who grew up with socialist realism, but," and Alexia finishes her sentence, "then saw Rodin." The couple also sculpted the diorama of a Koryak reindeer herder camp that we will see downstairs in the permanent gallery. Each figure in the diorama has a living counterpart, someone known personally to the sculptors.

The wooden statues in some ways resemble the socialist realist evocations of happy ethnic minorities that Laurel has seen in China. These sculptures seem respectful of their subjects and fit more harmoniously with the displays, but they are still troubling to an American curator's eye. Museological conventions are different in Russia than in the United States, even as both traditions are changing. Professional subcultures have their own unstated rules and assumptions. While it is no longer unusual for an American museum to display yesterday's "artifacts" as "masterworks by Native artisans" acknowledged by name, we do not make easy combinations of "art about" and "art by," save to deconstruct the colonial premises of the former. Most American curators are painfully aware that any representation of Native people is fraught with questions of relative power, that the non-Native witness, ethnologist, or curator is always suspect. Even so, Laurel continues to write both ethnographies and museum labels, albeit more self-consciously aware of her own position than she would have been twenty years ago. She wonders, is exhibiting the work of non-Native sculptors long resident in a Koryak town so very different from quoting a work of ethnography in a museum label—a common and respectable practice in Western anthropology museums?

Figure 27. Exhibit of contemporary handicrafts in the Petropavlovsk museum. The sculpture portrays a group of dancing Koryak. A Koryak hide rug hangs on the far wall behind the sculpture. (Photo by Laurel Kendall)

Our tour of the hall begins with a luminescent case of carved ivory. There is not a single piece of overly decorated scrimshaw or Uelen-style realist sculpture in the lot. The most memorable piece is of a small squatting figure, an expression of inner calm on his upturned face. Margarita Ivanovna tells us about some of the artisans whose work is on display, particularly the Itelmen (Bogoras's "Kamchadal"), an indigenous group that historically relied on subsistence fishing and once populated the entire central and southern areas of the Kamchatka peninsula, with some communities in the northwest as well. One community of Itelmen to the northwest of Petropavlovsk is attempting to revive its craft, although not necessarily in traditional forms. The author of the wonderful squatting figure probably saw something like it in a book or a museum, Margarita says. Perhaps a Japanese netsuke was his inspiration.

One of the carvers learned his craft in the Uelen workshop because there was no one left in his own Koryak community to teach him. His piece, a deer, does not have the complex, often fussily overdone tangle of antlers that one would find on a Uelen piece as a demonstration of the carver's virtuosity with an electric drill. This piece is small, delicate, and elegantly simple.

Encouraged by our questions, Margarita Ivanovna abandons her script and tells us about her work. She came to the museum in 1966 as an art historian and has been working with Native artisans ever since. Her particular passion is for the people and handicrafts of the Karaginsk District in the northeast, near the Bering Sea, where she has done her most intensive fieldwork. She invokes the beauty and integrity of Karaginsk handicraft at every possible conversational opening. The residents of the community in which she originally lived were subsequently scattered by the forced relocations that took place throughout Siberia and the Russian Far East off and on from the 1950s to the early 1970s.

In a 1957 decree, the Soviet government recognized "mistakes" it had made in the North in collectivizing herding and hunting and in disregarding Native heritage. After decades of imposing assimilation on indigenous peoples through residential schools, Russian language monopoly, and the collectivization of Native subsistence practices like hunting, reindeer herding and fishing, the government made an official about-face. Although the assimilation policies continued, countrywide programs began to preserve or revive elements of Native cultures, including dance, handicraft, and native language use —tangible, visible evidence of the government's new commitment to "diversity" within the borders of the Soviet Union. By the early 1960s, young, socially conscious, and energetic "cultural workers" had arrived in the North with a mandate to preserve "traditions" and popularize folk customs, dance, and handicrafts.

One of these inspired culture workers was Margarita Ivanovna. When she arrived in Kamchatka, Native handicraft was considered "dirty" and "backward," a view that even the Native artisans had begun to accept. To counter this, the young Russian intellectual wore Native dress and danced at festivals. With a smile, Margarita Ivanovna mimes the gestures of a Koryak dance. "I was young and slender then," she says with a laugh. This leads her to a reverie on body types: the Koryak, Even, and Chukchi are slim, whereas the Itelmen are fat. This is not to say that they are unattractive. This pleasingly plump woman recalls with a sigh that some of the early explorers were attracted to Itelmen women.

Until Margarita began collecting, there were no contemporary examples of any Native handicrafts in the museum and very little clothing. Margarita Ivanovna collected the best work that women produced under the stimulus of a special order from the museum. We see examples of contemporary hide embroidery in bright colors. The thread is commercially manufactured, but the patterns are traditional and the artisans still incorporate delicate wisps of reindeer beard. Margarita Ivanovna observes that the Koryak have been using cotton and silk thread for nearly a century. She points to one of the many rugs hanging on the wall, a carefully constructed patchwork of fur. Jochelson wrote about Koryak rugs, she tells us, but when she first visited Koryak communities in the 1960s, they were no longer making them. Like the Russians, they covered their walls with manufactured rugs for warmth and status. She encouraged local artisans to begin making fur rugs again and gestures proudly to the results, numerous examples of imaginatively patterned fur rugs hanging on the walls of the gallery. One of the rugs commemorates the three hundredth anniversary of the founding of Petropavlovsk in 1990. There is a silhouette of the map of Kamchatka in the center field.

In a case full of clothing, a reindeer head pelt becomes a jolly child's cap with the little ears pointing up. As she points to favorite objects, Margarita Ivanovna sometimes thwacks them with her pointer in enthusiastic emphasis. Alexia asks if Margarita Ivanovna has seen any changes in style owing to the market economy. She says that it takes so long to make a good piece that market demands are not a factor, but she will have more to say on the subject of the market later on.

The entire collection of contemporary handicrafts was exhibited widely in the early 1990s, not only in Russia but also in Sapporo, Japan, and at local culture centers throughout Hokkaido where dancers performed and the Karaginsk artisans demonstrated their work. Japan's indigenous Ainu, with their resurgent ethnic pride, have provoked curiosity on Hokkaido about their northern neighbors. Many pieces from this museum also toured the Russian Far East as part of the Smithsonian's "Crossroads of Continents" Siberian exhibition. Margarita Ivanovna has been the go-between for numerous exhibitions and performances. These occasions enabled the artisans to stay in touch with one another after they had been scattered by relocation. Exhibitions were reunions that gave them all an opportunity to see each other's work, keeping their competitive spirit alive. The Ministry of Culture and the local Union of Artists, which recognized highly accomplished artisans as its members, had once been able to finance all of the travel, both for the artisans and for Margarita Ivanovna herself. Around 1993 this mobility became a casualty of the new market economy. Margarita Ivanovna has not been able to go to the villages since 1995. In 1997, she and the artisans traveled to Moscow together to participate in an exhibit of contemporary Northern culture celebrating the 850th anniversary of the city. On this memorable trip, they were all received by the mayor.

The Moscow trip was their zenith. By 1995, the museum could no longer afford to buy the artisans' work. Then the American dealers arrived, mostly from Alaska. Margarita Ivanovna believes that because the dealers understood the market as no one in Kamchatka could, they turned a huge profit. But dealer visits are sporadic. There is no steady market for quality handicraft. The artisans are still invited to give public lecture demonstrations every now and then. Sometimes their appearances are combined with tours by a Native dance troupe, as when they went to Japan. Margarita Ivanovna is frustrated that she can no longer buy and protect good pieces within the museum. Quality work is disappearing from Kamchatka. In almost the same breath, she asks if we are interested in buying artifacts. We give our usual demurrals and denials. "But how could you resist them?" she asks, grinning at the lovely tunics and hats in the exhibit case.

We meet the vice director, Elina Effimovna Ponomarenko, who is short and thin and has jet-black hair. She drums her fingers on the table when impatient, and flashes between coldness and warmth throughout our encounter. Her initial reaction to our visit is, "But we already know all about the Jesup Expedition. We've read what's been written." Trained as a historian, she specializes in Kamchatka history, about which she proves to be quite knowledgeable. As she tells us later, her position requires broad interests, including ethnography.

Settled at a long table near an electrical outlet in the director's office, Alexia plugs in her laptop for the demonstration. Margarita Ivanovna and Elina Effimovna peer into the tiny screen, intense in their scrutiny of the objects. They flex their knowledge and sometimes spar with each other, challenged because, in addition to obvious gaffes in the AMNH catalog, some of the pieces that Jochelson collected incorporate Even design motifs on typically Koryak style clothing. "This is not typical." "This is not traditional." Since these are some of the oldest surviving pieces from Kamchatka, Laurel cannot hold back from asking, "But what, then, is 'traditional'?" Elina Effimovna gives a perfectly materialist answer, "Traditionally they just used hide and sinew." But what is in a name—"Even," "Koryak," "traditional"—when people live close beside one another, intermarry (as they did in at least one of the communities where Jochelson worked), and mutually admire each other's sense of style, flattering by imitation? It is sometimes suggested that the ethnographers' and the Russian state's official designation of ethnic groups sharpened peoples' sense of identity and ethnic presentation such that a proper Koryak artisan would now never dream of putting Even-style beadwork on her tunic.

Margarita Ivanovna and Elina Effimovna suggest that AMNH round out its collections with contemporary material as they have done. Margarita Ivanovna, who just a short while ago was lamenting the disappearance of contemporary work from Kamchatka, puts in a pitch for her beloved Karaginsk District as having the most interesting decorative work. Elina Effimovna tells her that she is biased.

In a warm rush of enthusiasm, Elina Effimovna takes us to the print shop and computer center next door to the museum where young computer wizards have the CD up and running. And although the museum does not have Internet access, the library nearby does. Can the artisans use the computer in the library too? Margarita Ivanovna replies, "This is their second home."

Now we tour the rest of the museum. The permanent gallery is bitterly cold and the lights have to be turned on for us. The exhibition includes the requisite natural history exhibit: a diorama of seals and seabirds, a killer whale skull, a heap of mammoth tusks, many fur-bearing animals. We feel as though we have been here before. Although devoid of a strong Marxist subtext, these exhibits betray no painful rethink of history or methodology.

Some Koryak masks on the wall resemble those Jochelson collected for the American Museum of Natural History one hundred years ago. He had sent his assistant, Axelrod, back to Paren, the Koryak winter village that had been deserted when his party passed through in the early autumn. Not only did Axelrod take the requested head measurements, "There he had the opportunity to see a mask parade and brought six masks to Kuel." Jochelson was ecstatic, "As no traveler has mentioned religious masks from Kamchatka or the Koryak of Kamchatka valley, I went to Paren to learn more about the custom and to take some photographs."[5] Jochelson subsequently described how the masked figures visited all the houses of a settlement and received presents of pieces of sugar or tobacco. Because these villages were deserted during the summer months, evil spirits had ample opportunity to gather there; the masked processions were intended to drive them away. Margarita Ivanovna says that the masks are still used in the Karaginsk District; she saw performances when once-banned Native rituals were revived during the 1960s.

Perhaps because her own efforts were a part of this story, Margarita describes the 1960s as an optimistic moment when Native cultures in the North engaged in the revival and development of Native arts. Alexia, sharing the view of many other scholars of Siberia, sees this same period as a time of rupture and as a time when Native people lost control over local subsistence practices and the nominal self-governance that had been in place. As the relocation policies from the 1950s continued, they disrupted village hierarchies, particularly as administrative positions in the larger collectivized farms were often filled by "newcomers," predominantly Russians and Ukrainians.

A collection of hats once worn by high-ranking Aleutiiq men is posed in front of a garish backdrop. Margarita Ivanovna says that the hats were made to resemble seabirds, and once she says it, the hats do take on the appearance of plump gulls. A dealer from Alaska told them that his offering price for just one hat would pay for a new museum, but even in their present difficult circumstances they would not part with a single hat.

We come to a section commemorating early expeditions, beginning with Bering's mid-eighteenth-century exploits. Bering named Petropavlovsk after his two ships, the St. Peter (*Svyatoy Petr*) and St. Paul (*Svyatoy Pavel*). The city is officially Petropavlovsk-Kamchatski, to distinguish it from another Russian town similarly named Petropavlovsk. But the illustrious Bering was not the first European to reach Kamchatka. Luka Morozko, a Cossack from Yakutsk, and Semyon Atlasov were among those who arrived and demanded that the Koryaks pay a tribute. From the seventeenth century Cossacks pillaged and exploited the Native people of Kamchatka, demanding tribute in fur. Native people offered periodic resistance. Most notably, in 1731 the Itelmen rebelled, burning Russian forts and killing Cossack soldiers. Ultimately, however, the

Figure 28. Jochelson photographed these masked figures in the Koryak village of Paren where masked processions were intended to drive away evil spirits that would have gathered in the village when it was abandoned during the summer. Both the American Museum of Natural History and the Petropavlovsk Museum have examples of these masks. (AMNH Library 1450)

Itelmen were outnumbered by Russian soldiers and the Russian empire was forcefully expanded.

Among early witnesses to life in Kamchatka commemorated in the museum, the most surprising are two nineteenth-century Japanese merchants who were stranded in the Aleutians and taken to St. Petersburg. They eventually returned to Japan, expecting to be executed under the Tokugawa Shogunate's laws prohibiting Japanese subjects from leaving Japan. To the contrary, they were spared to write the first account of travel in Russia in Japanese. Elina Effimovna warms to the topic, reeling off the authors and titles of dozens of works on the period.

By the late eighteenth century, Petropavlovsk had become one of Russia's major Pacific sea ports, a starting point for expeditions to the Aleutian Islands and Alaska, as well as a center for the trade in sable fur, but the settlement remained small. Even in the late nineteenth century, the town's population consisted of just several hundred permanent inhabitants. In 1865 when George Kennan landed in Petropavlovsk, his first stop on the Russian-American telegraph expedition, he described the sleepy atmosphere of this important Russian outpost where several German and American merchants were living and trading in sable. Bogoras and his wife passed through Petropavlovsk on their journey north from Vladivostok to Mariinsky Post in 1900. These days, Japanese fishing interests have replaced the fur trade.

The Jesup Expedition is here as well, with some familiar photographs and photocopies of the cover of Jochelson's monograph *The Koryak*. Margarita Ivanovna cannot resist pointing to a photograph of net fishermen and noting that they still use traditional techniques like this in the Karaginsk District. Of course, we have to pose for a photograph in front of the Jesup material, Russians and Americans together. In a serendipitous genealogy of intellectual history and museum collecting, these are our common ancestors.

The water in the samovar is boiling in the director's office and tea is served, with crisp new handkerchiefs as an impromptu tablecloth. From the wrapping, Laurel suspects that these were gifts from visiting Japanese. Over tea, Margarita Ivanovna and Elina Effimovna talk about the many tour groups that visit Kamchatka in the summer from Japan, the United States, Finland, Switzerland, Germany, and Poland, and some still from within Russia. Margarita Ivanovna is impressed by the wealthy elderly foreigners who have the resources to travel the world in style. She says that the silver-haired tourists make the local pensioners envious because their own resources shrink with each passing day. Soviet society had promised them security in their old age, but those guarantees are a dead letter now. Elina Effimovna says, "These are tough times. Things will get better." Margarita Ivanovna rejoins, "But this is the time we are living in," and lists the floods and droughts that have occurred this year.

They tell us that Vladimir Nutalyugin, the director of the Palana museum with whom we have exchanged correspondence, has described us as two Americans who are retracing Jochelson's expedition. We all laugh at this overstatement of our very modest travel plans, a long way from walking in the footsteps of giants. We talk of Russian and American colleagues that we know in common. Margarita Ivanovna again fondly recalls her golden time in the 1960s and 1970s when she could spend nine months of the year in expeditions, travel, and research.

On our way back to the hotel we check out one of the galleries in town that Margarita Ivanovna told us sells quality handicrafts from artisans known to her. It is filled with jewelry, birch bark containers, dolls, and paintings, gift items from all over Russia. The nice assortment of small mammoth ivory carvings includes some key chains reminiscent of the elephant bas-reliefs on the walls of the African mammal hall in the American Museum of Natural History. The proprietor assures us that these are made from mammoth ivory, not walrus tusk, and that she can provide us with the appropriate certificates to show that we are in compliance with U.S. customs regulations regarding trafficking in endangered animal parts—"to avoid trouble with Greenpeace."

Alexia overhears some other customers discussing the purchase of farewell gifts, more European Russians leaving the North who will inevitably carry back small oil paintings of local scenery. To complete our own transactions, we must saunter back to the G.U.M. where, again, the exchange window is closed, and once more one of the vendors helps us out.

The guidebook describes a Korean restaurant in a vast concrete expanse of hotel, away from the harbor and difficult to find. It looks fancy, with glossy dark lacquer tables and high-backed chairs like an expensive Chinese restaurant elsewhere in the world. There are flowers on the tables and a reasonable number of guests in the dining room. This looks promising. Alexia reads the Cyrillic transcriptions of the Korean dishes and Laurel translates them from Korean into English so that Alexia knows what to order in Russian, a cumbersome process that further whets our taste buds. But no, it is to be a replay of last night. The Koreans pulled out but a month ago; there is no one left to prepare Korean dishes. They were from the North and have gone home to face a famine.

We order a good bottle of red wine, which makes our mediocre seafood salad more enjoyable. Still, we do not linger as the dance floor fills up with what has turned into a ruckus of an anniversary celebration. As during the Soviet era, few people go out to enjoy a quiet evening at a restaurant. Restaurants are for either New Russians or organized crime types transacting informal deals. Others reserve them only for special occasions; we are reminded of the Pizza restaurant in Anadyr, where noisy birthday celebrations were so popular.

On our way out, we see a freezer marked with the unmistakable logo of Dove ice cream bars. Could this freezer in Kamchatka's premier former Korean restaurant actually have American vanilla ice cream and rich chocolate coating on a stick? "It's just an advertisement," the cashier tells us. Of course. They melted along with the optimistic moment that had brought joint venture restaurants to Kamchatka.

The taxi driver who takes us back to our hotel has been watching a portable television and is irate with the government. Accounts are frozen. Only 500 rubles a day can be removed from the bank, and U.S. dollar accounts at private banks must be transferred to rubles at *sberkassa*, government-owned savings banks, at the ridiculously low rate of 9.33 rubles. The driver tells us, in disbelief, that the official rate is already closer to 14. The evening news will peg the Moscow rate at 16 rubles to the U.S. dollar, but not for long, it is assumed. Despite the inflation, the shopkeepers seem indifferent to raising prices, either because business is so bad that any sale helps, or because it would be impossible to keep up with the changing rates.

The next day, Saturday, dawns bright and clear. Alexia again tries to reach our contacts in Palana, and again the call does not go through. We spend the morning at the museum with Margarita Ivanovna. She takes us back into the contemporary handicraft exhibit. "But didn't we see this yesterday?" "There's so much more to see." She does not have her pointer and we have more of a conversation.

Margarita Ivanovna proudly calls our attention to a case containing some of the work by Natasha Yevgor, a Chukchi woman married to a Koryak. Natasha came to live with Margarita Ivanovna while attending art school in Petropavlovsk. This formal education gave her a new perspective on her work. She began to harmonize colors and shades, rather than boldly mixing oranges, blues, and reds in her beadwork, as most of the older artisans do. Margarita Ivanovna is almost maternally proud of Natasha's work for respecting both tradition and modern style. The examples of her work in the case combine several shades of red with white accents for a very rich effect. One piece is Natasha's own handbag, very carefully designed with a subtle interplay of color. Laurel's favorite from the display is a beaded tobacco pouch with a polka-dot pattern, made in the early 1920s with just a whisper of Art Deco influence blown in from far away. One of the robes boasts an elaborate beadwork belt fastened with a European buckle. The artisan made the belt for her own husband. We wonder if such nontraditional forms as beaded handbags and belts become "authentic" when it can be claimed that they were personal possessions.

Another vitrine displays bags and pouches made out of seal flippers stitched together that resemble gray pumpkins. In the past such bags were used to store small sacred objects, but now their purpose is decorative. They demonstrate the artisans' skill in working with small animal parts. One of the bags has a plastic bead toggle. Margarita Ivanovna thinks that these would be interesting to American collectors. Laurel tries to explain how Americans consider seals "cute," and suggests the hacking off and stitching together of their flippers might not have a broad market appeal. "It would be appropriate for museums," Margarita Ivanovna says, "and for special collectors." The art of making seal flipper bags was revived in the 1970s, and Margarita Ivanovna had a hand in it. In the Penzhinsk District she saw a very old bag made with seal flippers and told the Karaginsk Koryak about it. They said, "We can do that." They had made these in the past. One of the artisans remembered that her mother used to sew them and asked the old people how to do it. By the time of Margarita Ivanovna's next visit, the following year, the bags were in full production.

Margarita Ivanovna has thought long and intelligently about the market. "You would be welcome to buy," she says. She contrasts the Olyutor Koryak who are "less assimilated" and produce their handiwork in a haphazard fashion with the Karaginsk women who are attuned to what connoisseurs expect of them, to what people consider the "typical" artistry of the area. Again, she favors "developed" (*razvitye*) handicrafts, the handicrafts she helped to realize, over the Western collector's preference for objects allegedly made by "less assimilated" or to other eyes "more authentic" Natives. We ask Margarita

Ivanovna about her own influence on Karaginsk handicraft production. Her answer is passionate. She insists that when she commissioned objects, she never told the artisans what to make, never dictated the terms of production. She has lived with these women for several months at a time, "giving them ideas."

Margarita Ivanovna regrets that only a very few young people are learning the leather-working craft. They think that working with hides is difficult and dirty. Occasionally, an artisan's grandchild might learn to work with pelts when three generations live together. Has there been a decline in quality? Yes, she has seen it. The young people want to earn quick money; they lack the skill and patience to work a large piece of hide, and they have no knowledge of how to do detailed work. All they can manage are the small bags and pendants, which they sell as novelties.

Is there anything equivalent to the handicraft training in the College of Folk Arts in Anadyr? No, not in Kamchatka. She tried, unsuccessfully, to get the local School for the Arts and the ones in Ossoro and Palana to establish Native arts programs.

She tells us the story of another of her protégés, Nadezhda Hilol, who teaches in the residential school system. When Nadezhda was a high school student in the Olyutor District, Margarita Ivanovna noticed that the Koryak girl was producing striking beadwork. She was surprised and disappointed that Nadezhda was going to Khabarovsk after graduation to study medicine. Margarita Ivanovna did not know then that Nadezhda herself was unhappy with this path. Her village was convinced that it needed a doctor, and according to Margarita Ivanovna, those who made the decision did not understand or value art. This system of education continues today throughout rural Russia. The district administrations evaluate which specialists are most needed in the area and they provide funding for training an allotted set of professionals, from doctors to English teachers to lawyers. With market reforms and the privatization of education, however, the majority of students pay something for their education, and correspondingly have more say in what they study. This was not so in Nadezhda's youth. She went off to study medicine and, on the very first day, fell sound asleep in chemistry class. In an era of greater mobility than the present, Margarita Ivanovna was often in Khabarovsk on museum business. On one of these trips, she looked up the miserable Nadezhda. Margarita Ivanovna brought her back to Kamchatka and found her a place in the art workshop that she had organized. Nadezhda eventually became the head of the workshop, a recognized master artisan.

In the 1970s, these art workshops (*masterskie*) were organized throughout the Soviet Union to produce folk handicrafts. Margarita Ivanovna describes the movement as part of a national effort to develop the arts in tandem with other domains of the Siberian economy. In her eyes, the workshops were a place where artisans were encouraged to do real handicraft and where their skills were recognized. Because Margarita Ivanovna had traveled among Native communities, she was familiar with all the best artisans. By bringing them into the art workshop system, she could win them recognition as exemplary artists representing their traditions. There were similar workshops in Sakhalin, Magadan, and other places all over the Soviet Union. The Uelen ivory-carving workshops are survivors of this tradition. Margarita Ivanovna started two local workshops. She would develop projects; the products that met the approval of the Kamchatka Department of Culture were then sent on to the Ministry of Culture in Moscow. Artisans at the site were provided with material and the master artisans made what they wanted. Their products were approved by the "arts inspectors"—Margarita Ivanovna was one—and then these works became the authorized prototypes that were copied by the junior artisans as in the Uelen workshop in Chukotka.

Margarita Ivanovna speaks of this work at great length and with considerable passion, perhaps in response to the looks on our faces. To our ears, the notion of an "art inspector" sounds perfectly Orwellian, and the idea of working from officially approved prototypes would seem to stifle any impulse of creativity. It all sounds so very Soviet, true to the Cold War rhetoric of our childhoods. And yet, the process is not unlike the certification of "living national treasures" in the very unsocialist polities of Japan, South Korea, and Thailand. In these places government committees confer recognition on master practitioners of traditional handicraft, periodically verifying that standards are being maintained, that ceramics, baskets, or masks are being produced in the manner and style that was recorded when the system started. The scholars and bureaucrats who initiated these programs in the face of rapid industrialization shared Margarita Ivanovna's desire to preserve what would otherwise be lost. True, in the Russian Far East, it was a colonizer's cultural policy directed toward its internal minorities, but an urban intellectual—Russian, Korean, or Japanese—is also very distant from a peasant artisan.

In less threatening times, some criticized the national treasure systems for the artificiality of their products and for stifling artisan creativity. In the Soviet system the master artisans, at least, seem to have had some room to create. There is nothing "natural" about elites' self-conscious attempts to "revive" and "preserve" traditions, and yet the workshops did maintain some tangible notion of Native culture in an era when so much else was destroyed. Now, as Native peoples are attempting to build identity and pride on shreds and patches of the past, who is to say that some of those fragments were not sustained in art workshops? If we did not value the naming and claiming of indigenous "culture," we would not be wandering the Russian Far East with our CDs of old beadwork and our catalogs of hundred-year-old photographs.

The art workshops also introduced innovations in production, such as mechanized tanning in Ossoro. "The Native people in Alaska do this," Margarita Ivanovna tells us. "It's the same thing." She acknowledges that, of course, handworked skin is much finer. She saw in Japan how entirely handmade products are carefully distinguished from those produced with mechanical interventions. Handworked pieces can command one hundred times the price of the latter. Even in Russia hand-loomed rugs from Central Asia are widely appreciated, but there is no equivalent appreciation and consequently no significant market for handworked crafts from the Russian Far East. And the issue is now moot. The workshop system has fallen apart in Kamchatka, even for the production of souvenirs. The artisans cannot get materials and no one pays them for their work. Margarita Ivanovna sees the master artisan system as having been possible only in an environment where culture workers and artisans were mobile, when there was money for travel expenses and fuel for the planes and helicopters, and when artisans could be aware of each other's work and compete to produce superb handicraft models.

How the workshop masters were chosen was a difficult issue. The decision involved taste, economics, and administration. The master was expected not only to be a fine artist but also to run the center. According to Margarita Ivanovna, local people were not interested in such work. She was constantly trying to persuade them that the art factories meant both jobs and the preservation of tradition. In the past, it might not have been so critical for a Native artist to be an effective administrator, but these days Native people are having a hard time adjusting to the new market economy. They are not used to working for money. No one is organizing a space for them.

If Margarita Ivanovna's comments have a patronizing ring to them, they are consistent with a line of argument that has emerged in recent years. The Soviet system has been criticized for creating a dependent population; people who have supposedly lost the ability to be innovative and resourceful. But if the system created dependency among indigenous Siberians, how does one explain the prosperous "New Russians," who do not seem to be suffering from "dependency"? A more plausible explanation for the difficulties with economic development in indigenous communities is the absence of infrastructure and financing for creative ventures for the vast majority of the population.

As Margarita Ivanovna speaks of the decline of the workshop system, tears of frustration and despair trickle down her cheeks. People say that the 1970s were a bad time because of the Cold War, she continues, but it was a boom time for the hunters and Native artisans. They were well fed then. Now youth, women, the elderly, and most of the men are unemployed. The educational system used to give priority to the children of reindeer herders, but now they have the least chance of all. Margarita Ivanovna is losing hope. She sees herself as having worked hard through all of her professional life for the people of Kamchatka. She is heartsick. She weeps in earnest. Laurel fumbles for a tissue.

Margarita Ivanovna is a native of Yaroslavl, a city on the Volga River in European Russia. When she breaks down like this, her daughter asks her why she is so upset about the Koryaks. Isn't she concerned about the fate of the Russian peoples back home? Margarita Ivanovna feels that the European peoples are more sure of their traditions, have more confidence in who they are. When she first came to the museum, a celebration was held for all the ethnic groups now resident in Kamchatka, including those who came from European Russia. People turned out in ethnic dress and gave costumes to the museum.

Her daughter asks her why she has no traditional outfit in the Yaroslavl style. Margarita Ivanovna sighs. Someday she will learn to make one for her daughter. Alexia asks if native dress is really so important for a sense of belonging. Margarita Ivanovna is not joking about making a costume for her daughter. She firmly believes that people need to know their tradition. In her view, ethnic conflicts occur when people have lost their sense of culture and fill this space with "simplistic nationalisms." As we exit the gallery, Margarita Ivanovna tells us to "watch out for the bear claw," pointing to one of the bearskins sprawled on the floor awaiting installation into the new exhibit.

We return to the hotel for our bags and are soon in the taxi heading for the airport and our afternoon flight to Palana. We felt smug for having bought our tickets to Palana in advance in Khabarovsk, but as we drive through Petropavlovsk we realize that we have been routed not to Palana but back to Khabarovsk, that we are on our way to the Saturday afternoon Khabarovsk flight. We ask the taxi driver to take us to the airline office, which naturally is not authorized to change tickets or issue refunds. The clerks send us to another office in another part of town. At the second office, there is much delay while they try to reach the manager, at home on a Saturday afternoon, to secure his permission to issue our refund. Wonder of wonders, after a long wait, Alexia returns to the taxi with the U.S. dollar refund in hand.

The bad news is that Palana flights have been backed up for nearly a week. Palana sits in the bowl of a valley that is often fogged in. To make matters worse, school has just started and parents are trying desperately to get their children back to Palana. There is an enormous backlog of reservations. They are using smaller planes now, because the normal demand is so much reduced in these pinched times. The smaller planes are less reliable, more dependent on good weather conditions, and hold fewer people We can get a reservation, but not until two days before our scheduled departure from Russia, and of course, owing to the weather, the reservation would be "iffy" in any case. If we got there on September 14, could we get out again in time for our flight home on the sixteenth? The ticket office personnel suggest yet another ticket office, one set up to deal with foreigners, that might be able to help us. We are grabbing at straws. The office is in an outlying hotel, not so easy to find, another concrete block sprawl. No luck this time either.

Back at our now familiar, overpriced hotel room we console ourselves with cups of coffee and the German chocolate Alexia picked up in the supermarket adjoining one of the ticket offices during her long wait. We take a long walk along the Pacific Ocean to clear our heads and consider our options. On the retaining wall by the beach, we see some graffiti. This turns out to be a me-

morial to Viktor Tsoy, the young Korean-Soviet pop star who died in a car ac-
cident in 1991. In the late 1980s and early 1990s Tsoy's group, Kino, was akin
to the Simon and Garfunkel of two decades past; Kino's music simultaneously
evoked a sensation of youthful angst and hope for a new, less rigid society.
Tsoy's lyrics were the stuff of Alexia's student days in Leningrad; for many
young people in Russia today Tsoy continues to represent a time of resistance
to the powers-that-be, but also a longing for a different kind of future. One of
Tsoy's songs calls out an anti-Afghan war text: "My blood type is on my sleeve,
my battalion number is there too . . . wish me luck in the battle . . . I just want
to stay with you."

A bottle of wine with dinner and hot showers help us to think positively
about our circumstances. We will try to fly standby on Monday morning, be
the first in line if need be. As there are no flights on Sunday, we may as well
take a day off and sample the hot springs at nearby Paratunka that Nikolay
recommended to us over dinner in Anadyr.

We are beginning to wonder if our rubles in hand will sustain us through the
next phase of our adventure. We do not know what the exchange facilities will
be like outside of Petropavlovsk. The ruble is at almost seventeen to the U.S.
dollar, nineteen to the dollar in Moscow, where shops have been stripped of all
durable goods being sold at the old prices, and long lines have formed outside
banks. We have not seen this scale of chaos, but the anxiety is everywhere. The
cab driver who drove us to the museum this morning told us that he is bracing
himself for a complete crash. He remembered how in 1992, when he was in
the army, his monthly paycheck was barely sufficient for him to buy a simple
pair of sneakers. He said he dreaded returning to those lean, hard times, but
he sees them on the horizon. Since 1994, people became used to a more stable existence; the ruble had remained around six to the U.S. dollar until this
crisis.

Sunday is a sunny, golden, early autumn day, perfect for the prospect at
hand. To catch the bus to Paratunka, we must first get to the terminal beside
the market. The hotel clerk tells us where to get the city bus. We wait, try another bus stop, wait, give up on it, and walk to the market, two miles away. At
the terminal, we learn that there has been no direct bus from Lenin Square for
awhile. "Has not been one for awhile" is becoming a standard Kamchatka re-
frain.

We find our bus amid the milling crowd, mostly women with empty pails for
berries. Vendors have set out small mounds of mushrooms and berries on the
periphery of the parking lot. We spend ten rubles on a quart of fresh raspber-
ries to eat on the bus. "Shouldn't they be washed?" Laurel asks. Alexia gives
her a "don't even think of it" look, then reassures Laurel that the babushkas
grow their berries in wild tangles without the expense and bother of pesticides.
As we enter bus 106, we each pay five rubles (less than fifty cents) and take our
places in the rows of velour-upholstered seats. At first, there are only five other

passengers, two of whom appear to be Chinese travelers. This is unmistakably a Korean bus with a legend over the windshield in Korean script, "Asia Bus— for happy travel!" but Laurel is probably the only rider today who can read this. The illegible legend has been encircled with a wreath of silver tinsel, a local touch. After her encounter with the Walker Hill Hotel bus in Khabarovsk, Laurel has seen Korean buses everywhere, buses proclaiming in Korean script that they will take their passengers to a housewives' school in Seoul's Yoido Plaza, to a Korean arts academy, and to locations in Cheju city, a popular South Korean honeymoon destination.

The city gives way to countryside, wooden barns, a grazing cow, even a horse-drawn cart. This is dacha country, pretty little wooden cottages with lacy trim and ugly tarpaper roofs. We transfer from the bus to a small van bound for Paratunka. As we drive out of the town of Elizovo we pass families out enjoying the Sunday afternoon; young fathers are pushing children in strollers. We hope to see one of the active volcanoes along the way, but the view from the paved road is obstructed by a dense canopy of trees. We pass a number of spas, some advertising casinos and nightclubs; one is called the Blue Lagoon. At the hotel we were told that although other spas might be more luxurious, the best and cleanest water is at a spa called Sputnik. The decisive judgment came from a guest in the hotel café who tests the water for the regional health department.

The van drops us at what the driver says is the Sputnik spa. To our left is a ramshackle farmhouse with a yard of cabbages; the cardboard sign hanging off the fence reads, "goat milk, 1 liter for 10 rubles." We hesitate for a moment, but just up the lane we see the sign reading "Sputnik" and advertising the services available: massage, hot springs, physiotherapy, and more. Sputnik once catered exclusively to the navy and its employees, but now it accepts any paying guest. In the late Soviet era of the 1970s, 1980s, and into the 1990s, each organization—the navy, a factory, an institute—either ran its own spa or arranged for access to such a place. Spas were part of the benefit package for employees, and people could arrange to spend days or weeks free of charge relaxing at these locations. Even reindeer herders would take a few weeks each year to rest and relax at a spa. Not all spas had hot springs, but the basic form was the same: a quiet place with meals provided where people could have access to staff trained in a range of restorative therapies, including massage and mineral baths.

The spa is old and a little bit creaky but freshly painted and immaculately maintained, much like an old but well-run ship. Lenin's portrait is painted on the exterior wall, looking purposefully over the garish plaster gnomes that line the drive. He is accompanied by images of two Young Pioneers, members of the children's division of the Communist Party, who are posed as if looking into the future. The Young Pioneers' slogan is inscribed in large block letters, "*Vsegda gotov!*" similar to the Boy Scouts' "Always Prepared!" A silver Toyota and a white Chrysler are parked below the figure of Lenin.

The spa is nearly empty and the attendant gives us a private dressing room for no extra charge. We spend a happy afternoon submerging in the hot mineral water, sunning ourselves on the wooden deck, reading, and resubmerging. From the condition of the wood on the deck, Alexia estimates that the spa was refurbished around 1994, more evidence of a now-vanished moment of economic optimism in Kamchatka.

Alexia strikes up a conversation with a middle-aged woman in a bright yellow bikini. Nina is spending a month in the spa for a cost of 456 rubles, not a bad deal even at the old rate. She is a doctor from a small town in the North, a place that used to have three thousand people but is now down to seven hundred. The sea is gradually eroding the land in front of her hospital. She says she is the only civil servant in the town who was given a vacation this year. A self-described workaholic, Nina had not had a vacation since 1991. The doctor seems perfectly blissful floating in the tank.

Nina speaks of her daughter and her efforts to enroll in university. Nina's daughter has just begun her second year studying psychology in a division of the naval academy in Petropavlovsk. Since psychology has been only recently reestablished as an academic discipline in Russia, Nina is worried about her daughter's prospects for finding work later. She is also worried about paying this year's tuition. It has been 5,000 rubles per year—at the earlier ruble rate, about $800 US—but she expects that it will now be prohibitively expensive. Even before the crisis, it was difficult to meet the cost of tuition, and most students worked during the day and attended classes at night. Her daughter now works as a janitor in a psychiatric center at night and studies during the day. Despite these problems, Nina is enthusiastic about the quality of education and is particularly excited that her daughter attends lectures given by a visiting American psychologist whose Russian-speaking wife provides translation.

Nina tells Alexia that she likes the sense of respect accorded to her in conversation with the dean of her daughter's institute, and she muses that perhaps this respect is related to her role as a paying customer. However, she laments the loss of the job "allotment" (*raspredelenie*) system whereby graduates were assigned a place of work. She confides that she is uncertain of her daughter's ability to find her own employment; this would involve a sense of self-promotion that her daughter lacks. Alexia has heard other anxious parents weigh the costs and benefits of a semi-privatized educational system in Russia in conversations she has had from Moscow to Krasnoyarsk to Vladivostok. Now ambitious young people are rarely viewed as a valuable government resource to be nurtured and carefully placed in communities in need of their skills.

Later in the afternoon, a group of brawny young men fill the large pool with splashes and loud conversation. A cluster of children, young enough to be suspected of pissing in the water but still very cute, inhabit the smaller, cooler pool. Foregoing yet another soak, we shower, dress, and catch another van in the still-warm late afternoon, feeling appropriately rejuvenated.

On the bus again, sitting in the far back, Alexia makes conversation with a sweet-faced couple. The wife holds a bunch of flowers from their dacha garden. A teenage son sleeps against the man's shoulder while a fluffy gray cat sits languidly on the boy's lap. They tell us that the cat goes back and forth with them like this to the dacha. Alexia tells them about our travels. They tell us that there is no longer any regular bus service to Esso. These days, one hires a helicopter or a microbus, and the road is mountainous, "like Switzerland."

Alexia hates mixing business with friendly interactions, but she decides that we are nearing a crisis. Since these seem to be honest, friendly people who might help us, Alexia asks if they know anyone who would be interested in exchanging rubles for U.S. dollars. The man says, not surprisingly, that yes, he thinks someone from his company might be willing to change money. We will call him later in the evening.

On the walk back to the hotel Alexia hears snatches of hushed and anxious conversations in the street. People are worried about how to pay for tomorrow's food. Prices for staples such as bread, milk, oil, and flour have risen two and three times in just a few days. Later, on a local television program, we see the Petropavlovsk mayor relate that he has been receiving letters from citizens threatening suicide (*samoubiystvo*) if he does not adequately address the issues of basic survival in a public statement. He urges people to stay calm and hold out for a couple of days when things should stabilize.

On the evening news we hear that tomorrow's official rate will be twenty rubles to the dollar and we pursue the possibility of a currency exchange with a complex series of telephone calls to our friend from the bus. The hotel is still calculating our room cost at sixteen rubles to the dollar, and we believe that we should aim for at least this in an informal exchange. We wait, as instructed, in the dark street in front of our hotel. Presently, a white Honda lurches around the corner and stops abruptly. Our friend, smiling, jumps out of the back seat and holds the door open for us. He and his wife wait on the sidewalk while we do business with his colleague. The fixer is hard-faced, with the spiky stand-up haircut of the upwardly mobile. He will not change less than one hundred dollars and gives us the unfavorable but tolerable rate of sixteen rubles. Grimacing, we do the deal. Our friends leave us with a shower of warm farewells as they drive away.

The next morning, anxious to be the first in line for the flight to Palana, we are out of the hotel at 6:10 A.M. It is still very dark and chilly when we arrive at the airport, which is locked. The taxi driver knocks on doors and finally rouses someone who lets us into the waiting room. The terminal is empty except for a little white terrier with a bloodstain on its flank who roams forlornly through the premises, probably the abandoned pet of a household that has left the area and moved back to European Russia. Eventually, a large woman descends the concrete stairs with ceremonial slowness and opens the door for the employees. Things start to hop. Laurel sits surrounded by our luggage (minus the big black bag, which we have filled with things we will not be needing for the next few days and stowed at the Oktyabrskaya). Our emergency rations and gifts for distribution are crammed into two small flight bags. Alexia goes to negotiate with the ticket desk. Laurel, alarmed by how swiftly she is moving though her stash of English-language reading material, recalls Kennan's late nineteenth-century travels in this part of the world. Staying in an isolated cabin en route to Esso, Kennan and his travel companion were so desperate for reading material that they spent the night reading the wallpaper—pages from a ten-year-old *Illustrated London News*—by candlelight.

It turns out that we cannot get a flight to Palana until September 21, when we intend to be back in New York. There is a daily microbus for Esso—also on our itinerary—from the center of Elizovo, the town beside the airport, but by the time we learn this, we have missed it for today. Alexia makes some calls, one on a whim to Margarita Ivanovna to see if she wants to go to Esso with us, but there is no answer at the museum or at her home. She is probably away at her dacha. Nelson Hancock, another graduate student from Columbia University who has conducted research in the area, had given us the telephone number for Vladimir Kolegov, the representative to the Koryak Autonomous Region in Petropavlovsk. Alexia calls him on the chance that he can arrange tickets to Palana, the administrative center for the Koryak Autonomous Region. She learns from his office that he is, at this very moment, in the international terminal of the airport, greeting official visitors. She goes off to find him. A youngish man with a moustache and wire-rimmed glasses approaches Laurel, speaking rapid Russian. She doesn't understand a word he's saying, but his tone is urgent. She produces two of the five phrases of Russian Alexia has managed to teach her. "I don't speak Russian. I don't understand." His English is similarly limited, but he makes an effort to speak slowly and carefully. "I am . . ." The name is incomprehensible. Could this be the Koryak representative, or is he some tour guide looking for his client? He disappears. A short while later Alexia appears. This was our man, Kolegov. His office had told him that a Russian-speaking American woman was trying to meet him in the airport. When he saw Laurel first, he was completely confused. Alexia overheard his desperate attempt to find someone who could speak English and introduced herself.

Vladimir Kolegov reappears, just as Alexia has explained this all to Laurel, and he and Laurel have a proper introduction. Kolegov thinks he can get us on a flight by the end of the week, once he has taken care of his charges, who must get back to Palana. He suggests that we go to Esso in the meantime. He gets us a good rate at the airport hotel for the night, although the hotel initially claims to be full. We present him with a copy of the *Drawing Shadows to Stone* catalog as an expression of profound gratitude.

The Kamchatka Airline Hotel is less luxurious than the Oktyabrskaya, but serves a very nice fish soup for brunch. Thus fortified, we head off to the bus station in Elizovo to make a reservation for tomorrow. The cashier's window is crowned by a surly sign, "We only sell tickets, don't ask us for information." A van driver outside offers to take us to Esso immediately if we are willing to rent the entire van. The idea appeals—we have been stalled for too long and are loath to lose another day—but we need more rubles. We go to the bank, which is out of rubles, as are the currency exchanges next door and at the airport. The predicted inflationary leap to twenty rubles per dollar has not happened; the Petropavlovsk bank rate is at sixteen to the dollar, but suddenly no one wants to buy dollars. Something must have happened in Moscow, but we have no idea what.

In search of rubles, we ride back to town with the only woman microbus driver on the Petropavlovsk-airport circuit. When we explain our predicament, she tells us she has a friend who sells cars who is likely to have a lot of cash. She takes us to an auto yard on the outskirts of the city. The friend will not trade for more than thirteen rubles to the dollar, well below the official rate. The driver thinks this is ridiculous. She points us to a currency exchange near the market, but they are out of rubles, like everyone else. We go back to the exchange window in the G.U.M. department store, but it is the same story there as well. A security guard has been posted today to discourage informal transactions. The vendor who had been so willing to change with us a few days ago is nowhere in sight. No one wants to do business. We try the bank across the street from the Oktyabrskaya. Some nature tourists we had met in the international terminal had been able to change their money there this morning. The pretty blond cashier is helpful. She tells us that rubles have been coming in dribs and drabs all day. She does not have anything right now, but we should try again before she closes for the day in fifteen minutes. We sit and wait while a stream of Russians approaches the window, similarly hopeful of changing dollars for rubles. A woman comes in, casts a glance at the rates, and turns and walks briskly out the door.

We are beginning to feel desperate. Perhaps this woman has rubles to trade. When Alexia follows her out of the bank and asks her, she is not interested in doing business but does explain that people are pulling money out to make purchases before prices rise against inflation—the best way to use their inflated currency. The woman says in a panicked tone that the entire city of Elizovo is informally trading at thirteen rubles to the dollar, at least five rubles below the bank rate. We return to standing in line and begin to wonder how we will pay our hotel bill.

At the last minute, the cashier calls us to the window and we are able to change $50 US, taking the edge off of our situation. Apart from dollar payments, we will live on this money for the next several days. We collect our extra bag from the Oktyabrskaya; we do not know when we will be back from Palana and, in case of a tight connection with our return flight to Alaska, want the bag to be conveniently stored at the airport. In the lobby, we chat with a student of

Slavic languages and culture from Oxford who is here to teach English. He is moving out of the posh hotel to humbler accommodations because his sponsors' accounts are frozen.

We haul our bag onto the city bus and then to the microbus stop at the terminal for a ride back to Elizovo. On the periphery of the market, we pass long lines at the bread kiosk, the longest bread lines Alexia has seen in years. Done in by travel, after stowing our bag at the airport, we overshoot our bus stop and walk back to the Kamchatka Airline Hotel amid flowering meadows. After our time in tundra towns, even a sparse showing of wildflowers is not taken for granted. We are almost too late for dinner, a tasty salad of buckwheat groats and cabbage, a pleasant change from hotel room picnics of bread and cheese or restaurant meals accompanied by blaring disco music. The empty dining room has a homey feel to it. When we compliment the cook on her mint tea, she gives us a big bunch of dried mint, along with some fragrant currant leaves, all from her own garden.

When we pay the hotel and dinner bill, we learn a bit more about how people are thinking about their futures here. The woman at the desk recounts how she came to Kamchatka from Bratsk, a city in central Siberia near Lake Baikal. She had a plethora of reasons to keep her in Bratsk—work in her field as an economist, a dacha, and good schools for her children. Still, when her parents died, one after another, and then her husband died, she decided to move to Kamchatka to be closer to her sister's family for support. As she explained it, in hard times like these, family ties mean more. She observes pragmatically that she is not getting any younger and her children could be brought up by her sister, should anything happen to her, "God forbid." She gave up quite a bit for this sense of security. Now she works here at the hotel desk, keeps an eye on things, and in all of her "free" time tends her garden and greenhouse to scrape food together for her family. This seems to be a common story.

We've been up since before dawn and are happy to call it an early night after cups of steaming mint tea, knowing that we will have an early departure tomorrow morning on the microbus for Esso.

Chapter 7

Esso and the Way There

Ulashkan, a Lamut (Even) man, told Waldemar Bogoras the following "Tale About Stingy Reindeer-Owners" in the summer of 1895. (The title was Bogoras's.)

The short days of the year had already begun, and the cold of winter had come. Then some (Even) met to live together. They pitched their tents close to one another, played cards, and had merry talks and joyful reunions. An old shaman, who had nothing to eat, had no joy. The wealthy reindeer owners gave him nothing, so stingy were they.
. . . The people in the camp played cards as usual, and laughed noisily. Then they went to sleep, the herd being quite close to the camp. In the morning, however, the reindeer were gone, and only numerous tracks of wolves were seen in the deep snow. The rich man had nothing left. . . . In ten days they had never a meal, and so at last they took to gnawing their own long hands.
The father wandered the whole day long in the open country, and found nothing. Finally, he stopped in the middle of the desert and cried aloud in despair. The Master of the Desert . . . came all at once from underground, and asked him, "What do you want?"—"My wife and children have had nothing to eat for ten days and they are starving to death. My hunting boots are full of holes, and I am unable to walk any longer."—"Do not cry!" said the Master of the Desert. "I also am the owner of reindeer. I will give you something to eat, but you must remember the ancient custom of the Lamut. When you have food, give the best morsel to your poor neighbor."[1]

Jochelson's tale captures the precariousness of this hunting and herding way of life, where a scattering of the herd could bring starvation, and an ethic of sharing one's food was also a survival strategy. The story also highlights the power of Even shamans, whom, Jochelson observed, the neighboring Koryak feared and respected. Jochelson would visit the Even encampments near present-day Esso on a future trip, the Russian Geographical Society's Aleut-Kamchatka Expedition of 1909-1911, but Jochelson and Bogoras frequently encountered reindeer-riding Even (formerly called "Lamut" or "Tungus") hunters and herders in their ethnographic travels, both before and during the Jesup Expedition. This tale about the dire consequences of refusing hospitality to strangers must have been particularly appreciated by a wandering ethnographer.

Afraid of missing the one daily departure to Esso, we arrive at the terminal at the center of Elizovo in good time for the nine-hour bus trip. The nine-seat

Figure 29. Portrait of three Even. Front-view and side-view photographs were intended to record physical types. The rich beadwork on Even hide garments is a continuing source of pride for Even craftswomen. (AMNH Library 1895)

microbus, more economical to run than a regular coach, is nearly full from the single stop it made before reaching us. Everyone seems to have as much luggage as we do. An elaborate edifice of bags and vinyl cases against the closed sliding door of the microbus will have to be disassembled and then carefully reassembled at each pit stop. We are at very close quarters inside. A burly young man tries to squeeze into the seat beside a petite teenager with braces on her teeth. At the driver's suggestion, he lifts the embarrassed girl onto his lap, where she spends the rest of her journey. At the first rest stop we will find this young woman quietly retching outside the two-hole outhouse, having narrowly escaped losing her breakfast all over her traveling companion.

Just before we leave, a woman approaches the microbus with a letter in hand and asks if anyone is going to Milkovo. Yesterday we were approached in the airport by a woman who wanted to know if the only obvious foreigners in the domestic terminal were going as far as Moscow. These handoffs are not a matter of confidentiality, a fear of censorship and scrutiny, as they might have been in another time. That would assume an efficiency of public service that the present moment lacks. Much to the contrary, people simply do not trust the reliability of the mail, and posting anything larger than a letter is prohibitively expensive.

One of our fellow passengers, an older woman in a tiger-print shirt with a brown beret on her lavender-rinsed tresses, is addressed by a more conventional-looking babushka, "Aren't you Nadezhda Pavlovna Chikisheva?" The better-dressed woman seems to keep the babushka at a distance, to patronize her. Alexia makes a point of engaging this lavender-haired woman in conversation as we bounce along the road. Yes, the woman was once a big name at Party headquarters in Esso, just as Alexia suspected. The rest of her story is more unusual. The woman identifies herself as Itelmen, but her stepgrandparents were American traders operating out of Petropavlovsk. In the 1930s, they were arrested and sent to the camps before they knew what was happening. She went to see her grandmother off at the boat to Magadan. The guard dogs at the dock attacked her, and she carries the scar to this day.

Laurel is amazed that a woman with this background would grow up to be a Communist Party hack. Alexia tells her that it's not unusual, that the Soviet experience was not the Maoist experience. Grandparents' "crimes" do not necessarily taint their descendants, and political repression is not the full sum of a remembered Soviet past. In fact, Alexia has met many elderly people throughout Siberia who are nostalgic about the Soviet era, despite the repression that many of them or their parents faced. It was the Soviet system that gave a Native woman, like our well-groomed traveling companion, a position of local political authority.

At the pit stop, we pile out of the van into the billows of morning fog that roll down from the hills, obscuring the surrounding volcanoes. Vendor women have met the microbus with trays of steaming piroshki. One type is filled with cabbage and the other with chopped eggs and potato; they are both delicious. The vendors ask us jocularly if in the United States we get our paychecks. Alexia tells them that if our employers did not pay us, we would strike. They tell us that even if they went on strike, no one would pay any attention to them. One vendor woman tells us about her sister who emigrated to Germany. The sister writes that were it not for her relatives still in Kamchatka, she would never give a thought to her old home.

The babushka has left the bus at the rest stop. Everyone makes minor adjustments for comfort, swallowing all the space she occupied as if she had never been among us. We are on our way again, serenaded by the driver's choice of golden oldies. Dead Elvis asks us if we are lonesome tonight. George Harrison is belting out Hare Krishna when a rear tire goes flat. Fortunately, there is a spare. We continue through a flat plain of birch, the leaves turning golden against a distant view of volcanic mountains. The road is far smoother than expected, and we are able to read our novels for the remaining eight hours of the trip. Alexia is tearing through *The Handmaid's Tale* by Margaret Atwood, finding this heavy allegory of universal women's oppression a bit dated. Even so, she is reminded of the rigid government control and concomitant public fear often encountered in former Soviet times. In her first trip to the

Soviet Union in 1987 one had to carefully consider one's reading material; a travel companion had taken along Solzhenitsyn's *One Day in the Life of Ivan Denisovich* and decided at the last minute to leave it in the transatlantic airplane's bathroom to avoid inevitable problems with Leningrad customs officials.

We lose most of the passengers in Milkovo, a tidy, leafy little town with a lot of low wooden houses, the sort of orderly place that one would expect to have a good public library. Milkovo has a population of about 9,000 people, 2,000 of whom are Itelmen. Nelson Hancock, who lived here during his fieldwork, says that the local library is quite active, sponsoring workshops on local history and traditional subsistence and artistic practices.

Milkovo may seem like a sleepy town, but for several weeks in the 1860s it proudly proclaimed itself as a place worthy of a visit from the Russian tsar— or so the inhabitants briefly thought. In 1864, the Western Union Telegraph Company began planning an overland extension cable across the Pacific and Russia; George Kennan traveled through Milkovo in 1865 as part of the survey team. To the surprise of Kennan's party, the whole population, including the Itelmen living there, gathered and a salute was fired. It turned out that a letter sent ahead to warn of the group's arrival had been misinterpreted by the village elders. Kennan was identified in the letter as a "telegraphist and operator"; not knowing what an operator was, the elders decided that it must mean "imperator" or "the emperor." The town was expecting the tsar of all Russia.

Our arrival meets with less fanfare. The driver drops us off at a roadside café where we have a tasty, cheap borscht lunch with the young man who had been carrying the carsick girl on his lap. He is the only other remaining passenger, returning home to Esso from Petropavlovsk, where he is the engineer of a fishing boat working for the Japanese. Everything is packaged here in Kamchatka with wrappers written in *katakana* for the Japanese market.

We take on another passenger, an Even man who keeps quietly to himself. Alexia manages to strike up a conversation with this haggard-looking traveler and learns that he has just been told that he has terminal cancer. He tells her he has had a long life; he is going home to die.

As we approach the mountains we have a second flat tire, not as serious as the first. It can be repaired without changing tires. We pass trucks filled with lumber. The driver says that there was a Japanese mill in the area, but he does not know if it is still in operation. Alexia surmises that this explains the good road. In her experience, growing up in northern Vermont, logging interests often made for decent roads, at least until the weight of the trucks took its toll. But the driver tells her that the well-graded road is more likely carefully maintained due to its use as a military thoroughfare.

We make a few stops at scenic spots along the road so that the men can enjoy a smoke. The most spectacular of these is above a dam. On the way to the observation platform, a tree whose limbs have been festooned with multiple colorful strips of rags reminds Laurel of shrine trees in Korea, trees to which one can bind restless spirits or make obeisance to various deities. Travelers to Mongolia have seen similar trees. We ask about the rag ties and get a pleasant but innocuous explanation. "Travelers tie strips of cloth to the tree as a wish that they will return to this scenic spot. Even foreigners tie strips of cloth to the tree." But there must be more to it. Alexia has seen these strips of cloth at ritually significant sites throughout Russia. In the central Siberian city of Krasnoyarsk, at a cliffside site commemorating those who had fought in World War II, the surrounding bushes and trees were heavily laden with swatches of bright fabric. She has seen these same strips of cloth tied to trees near the site where the celebrated (but once underground) poet Marina Tsvetaeva is buried south of Moscow. People say that this practice has deep roots in Russian pre-Christian practices.

As we approach Esso, we begin to get nervous. Thus far, in the sheer pleasure of being in motion again, we have avoided thinking about what might be waiting for us. Our calls to the museum never went through. The driver has assured us that there is a hotel. Given Alexia's research experiences in another small Siberian town, we expect no running water, a cold room, and hallways full of drunk itinerant men. After nine hours of travel, the microbus pulls up beside a sprawling wooden structure. The "hotel" is indeed a truckers' dormitory. But not to fear: we are immediately commandeered by Lyudmila Ivanovna, a brawny blond with fierce eyes who insists that we will be more comfortable in her apartment, which seems a favorable alternative to the truck-stop hotel. Travelers come here for the mineral springs, and Lyudmila is more than ready for whomever might show up on the microbus. She tells us that she can comfortably accommodate up to seven guests. At one hundred rubles a night, the offer seems reasonable, the more so when she tells us that the truckers' dormitory has only an outhouse. We go off with Lyudmila in her small silver car, a second-hand Japanese model.

Lyudmila's apartment, on the second floor of a two-story wooden four-unit building, is spacious and clean. Similar buildings line the street, each with a patch of garden at the front and back. Late berries and some unrecognizable blue flowers bloom in front of Lyudmila's house. The apartment is fragrant with drying mint. Best of all, houses in Esso are heated with pipes of warm water from the mineral springs. On this mild day, with an abundance of piped heat, the windows are thrown open to the late afternoon light. From our window, Esso is a pretty rural town of wooden houses, gold-leafed birch trees, vegetable patches, and a mountain vista in the distance. Sixteen hundred people live in and around the town. Nearly one hundred Even are directly employed in reindeer herding and its administration in the area.

The several beds crammed into her guest room are freshly made, each with a clean towel set out on an immaculate turned back top sheet, as in a hotel. She says that she puts everyone up, even Australians and Japanese. A Japanese group had stayed with her just recently. They were very tidy, and each one gave her a small gift when they left. The giving of *omiage* is a Japanese custom, but we take the hint.

Lyudmila is partly deaf and raises her voice to aggressive decibels when answering simple queries, even sometimes when talking to herself. She was a navy cook and swears like a sailor. She says that she had no problems dealing with the crew; it was the big pots that were tough to handle. She moved here because the air pollution in Petropavlovsk was aggravating her asthma. She smokes like a chimney, burps with gusto as she chews raw oats (part of her "personal diet program," she tells us), and, we find out later, snores loudly.

Lyudmila cooks us dinner. Alexia, who thinks that her quoted price of thirty rubles a meal is too high, is delighted to reply when Lyudmila demands to know how much we paid for lunch. Twenty-two rubles for both of us? She sputters that perhaps the prices haven't yet risen in Milkovo. She serves us a hearty chicken soup, complete with fat chicken legs, an American import dubbed "Bush's legs" throughout Russia following a trade deal cut during the first Bush presidency.

After dinner, Lyudmila suggests that we go for a swim in the hot spring, two immense but shallow pools, each covered with a layer of dead bugs and a little slimy under foot. Even so, it is lovely to soak in warm, purportedly curative waters in a mountain setting in the fading golden light of an Indian summer day. The spring seems well maintained, despite the bugs. There are small cabins above the far bank and Russian tourists are in evidence. Our microbus driver is also in the water. He banters with Lyudmila, who takes a quick soak before driving us home. Without her elaborate wig, in cropped red hair and wrapped in a terrycloth robe, Lyudmila bears some resemblance to a burly prize fighter.

Back at Lyudmila's, inspired by abundant hot water, we hand wash our laundry, tackling jeans encrusted with dust from the trip up here. In the bathroom, Alexia notices the gigantic, heavy-duty stainless steel storage vats, typically filled with dairy products such as milk and sour cream. Judging by the smell of hops, these are being used to brew beer or maybe *kvas*, the beer-like substance brewed throughout Russia and enjoyed in warm summer months.

Alexia locates the home telephone number of the museum director. She learns that the museum telephone has been disconnected for months and that the director is in Petropavlovsk for the next several days. The director's wife thinks that the vice director, Sergey Adukanov, goes to the museum at eleven each day, that we can probably meet him there. This is a New York connection. Sergey is a professional dancer who performed with the troupe that came to the American Museum of Natural History for the Jesup Expedition centenary in 1997.

The next day is cooler and overcast. On our way to the museum, we pass a rusted memorial to the veterans of World War II. The museum is new and in far better shape, a wood-shingled complex of buildings with quaint cupolas designed in a style typical of seventeenth-century architecture of the European Russian North. There is even a shingled, cupolaed covered bridge over a stream. The architectural inspiration for this museum comes from historic towns to the north of Moscow, like Voronezh, four thousand miles from here. It is an odd choice for a local history museum in the Russian Far East. Alexia thinks of the incongruity of Han Chinese architecture scattered in outlying regions of China, such as Xinjiang Province, where they remind the Muslim Uighurs of Beijing's presence.

An English-language signboard advertises the museum's ethnology and natural history exhibits and promises displays of "authentic shamanic paraphernalia." Unlike other museums on our itinerary so far, the museum is billed as an "ethnographic" (*etnograficheskiy*), not "regional history" (*kraevedcheskiy*) museum. The signboard indicates an effort to appeal to Western tourist sensibilities.

The first building in the complex is locked. Just inside the doorway of the second building a slim young woman with long dark hair tends the admissions desk and seems to resent our intrusion into her solitary morning musings. She tells us that Sergey, the vice director we had hoped to meet, is away with the folk dance troupe, Nomads, and will not be back for several days. No one else can possibly deal with us. She is not authorized to guide us around the museum, but we are welcome to look. On second thought, she says we will be better served if we go to meet the director of the House of Culture. She recommends that we go over there immediately, before everyone takes off for lunch. We make arrangements to come back at three after her own lunch break and head for the House of Culture, an ugly concrete structure looming up over a town of attractive wooden buildings.

Inside the barren lobby, we go up a dank stairway and into a bright, tidy room where a buxom young Russian woman with a short haircut sits behind a desk. Alexia introduces us. On hearing Alexia's name she says, "Oh, I've been hoping to meet you!" This is Lena Zlodnikova, the director of the House of Culture. She tells us that Sergey Adukanov and Galina Fedotova, another dancer known to us from the American Museum of Natural History performance, have gone to Kovran to take part in the annual Itelmen festival, along with many local artisans. Viktoria Petrasheva, the Itelmen scholar-activist whom we have both met in other places but missed in her hometown of Petropavlovsk, would be there. Because times are tough, the House of Culture has not been able to send the entire dance troupe, but there was space for two dancers on an accommodating helicopter. For want of more efficient transportation, some of the local artisans have gone off to Kovran on horseback or piled onto the tops of the all-terrain, tanklike tundra vehicles (*vezdekhod*, or "goes everywhere") and made the ten-hour trip.

As in Providenia, this House of Culture runs on a tour group connection.

Lena works with a Petropavlovsk-based enterprise called Lena & Friends. She shows us a glossy brochure that promises "culture and trekking, skiing and hiking." The tour package includes accommodations, cultural performances, and meals. Lena tells us that we should have arranged our Kamchatka travels through them. This is the first whisper of Lena's pegging us as tourists rather than as colleagues whose instrumental possibilities are not so directly translated into cold cash.

Kuril Ichanga, the lithe, curly-haired Even dancer with a dashing hint of a moustache who also performed in New York, is delighted to see Alexia again. On hearing that we are trying to get to Palana, he says mournfully, "Don't go there, Alexia. There's no heat in Palana, no electricity, no telephones. The whole North is falling apart. Don't go to Palana." The plight of Palana, capital of the Koryak Autonomous Region, had been featured in a television special just a few days before.

Lena has other plans for us. We can hire a helicopter and take two more of the troupe with us to Kovran. Kuril can go with us and take his video camera. We have been blocked at every turn. Days of trying to establish telephone contact with Palana got us nowhere. In Esso the museum director is out of town. Two people we want to meet are in Kovran, and the festival itself would be an example of cultural revival in Kamchatka in the company of participants. "We'll do it." "Yahoo!" shouts Kuril. We will go to the heliport and make arrangements. Lena calls the car after we have agreed to pay for the gas required to get us across town and back. Lena tells Kuril to have the samovar ready for tea on our return.

Riding across town, we ask how Esso has managed to keep its electricity when so many other towns in the North have lost theirs. Lena says that the hydroelectric plant, running on power generated by the dam we saw yesterday, saves them. Lena tells us she can find us a more comfortable place to stay than with Lyudmila, of whom she does not seem to approve.

The Esso heliport is a single, small, sky-blue wooden house with a tower and a detached banya, the pilots' own steaming Russian-style sauna. There are three cars in the lot but no drivers can be found. Lena sizes up the situation. "They've all gone hunting. We'll try later when we hear the sound of a helicopter coming in." A gusty cold wind is blowing and we are happy to get back in the car. Lena takes us to two sparsely stocked shops where we buy things for tea: two bags of the ubiquitous wrapped Russian hard candies, chocolate, apples, a box of Twinings tea, and some cheese. It is understood that we will subsidize this repast. Lena adds a fifteen-ruble pack of Camels to our purchases. She says that her inability to buy decent cigarettes is the most difficult thing about the current crisis. Alexia recalls that in the microbus she heard a radio announcement that the old Soviet brands such as Kosmos, the cigarettes she used to smoke when she was a student in Leningrad in the late 1980s, are again being sold in large numbers. Alexia had emitted a groan and wondered who had thought to stockpile these. Beginning in the early 1990s these Soviet-era brands seemed to disappear in the wake of more popular imported brands like Marlboro, Camel, and Winston. Alexia was probably not the only passenger thinking nostalgically of times synonymous with these awful Soviet fags.

Back at the House of Culture, Lena bustles over the tea things in the kitchenette of the social hall, cutting cheese and apples. The hall is a spacious, comfortably furnished room where cultural programs are held and Native women do beadwork. Kuril is proprietary; he calls this large room his dance studio, but this space also functions as a café and discotheque. Stars twinkle from the ceiling and there is a small mirrored platform stage equipped with a heavy-duty amplifier system. As in Providenia, tour groups are entertained here and this is prime space for local celebrations of birthdays, weddings, and anniversaries. Indeed, it is the only space of its kind in town, they tell us with undisguised pride; New Year's parties are booked by early October.

Over tea, Lena talks about some foreigners currently living in Esso. An American entrepreneur has taken up residence to open a hunting camp. His campers pay $4,000 a person for a tour package, including a performance by the folk dance troupe. The House of Culture receives five hundred dollars for each forty-minute performance. Then there are the two students from Cambridge University, Alex Fox and Emma Wilson, who are doing an environmental impact study. The area has been declared a national park and there are restrictions on hunting and fishing. Lena hopes that an influx of tourists interested in "folk life" will give people new possibilities for earning income.

At one point, Lena dashes out and returns smiling, with a few examples of the precise beadwork they sell after tourist performances, the ubiquitous sun disks, or *solnyshki*, on thongs and a bead and leather bracelet. We do not bite and the items are whisked away. She talks now about her desire to put Lena & Friends in touch with tour agencies. When our museum colleague Teddy Yoshikami visited Esso the previous year to arrange the folk dance group's New York tour, she mentioned to Lena that she has contacts with the tourist industry in Japan. Lena is anxious to pursue this lead. The company in Petropavlovsk is going to create a Web site for the House of Culture. The Rotary Club in Canada has financed an e-mail connection at the post office.

Rotary also sponsored a tour by children from the local arts school who gave forty-two performances in Canada. We had met the director of the troupe just that morning outside Lyudmila's building. He was wearing a "Beautiful British Columbia" sweatshirt. Lena tells us that the children all came back fat from Canada, and everyone wondered what they had been fed. There was a story about a pile of bananas that disappeared, was replenished, and disappeared again until the insatiable children were given free reign of the pantry and allowed to gorge themselves. The children had also been taken fishing in a stocked stream, but when one of these resourceful children from the North caught a big fish and was anxious to have it fried up, he was told that the pond was stocked only for sport. He would have to throw the fish back in but could have any fish he liked from the supermarket.

Kuril shows us a video from his "expedition" this past summer. We see our friend Erich Kasten, a German anthropologist who works in Kamchatka, leading his horse to drink from a forest stream. For Kuril, the Even videographer, German Erich is the exotic attraction. They fished, they visited some Koryak, they traveled eighty kilometers from Esso on horseback. There is an interview with a babushka-farmer-hunter who is so much an expert on the local terrain that she advised a team of geologists mapping the area. The tape, edited with a sonorous narration and schmaltzy background music, was screened as a special event at the House of Culture.

Kuril carried his video camera throughout the dance troupe's New York tour, returning with ample footage of the American Museum of Natural History. This tape was also the subject of a special program at the House of Culture. The old ladies were amazed by the excellent condition of hundred-year-old fur and beadwork. Kuril told them about museum storage areas where heat and humidity are maintained at a steady rate. He says that the women all bent their heads close to the monitor. These women, members of "the Club" at the House of Culture, are the perfect audience for our CD. Their monthly program includes storytelling and programs on folk culture for children. For one session given over to the telling of local history through the lives of ancestors, one of the women diagrammed her family tree in a huge wall poster.

The old women also teach beadwork, not just the technique but also the local meanings that are encoded into the pattern. Later, Kuril will show us his own beaded dancing belt, pointing out the rhomboid shapes that are worn only by members of his clan. His sister had explained this to him when she gave him the belt, and he is proud of this knowledge. Many Even do not know the significance of the patterns.

Recalling our conversation with Margarita Ivanovna in Petropavlovsk, we ask about the fate of the local artisans after the collapse of the state system of workshops. Of course this is a problem. The artisans do some work on commission from Petropavlovsk, making only four thousand rubles a robe, less than $500 at pre-crisis rates, for the time-consuming and highly skilled work of tanning, trimming, and beading. They used to make things for the Petropavlovsk museum, which has not been able to commission anything for the last few years. Sometimes they make practical hide gear, tunics and boots, for hunters. We can imagine a brisk trade in the future among the well-heeled back-to-nature types who will patronize the American's hunting camp. The dancers in the troupe give the artisans a small but steady business in Even and Koryak robes. Although it seems de rigueur that a Native dance troupe should make at least some appearances in traditional hide and beadwork garments, many performance costumes are now made of fabric, fringed and beaded to resemble hide garments. As Margarita Ivanovna told us, the tourist market is only for smaller things, the medallions and bracelets, or at most an elaborately beaded headband.

The tannery and leather workshop in Anavgay closed two years ago when it was unable to pay a rent debt—a casualty of the end of the state farm system. Kuril has heard that local interests are trying to start up the workshop again, tanning hide for boots and jackets. Kuril sees this project as a way of addressing the acute problem of female unemployment in the town and neighboring communities. In the Soviet period throughout the North, Native women left the reindeer camps to stay in the towns with their school-age children and take up work created in the state service and administrative sectors. The few women "tent workers" in the camps were once compensated as part of the state farm system, but these jobs have disappeared. Since the government infrastructure in town collapsed there are fewer jobs for Native women. Native men are still concentrated in herding, hunting, and fishing, but they are barely compensated for their efforts.

Lena thinks that she hears the distant sound of a helicopter and hastens to the telephone, but she can rouse no one at the airport.

Kuril brings out the House of Culture's few examples of old hide costumes. A finely worked child's garment from the Olyutor or Karaginsk District in northeastern Kamchatka was worn for dances; Lena and Kuril consider it an especially well-made example. There is a mismatched Even costume consisting of a coat and apron. The coat is a recent product made of mechanically tanned hide that is too smooth and shiny. The apron is an older piece; its metal decorations include buttons from Soviet-period uniforms with hammers and sickles stamped onto them—an appropriation of state uniformity to the unique designs of an Even craftswoman. Kuril says that the designs on the older garments and the means of reproducing them are not taught anymore, and may no longer even be known.

Next they bring out the bead supply and we have a long discussion about the difficulty of keeping the local artisans supplied with beads suitable for their work. This is an old story; beads have been a popular global trade item at least since the Age of Exploration. The House of Culture provides beads for all of the work that it commissions. Five years ago they got a good deal on the purchase of thirty kilos (about sixty pounds) of unsorted beads. They had long sorting sessions with the beads spread out on the big table in front of them. Lena describes this process as a "kind of meditative discipline." They have also tried working with inexpensive beads from Taiwan and Malaysia, but these beads are painted and eventually lose their color. When the school children went to Canada the director brought back a supply of beads worth $400 US. There is also a stash of Japanese beads in the various pastel colors favored by contemporary Japanese taste. Lena says that the colors are wrong for the artisans' work, but some of these beads seem to have been worked into pale laven-

Figure 30. Kuril Ichanga proudly displays a hide robe belonging to the House of Culture in Esso. The old robe is a model for artisans attempting to maintain traditional handicraft. Kuril's "voyage" sweatshirt is a souvenir of his performance at the American Museum of Natural History. (Photo by Laurel Kendall)

der combinations on the made-for-tourist pendants she showed us earlier. We realize that we are talking with people who really know their beads.

Kuril claims that the preference of the "old folks" is for the contemporary uniform American-made beads, which they work into precise symmetrical geometric patterns. To our eyes, the results are far less interesting and beautiful than the ever-so-slightly irregular beadwork on the old robes and aprons. Approximations of the old beads are manufactured in India and China, but having worked with smooth, perfect beads, the artisans have no interest in an aesthetic of imperfection.

Considerable resourcefulness is needed not only for the beads but for all of the materials that they work on. A hunter who saw one of Kuril's videos provided hides in exchange for a video about one of his hunts. Kuril shows us suede that they bought in Alaska on the way home from their tour because the tannery in Anavgay had closed. The quality is not very good, and the pieces can be used only for aprons.

On the way to the costume room we pass a workroom where Nina, a young artisan, is working on one of the costumes for the troupe's seagull dance. The gown is made of heavy white crepe, an approximation of pale hide, but the lighter fabric is effectively deployed in this airy, graceful dance. Most of the costumes are made of cloth, some of shiny satin.

During the American tour, Kuril made friends with a "Native American" and swapped beaded headbands. The exchange had been the occasion for a long discussion about beadwork. Kuril intends to commission a new Even headband, but he has not yet had an opportunity and still wears the Native American headband when he dances. He shows us the difference between women's and men's headbands and speaks of his dream of visiting Native American (especially Yupik) communities to learn how these people transmit their culture to the present generation.

Kuril was born on the taiga and lived there until the age of seven, when he was sent to residential school. He describes his seven-year-old self as a "wild kid," afraid of everyone. In those days, the school did not teach dance and discouraged students from speaking their native languages. "They would hit you over the head for speaking Even." Now he swats his own students for using Russian. Even should be spoken at home and among other Even. He also teaches something he calls "tourism," which sounds like basic wilderness survival skills: how to orient yourself without a compass, how to build a fire, and so on. He has been doing this for three years but tells us this sort of instruction has been around since his own youth.

Back in the social hall, we view a very long video of the all-Kamchatka tour their troupe made after their return from New York. Lena and Kuril interject comments as we watch a montage of travel, performance, and post-performance celebrations, partying in Petropavlovsk at the end of the tour, warm hugs on a dark snowy street. The performers were told, on undertaking the tour, that they would not earn any money but would have a really good sex life, or in Russian *polovaya zhizn*; this expression was a pun for "sleeping on the floor," which they did often enough. People thought that they were mad to do such an ambitious tour in hard times. How would they pay for gasoline? There were times when they were not even fed. In one House of Culture, so old-fashioned that the spectators still sat on benches rather than chairs, the stage was so rickety that it nearly broke through from the weight of dancing feet. In Petropavlovsk, Ekaterina Gil, formerly the premier dancer in Mengo, Kamchatka's professional Native dance troupe, put up fifteen people in her small apartment. The driver of the Esso dance troupe's large rented jeep was so pleased to be part of the tour that he painted their name, *Nulgur* ("Nomads" in Even), on the side of his vehicle. Now people think that the group has its own vehicle, but this is far from the case. At the end of the tour, an Icelandic man associated with a tour agency gave them the money for the gas they needed to get home.

We see taped replays of dances that were also performed in New York, the lyrical seagull dance (which bears no small resemblance to Swan Lake), the frenzied exorcism of an evil spirit, and a rambunctious courtship dance that ends with the lively girl placing a pendant around the lively boy's neck and the boy draping her neck with a pelt. These are polished pieces influenced by professional standards and the cultivation of "Native dance" for general audiences. The dancers have been carefully trained and are very skilled. Even so, like many other folk dance groups they find it necessary to pander to perceptions of themselves as excessively libidinous and simultaneously antiseptically cute. The Soviet conservatory system and the role of professional dancers in preserving and "developing" Native dance have been both a blessing and a curse.

On tour, the Esso troupe had many emotional experiences. In Milkovo they joined with other groups for a performance honoring the artistic director of the Mengo troupe, Alexander Vasilevich Gil, who died in 1990. Gil's widow, Ekaterina, dances with the Nomads group in Esso. In the memorial performance, people wept during her rendering of the seagull dance. In Ust Kamchatsk their opening performance was greeted with shouts of "Chukchis get out!" ("Chukchi" is a term broadly used as an epithet for Siberian Natives. Throughout Russia the "Chukchi" are the target of the local equivalent of "Polack" jokes.) At the end of the first number, however, there was a stunned silence, and at the end of the program people were pounding on the stage and asking for more. In Pluche, an Itelmen town, they were treated to a huge banquet. At an officers' club, where they were originally given a cool reception, they were lauded after the performance as being "As good as Mengo," a statement amended by an officer's wife to "Better than Mengo."

After more than an hour of video, we realize that the afternoon is slipping away and that we really ought to get back to the museum. Lena insists that we at least sit thorough a number choreographed by Alexander Vasilevich Gil, performed in memoriam in front of his portrait and a vase of flowers. Finally extricating ourselves, we bolt to the museum and find the door padlocked with a sign, "Closed early today at 4:30." The admissions attendant let us down. She knew where we were, had herself sent us there. Why didn't she let us know she was leaving? A group of German vulcanologists is pacing the museum porch, similarly disappointed but hopeful that the delinquent custodian can be found. We try to change money with them, but they have worked out their finances very carefully and have no rubles to spare.

We go to the phone station and leave a message for Vladimir Kolegov, the Koryak representative, informing him that we will not be trying to get to Palana on Friday after all. Then we agonize. Are we really giving up on Palana? On the one hand, we have been in touch with the local museum there for almost a year through anthropologist Alex King and his wife, Christina Kinkaid. The Palana museum had even offered to sponsor our visa. On the other hand, even after days of telephone calls, no one has answered the telephone at the museum, and Alex, our local contact, is not picking up either. We had been disappointed in Esso. Would we find a padlock on the museum door when we got to Palana? And having gotten there, would we be stuck for days and risk missing our flight home? After Providenia, this was no abstract speculation. In Kovran, people will be "doing the work of culture," and there will be people there we ought to meet and have missed in other places. But there is no museum in Kovran, and we feel huge pangs of guilt at the prospect of deviating from the itinerary so carefully worked out in our grant application. It is also possible that we might be stranded in Kovran.

We return to the House of Culture, where Lena makes one more—successful—attempt to reach the airport. She learns that a round trip to Kovran would cost us about $1,500 US. We go to the airport with her, but the pilots are noncommittal about flying. There has been only one flight today, and even that was considered risky. Hunters have already chartered the first flight for tomorrow. We ask for clarification of the cost of going Saturday and returning the next day. This is, for the pilot, two round-trip flights, one to drop us off and one to bring us home, a total of $3,000 US unless we go for one day only. The sum seems excessive for a journey, especially for one not on our itinerary. We say that we will consider going for a day. We want to get in and out as soon as possible, to minimize the chances of being stuck there. It is in Lena's interest to make the trip on Sunday, at the end of the festivities, and get her people home on our nickel. We are beginning to feel railroaded. On the drive back to town, Lena reminds us that the airport is closed on Sunday, that we would have to go up on Saturday and return on Monday to meet her needs.

In the car Lena suggests that we visit a private museum run by an acquaintance of hers in his apartment. She tells us that there will be a small admission fee. How much? Fifty U.S. dollars for the two of us. At this point, we tell Lena that anyone who thinks they can charge a fifty-dollar admission fee for a private "museum" is not a member of the museum world as we know it. She adopts her soft, conspiratorial voice, the voice she had used with the helicopter pilots, and tells us to come along and see what sort of deal we can cut. We tell her firmly that we don't want any part of it, that the suggestion itself is insulting. The proposal becomes even more ludicrous when we learn that the "private collection" is of taxidermized beasts. She leaves us huffily, taking with her the last remnants of our desire to go to Kovran.

The rest of our evening is given over to telephone calls to Petropavlovsk as we try to track down the director of the Esso museum and Kolegov, to see what our chances are for actually getting a flight to Palana. The director cannot be run to ground. Alexia does get through to Kolegov around 11:30 P.M. He tells us that the planes have been grounded for the past two days and everything continues to be backed up. He tells us not to rush back to Petropavlovsk, for he has one very promising bit of information for us. A privately chartered helicopter will touch down at Esso at noon tomorrow, en route to Palana. We should try to talk our way on.

Lyudmila offers us a late-night treat of blini filled with fatty meat and saturated with grease. Laurel is unable to finish hers. "Then you can just eat it for breakfast!" Lyudmila tells her. True to her word, she plops the now-cold confection on Laurel's plate in the morning. When Lyudmila leaves the room, Laurel hastily stows it deep in the trash basket and is smiling sweetly when Lyudmila returns. Lyudmila stalks to the trash basket. Laurel holds her breath, but her maneuver was effective. The evidence remains hidden.

Lena has told us that she is usually in her office by nine, and we intend to stop by on the way to the museum to show her how to operate the CD on the laptop computer. On the way, we try to send a fax to New York from the town's telephone office, but it will not go through; they do not have a direct-dial system, and it is difficult, if not impossible, to send a fax via a trunk call connection. At the telephone center we get into a conversation with a pretty eleven-year-old who lives on our street and knows all about the two British researchers. The girl is slim and blond and wears a short dark skirt over her long and dirty legs. Her bare feet are stuffed into dressy black pumps. She tells us that yesterday and today are school holidays so that the children can help bring in the potato harvest. Since this year's crop was poor, her work is already done and she intends to spend the day reading Tom and Jerry comics. Her father has run off to Ukraine, but she has a grandmother and a grandmother not-by-blood who lives on Lyudmila's street, and do we believe in God? She is Russian Orthodox and knows of no other religious groups in town.

We go to the House of Culture hoping for a quick in and out, knowing Lena is going to be displeased when we tell her that we are not going to Kovran after all. She is not there. A group of people are in the social hall watching television, news features on the military training of "special forces" and on the growth of prostitution in the south of Russia. They tell us Lena has gone to "Party headquarters," meaning the municipal building, but the old language sticks.

We talk to Nina, the slim woman with Cleopatra eyes whom we saw at work beading yesterday. She is dressed in a cut work blouse, a pink and white patterned sweater, and athletic slacks, a woman who takes some trouble with her appearance. She tells us that she only began beading when she came here to Esso from the south and noticed that the old women spent a lot of time doing it. She used to be married to Sergey Adukanov, the lead dancer, whose mother is a respected artisan. She tells us that she has two sons, ages twenty and twenty-five, by her first husband, and a five-year-old from her marriage to Sergey. She moved here with Sergey five years ago to be near Sergey's parents. She began beading seriously two years ago. In the past, she had made only fur hats and boots. She works mainly for the House of Culture.

Lena arrives and then Kuril. Of course Lena is seething, not only with disappointment at our plans to go to Palana but also because she has already organized our life for the next two days. There is to be a presentation in the library and a meeting with the babushka artisans at five. Tomorrow Kuril will take us to Anavgay. Of course, this would all have been wonderful and we are surprised by her efforts, but not derailed. We bestow our small gifts (a fish line for Kuril, a clear file and pen for Lena) and remind Lena of our willingness to carry the tour brochure to our colleague Teddy. We do what we can to preserve the semblance of an amicable collegial encounter. Even so, because we have spent the better part of the morning waiting for Lena, we must simply leave the CD in her hands and head for the museum in the hope of seeing the exhibits before going to the airport. We leave her with a smile.

Kuril walks with us to the museum. He was supposed to spend the day berrying with a group of Russian tourists but somehow missed the connection. He is philosophical about the missed trip to Kovran and says that in the North opportunities surface and disappear. Then he talks about problems that are linked to the wildly bloating U.S. dollar, "Why should it behave like this?" We realize that we, too, have been anthropomorphizing money, but in our eyes the ruble is the capricious entity.

Kuril leaves us at the museum. The beautiful but cold receptionist still seems surprised and put out that anyone would actually want to enter the museum. We are negotiating our admission when Kuril returns with Alex and Emma, the two Cambridge students. They tell us that they were in the municipal building this morning and heard Lena talking us up and describing our computerized collections. We relate our embarrassment on learning that Lena had cooked up a full itinerary for us when we had already decided to leave at noon and bet that they will get an earful at the House of Culture later on.

The museum reception area is a shop. As elsewhere, there are not-very-memorable oil paintings by local artists and handicrafts, some more imaginative than others. The prize would go to a pair of spike-heeled sealskin boots. The ethnography collection is in the building shaped like a church, a hexagonal structure covered with wooden shingles. A mock-up of an Even encampment claims the center space with artifacts and vintage photographs, some dating from the 1950s, on the walls. By now we expect a tent structure, which seems to be requisite in all local museums. In this one, the tent entrance faces the door, and a wooden plaque above the tent opening says "Welcome!" in several languages, including German and Japanese.

In one corner we find a glass case devoted to shamanic paraphernalia. It is one of only two glass cases in the entire hall; everything else hangs in the open air. This treatment is one indication of the respect now accorded shamanic artifacts, as is the "no photography" sign, attached to this case alone. The label describes shamanism as a general phenomenon, shared by all of the people of Siberia, and trance as a type of "meditation." Alexia attributes this unusual explanation to a longstanding Russian interest in Eastern religions and the widespread popularity of New Age jargon in Russian speech; alternative medical practices are infused with words like "karma." According to the label, shamans were active in this area until the 1950s, when even isolated herder communities came within reach of the Soviet state. The items in the case—shamans' hats in four styles and a drum and its beater—are original. The drum and beater were found in a dilapidated house, probably in an abandoned village, in 1974. The weathered drum is in remarkable condition and must have been tenderly repaired. The label suggests that this equipment might have belonged to the last shaman in the area. More surprising, we see a photocopy of one of Jochelson's illustrations and a label linking this drum to one that the vice director examined in the vaults of the American Museum of Natural History during the dance tour. It is a small world indeed.

Old pieces and newer ones are hanging on the wall. The object names are given in Even, as well as in Russian, and some of the donor and artisan names are given. Unfortunately, many of these pieces are driven straight into the wall with nails. The receptionist sits at a desk in the corner of the room, tidying her ledger while we tour the hall. Alexia tries to warm her to a conversation about the museum, but gets nowhere.

We go back to Lyudmila's and pack up our things. We have mixed feelings about Lyudmila. Yesterday, Lyudmila upped the price of our food, raging about the cost and bother of finding vegetables to feed us. She continued to rage, even after we had met her price, as if her "off" button was broken and she would rant on until her battery went dead. She talks to herself, loudly, and has the television blaring past midnight. Laurel tunes it out as noise, the way she tunes out incomprehensible ranting on the streets of New York. Alexia does not know how to respond to these streams of obscenities that were not necessarily addressed to us. This is the type of language you might hear in a raucous bar, but not in a Russian home.

Lyudmila has agreed to drive us to the airport. We hold our breath when she turns the ignition key; her car engine has been misbehaving and it is a matter of faith and prayer that the vehicle will actually move. It does.

Lyudmila likes the lavender scarf that Laurel drapes over her shoulders on the way to the airport. She fingers it and tells us that maybe she likes us after all. We have a final image of Lyudmila, wrapped in the lavender scarf, striking an imposing stance for our camera beside her shiny silver car.

We sit by the side of the airfield. The pilots are friendly and tell us that if we cannot get on the charter flight, maybe we can get to Palana on a cargo flight a few hours later. We try to be optimistic, but this is not easy. The Esso airport is where our friend David Koester spent nine days waiting for a flight out earlier this summer. A slim man with short silver hair and a blue denim jacket arrives on a bicycle and tries to sell us souvenirs from the attaché case fastened to the back of his bike. He extracts the usual Soviet-era medals and beaded pendants and one seal-fin pouch like those we saw in the museum in Petropavlovsk. He tells Alexia his hard-luck story. He grew up in the area and knows it well. As a young man in the 1970s, he traveled far and wide during hunting expeditions and has good contacts in all of the villages. He gave up a

Figure 31. Lyudmila the former navy cook stands beside her car to bid us farewell at the heliport. The chiffon scarf was our parting gift to her. (Photo by Alexia Bloch)

job in Petropavlovsk a few years ago to come back to Esso with the promise of a better job in the city administration. He had been told that the job's present occupant would soon be history, owing to his strong Communist Party ties. But by the time the aspirant had relocated to Esso, a past Communist identity was irrelevant. The former Communist incumbent was solidly in his job. Alexia has seen this sort of thing in central Siberia as well. All too soon, people missed the Communists for what they remembered as administrative competence. It is not clear what he does now for a living, apart from hawking souvenirs to the passengers of passing charter flights. He is on hand later as a quiet partner to the negotiation for our transportation to Palana. Like so many people in this town, he has a hand in the tourist trade.

We hear the sound of a propeller and then huddle away from the whirl of dust it leaves as it sets down. Perhaps half a dozen well-dressed people emerge from the helicopter. Sergey, the affable pilot, tells us that the flight has been chartered by the head of the largest fishing company operating in Kamchatka, Marina-ich. For $120 US, which Sergey quietly gestures that we must pass to his silver-haired friend, we can board the flight. The chartering party has probably just indicated their willingness to take us on and turned a blind eye to the exchange of cash. As to how many hands might claim a part of our fee, we can only guess. Alexia says that this happens all the time in the North. We will see much more of it before we are home again. The good news is that we have paid in dollars rather than with our dwindling supply of rubles. The best news is that we are on the flight, in motion again.

Chapter 8

In the Entourage of the Fisher King

While among the Maritime Koryak, we lived most of the time in their underground dwellings, which are reached by a ladder leading down through the smoke-hole. It is almost impossible to describe the squalor of these dwellings. The smoke, which fills the hut, makes the eyes smart. It is particularly dense in the upper part of the hut, so that work that has to be done in an upright position becomes almost impossible. Walls, ladder and household utensils are covered with a greasy soot, so that contact with them leaves shining black spots on hands and clothing. The dim light which falls through the smoke-hole is hardly sufficient for writing and reading. The odor of blubber and the refuse is almost intolerable; and the inmates, intoxicated with fly agric, add to the discomfort of the situation. The natives are infested with lice. As long as we remained in these dwellings we could not escape these insects, which we dreaded more than any of the privations of our journey.

—*Jochelson cited by Boas in* American Museum Journal, *October 1903*

During the first half of the winter 1900-1901, the Jochelsons carried on their expedition work in Maritime Koryak villages on Gizhiga and Penzhina bays. When they had their reunion with Bogoras in Kamenskoye, they were in the northwestern most corner of the present-day Koryak Autonomous Region whose administrative capital, Palana, is our destination. The second half of the winter, they turned inland to the camps of the Reindeer Koryak, trading the dark and odorous, but well-insulated underground homes of sea mammal hunters for the herders' frigid tents: "The winter tents of the Reindeer Koryak are so cold that we could not work in them; therefore we had to put up a tent of our own. It was furnished with a small iron stove, and there we carried on our ethnological and anthropometrical work. At night, however, the tent was very cold, and we slept on the snow, covered with fur blankets. Several times we were exposed to snowstorms, and had to wait under our blankets, covered with snow, until the gale was over."[1]

Jochelson described their method of work: "Mr. Axelrod with Mrs. Jochelson's help took anthropometric measurements, I wrote down Koryak tales, collected ethnological material, bought artifacts for our collections, cast plaster masks and had songs and shaman's chants taken down."[2] The Koryak in Kuel were receptive to the work of early professional ethnology. Jochelson found them,

Figure 32: Maritime Koryak stand beside the smoke hole of a subterranean winter house. One entered the dwelling by descending through the smoke hole on a ladder. In his correspondence, Jochelson described the misery of a residence in these dark, smoke-filled, but efficiently insulated dwellings (AMNH Library 4140).

"much friendlier and gentler than I had expected. With presents we could do more work with them. . . . But they could not be persuaded to do anything that might interfere with their customs or their religion; e.g. make fire with a wooden fire drill at an improper time and place, sell their old treasured idols, or part with their family (shaman) drum, or let us have the cloth in which they wrap the dead before cremation, or have a parade of masks to scare off evil spirits."[3] The Koryak of Kamenskoye, in contrast, had reservations about the Jesup project, "[They] don't like to be measured, especially the women, although they are offered presents. Older people stop the younger ones from singing into the phonograph saying the 'old one' as they call the phonograph will take their voices and they'll die."[4] In our travels, we will encounter some present-day Koryak who are also dubious about the intentions of ethnology, but for different reasons.

We are catapulted into the midst of a party of New Russians on a spree. Alexia has flown under all kinds of conditions in the North, including many times with schoolchildren returning home to reindeer camps for summer holidays, once with a corpse, and another time with a huge dead white wolf. This is by far the most elegant helicopter flight she has taken, with wine and hors d'oeuvres and an "Oriental" carpet on the floor, a flying magical carpet. A distinguished-looking man with iron-gray hair and a tweed jacket serves slabs of spiced salami and slices of cucumber on rounds of bread. He passes a dainty appetizer to each of us. This is followed by a circulating tumbler of vodka and a glass of wine for the "ladies."

We are brought into the circle, and although we do not realize it at this moment, we will spend the better part of the next two days there. We scrutinize our fellow passengers: the man on our left is wearing a stylish black shirt and checked sports coat, unexpectedly dapper for a helicopter ride in the Russian Far East. He bears a slight resemblance to Prince Charles but without the jug ears and seems to be the company go-fer. His name is Vladimir. Consistent with his task of making everything run smoothly and keeping everyone happy, he affably describes for us the identities of our traveling companions, ever eager to talk up the company, Marina-ich, the largest fishing industry in the North, profitably dealing crab to the Japanese market.

The director is short and swarthy with a silver whale affixed to his tie. We initially assume, from his jet-black hair and almond eyes, that he is Koryak, but he would be the biggest-bellied Koryak imaginable. He is, in fact, a Kazakh from the far west of the former Soviet Union, one of the most successful of the Kazakh businessmen who are prospering in Kamchatka. The party includes four company representatives, the silver-haired man, Vladimir, the director (Olzhebay Kasenovich Shamangarinov), and a bouncy blond woman (Lena) who exudes poise and confidence and provides a shoulder for the boss to sleep on. Is the novelistic imagination disappointed when we realize that she is his wife? Then there's a white-haired judge from Moscow, dressed in denim, who is also a poet and passionately engaged in the revival of romance ballads. He and his charming wife, Galina, a physician, seem to be the emotional center of this diverse party. Their attractive twenty-something daughter is accompanied by the equally attractive daughter of one of the judge's university classmates, now living in Petropavlovsk, who works in the tourist industry. A sweet-faced, dark-haired woman of a certain age is, we are told, a well-known singer of romance ballads. Lidia Nebaba resembles the middle-aged Shirley Temple Black, and speaks with a soft, sweet voice, like the grown-up child star when she introduced fairy tales on television. Her accompanist, a lithe young man who also plays a mean classical guitar, is yet one more Sergey. They are on a tour of Kamchatka, sponsored by Marina-ich through the initiative of the judicial poet who networked the connection to the company through his former school friend in Petropavlovsk. The party in the helicopter also includes a representative from the Koryak village of Voyampolka where, we now learn, we will make our first stop. One hundred years ago Bogoras spent the night in this village perched on the northwestern edge of Kamchatka, on the shores of the Sea of Okhotsk.

The go-fer describes the village of Voyampolka as a hell hole (*dira*). Marina-ich is required to invest in an impoverished community, and this is the village they were assigned. The company built a school there a year ago out of parts flown in from Canada and assembled by Canadians, also flown in. In return, Marina-ich receives favorable fishing quotas in the Koryak Region. The go-fer speaks with pride of the company's good works, claiming that the community was falling apart until the company built the school. Now Marina-ich is thinking of building a water tower because the village has no immediate supply. The task today is to deliver a furnace to replace the one that went out in January, just five months after the new school opened. The children had to be farmed around to houses for lessons. (We will learn this brief history of the original furnace from a woman in the village, not from the go-fer.)

When the helicopter lands, all of the village children gather. Alexia says this is a typical Northern village scene. The judicial poet rises to the occasion and bursts into song. He reaches out his hands and, singing, leads them in a ring dance. The sweet-voiced folk singer joins in. The furnace is unloaded and the crowd moves off in the direction of the school. Passengers, children, and villagers, mostly women, mill around outside the school building while the director and his immediate entourage go inside to inspect. It is overcast and chilly. Someone hands us pinecones and we sit, popping the soft nuts from their woody shells, enjoying this basic Northern snack. Eventually, in response to some cue that is imperceptible to us, the children all sprint toward the village's House of Culture, and we follow the milling crowd.

It is cold inside this simple building and, in the fading afternoon light, gloomy This village has been without electricity for nearly six months. With the economic downturn of recent weeks, the desperate situation the previous winter will be replayed with even greater severity in the coming winter. Cash-strapped districts are finding themselves unable to buy and transport fuel—oil and coal—for heat and electricity. Villagers quietly comment that they have been dragging wood from the sparse taiga more than two kilometers away. They do not know what will happen when the wood supply is depleted.

The walls of the House of Culture are painted with murals of abstracted Native life; they are of a piece with the decorations in other public buildings we have seen, a local rendering of the Soviet legacy in public culture. The hall fills. The folksinger will perform, but first the boss makes a speech. Yes, times are hard, but they will get better. It is true that the villagers no longer have electricity, but we have all lived through times of hardship and scarcity. Marina-ich will help them, but the company must also spread its benevolence among villages.

There is surely a subtext here. The people in this village must have been mightily annoyed when the furnace went out in January. The boss insists that his is not a cosmetic philanthropy. Does he protest too much? He reminds them that his company has provided a new furnace, that it has not forgotten the

Figure 33. The arrival of a helicopter is an exciting event in an isolated Northern village. Children in the Koryak village of Voyampolka have rushed out to meet the Marina-ich party and have been encouraged by their high spirited visitors to join in a ring dance. (Photo by Laurel Kendall)

community. Whatever the motive, this is a remarkable encounter. It would be utterly impossible for a Kazakh doing business with Japan to address a room full of Koryak had they not shared decades of Soviet cultural practice. Even so, his audience is mostly women and children; there are very few men. Are the men less interested in folk songs—or perhaps just less willing to be patronized?

And then, the concert. The folksinger has draped a lacy white spangled shawl over her sweater and slacks, a simple but effective transformation from travel wear into theatrical glitter. She is extremely sweet and earnest, telling her audience that this is the first time that she has ever been in a Koryak village. She will sing her music today, but she knows that they have their own music. She hopes that they will never forget the spirit behind the songs of their own people. Then she sings several pieces with a pretty and well-trained voice. As an interlude, Sergey, the virtuoso guitarist, plays a solo, a tango.

How uncanny this all is. The library mural in Anadyr has come to life, transformed by the present moment. Where the Soviet system bestowed enlightenment from the air, lowering books into the hands of Native people, the new capitalists drop tango from the skies. The performance ends with a roaring round of applause and we are all ushered into the largest house in the village, a clean and comfortable house, very different from the Jochelsons' accommodations in Koryak villages long ago.

The local women have prepared a feast for us out of ingredients that were flown in on the helicopter. There is a hearty soup, potatoes in a spicy sauce, piles of fresh bread, and crab cake which, the go-fer tells us, is a special Marina-ich product. It is a tasty meal, but eaten in haste. The boss announces that it is time to leave, and the go-fer makes certain that we move quickly; the pilot is anxious to make it to Palana before dusk.

There is a thrilling vertical liftoff over the taiga in autumn colors, lush green, yellow gold and red, giving way to the moonscape tundra. We arrive in Palana just at dusk. It is a city of gray concrete structures, mud, rain, and damp. From the airport bus we see a bare bulb burning in one of the dingy airport buildings. At least the electricity is back on up here.

We are all staying in the same rambling and nondescript gray concrete hotel, the tallest building on Lenin Square at the center of town. Amid the flutter of securing rooms, we meet a man from the local Department of Education who is involved with arrangements for Lidia's concert this evening. Of course he knows Nutalyugin, the director of the Palana museum, knows him well enough to know that Nutalyugin does not have a home telephone. Off the top of his head, he provides the telephone number for Raisa Avak, director of the Department of Culture, who has been advised of our visit. He tells us that she has been ill. We assume that this means she will be at home, but there is no answer when we telephone. We wonder what to do next. Should we take a taxi to Nutalyugin's house? What if he is away at his dacha? In all the adventure of getting here, we have forgotten, for a few hours, our basic dilemma: will there be anyone at the museum who is willing to talk with us? Will they all be away on vacation? How do we find them in a strange town? Then, as happens in small towns, the receptionist makes a suggestion. She tells us that she knows the museum librarian and can call her at home. Yes, the museum telephone went out of service a while ago. We are clutching at straws, willing to try anything. Wonder of wonders, this is a direct connection with Tatyana Volkova, the librarian turned museum registrar. We know of her through Christina Kinkaid, who worked with Tatyana during her year here with her anthropologist husband, Alex King. Tatyana has been waiting for us.

She is willing to meet us at 8:30 the next morning at our hotel to maximize our time. We can fly out with the helicopter later in the morning and not risk getting stuck in Palana should the weather change again. She will send messengers to Nutalyugin's and Avak's homes to advise them of our presence, but she thinks that Nutalyugin is indeed at his dacha. Alexia assumes that despite our earlier correspondence, Nutalyugin left town because he knew very well how difficult it is for people to get to Palana. He probably assumed that we would never make it, and he was almost right.

Our situation settled, we walk through the rain-soaked streets and examine the shelves of the local store, surprisingly better stocked than the shops in Esso. As an administrative "center," Palana has storage sites. When the ruble was inflating, nothing was shipped out from Palana, but the local stores could weasel supplies and their shelves were always stocked. We purchase two overpriced apples as a breakfast provision.

The pilots have asked us to join them for dinner. They have reserved a table at the local restaurant adjoining the hotel. We have agreed to meet them thinking that, in anticipation of a return flight, we ought to try to be charming, and maybe they will be willing to change money with us. But they stand us up. We munch the salad that has been artfully set out on the reserved table, dining in candlelight because the electricity has gone out. Eventually, a pilot staggers in to report that they had all gone to Lidia's concert but would join us in a bit. His ruddy complexion belies the claim of music appreciation and this is the last we see of any of them that evening.

After dinner we are shown to one room on the hotel's fourth floor, but it turns out there are no blankets there. When the concierge cannot locate spare blankets we are shown to another room, equally spartan, furnished with just a table and two beds with thin mattresses supported by boxsprings. There are no towels, but there is running water, even if it is cold. Our room is an icebox. We borrow a tea kettle from the receptionist and fill the room with steam to create a vaporous illusion of warmth as we bundle into all possible layers of clothing and try to sleep. Things might have been better had we realized that the small topmost window, the *fortochka*, used throughout Russian construction to allow for fresh air, was wide open.

We wake to a clear, bright sunny day. We are slowly assembling ourselves when Tatyana Volkova knocks lightly on our door at 7:30. She has seen that it is a clear day, that we are likely to be able to leave, so she has come for us even earlier than arranged. She sits on the bed politely thumbing our gift of the *Drawing Shadows to Stone* catalog. Christina had already given the museum a copy; we should have realized it. Tatyana is completely at ease as we disjointedly finish dressing and packing. She helps us bundle our bags downstairs and stow them with the receptionist.

Tatyana Volkova is a warm, slightly dumpy woman with lively features and a clear intelligence and energy. We suspect she is the real mover in the museum. Her husband is a representative in the Regional Duma, the parliamentary body governing the Koryak Region. We had expected Tatyana to be Koryak like the director, but she is Russian. Tatyana is formally trained as a librarian and self-trained as a bibliographer of local history. The museum's historical archive is her work. Originally, she had come to the Russian Far East from central Siberia for a reasonably comfortable position in Petropavlovsk. Almost immediately she was told that someone with her skills was urgently needed in the Commander Islands, where she spent ten years in the town of Nikolskoe. Her children were born there and thought their mother was an

Aleut (Aleutiiq). After the Commander Islands, she lived through several harsh winters in the Olyutor Peninsula. In all, she has spent twenty years in Kamchatka, but this is her first year in Palana.

Tatyana suggests that we pay a courtesy call on the Department of Culture just across the square from the hotel. Access to their fax would make communication between us so much easier in the future and, as we have already learned, friends in high places can help us find space on flights. But the Department of Culture is inexplicably closed this Friday morning.

Tatyana takes us up a muddy road to the museum, a small wooden building surrounded by trees. This building, which the museum has occupied since 1971, has served a variety of municipal needs, once as a dormitory, another time as a school classroom. It is a small, local museum and does not have a trained specialist on staff. The director studied "agriculture"—probably reindeer husbandry—but became passionately immersed in researching and recording the Koryak language. This is getting to be a pattern. Vladimir Etylin's son in Anadyr was a reindeer veterinarian turned Chukchi lexicographer. In these efforts they are cousins to all those Ainu amateur linguists Laurel met a few years ago in Hokkaido, passionately bent on recording the fading speech of the elders as a way of grabbing hold of a past, a culture, a sense of self.

The staff also includes a tour guide educator who was trained as a musician, the lovely blond Vera who soon joins us. She was born in Tuva, in southeastern Siberia bordering Mongolia, and her siblings live all over the United States. There is also a docent who doubles as a bibliography assistant and works with the Koryak language, but he is away in Esso right now. He is frustrated, Tatyana says, because the daily round of museum work allows so little time for research. Because half of the staff is engaged in linguistic research, we mention the recordings that Jochelson made with wax cylinders a century ago. Upon our return to New York we will send them copies via colleagues departing for Kamchatka.

We go into the small ethnology hall and see the sort of display we would expect to find— Koryak and Even costumes and a range of objects of daily use. The most stunning part of the ethnology hall is a diorama by Pirozhenko and Krupina, who did the sculptures in the Petropavlovsk museum. They made this diorama in the 1970s, fashioning each of the figures after actual people then living in the Koryak fishing camp of Naya. The backdrop is a Kamchatka scene of striking purple mountains.

We are running out of time; we have to be back at the hotel by ten if we want to fly out in the helicopter. We go to Tatyana's office and set up the computer on the desk that Tatyana describes as "Christina's spot." Today, for some reason, the CD player refuses to respond. Not only is this a disappointingly brief visit; we aren't able to perform. Back in New York we will learn via e-mail that Alex King was able to get our disk up and running. The museum will lose direct access to the Internet when Alex leaves at the end of the month; the cost of arranging their own connection is prohibitive. They might be able to use the CD in the Department of Culture. Since we cannot perform, we talk. Viktoria Petrasheva, our mutual acquaintance from Petropavlovsk, was here recently with Dr. Watanabe, a Japanese researcher from Hokkaido. Dr. Watanabe, they report, carried a huge backpack and kept asking of the objects, "Is that traditional?" probably because this collection was made relatively recently, beginning in the 1960s.

Tatyana shows us a colored brochure that Christina had worked on and then, apologetically, gives us a black and white photocopy of it. They cannot afford to produce the color version anymore; they have only the one copy left. But that is not as bad as it gets. They catalogue their collection on cards, a standard method, and in the past when they ran out the supply would simply be charged to a museum account with the local Department of Culture. Now it is no longer possible to charge supplies, and they have no money to buy, so they have done without since January. This hobbles Tatyana's efforts to systematically catalog and inventory a collection that had been only sloppily recorded in the past. Since 1995, they have had no direct municipal financing for the museum. As elsewhere, they get lighting (when the town has it) but, as in Esso, they have not been able to maintain their telephone. Here Tatyana launches into a familiar litany of how people struggle to get by in the North, living on the fish they catch and what they grow in their gardens.

By now we are walking back down the muddy road to the hotel under sunny skies. Tatyana tells us that it looks as though Yevgeny Primakov will be accepted as prime minister to fill the void after Anatoly Chubais's dismissal earlier in the summer. Just eight months later Yeltsin will replace Primakov, this time with a former KGB operative, Vladimir Putin. On this September morning, Primakov's appointment is a cause for optimism since the Duma, the national legislative body, likes him. As a hopeful sign, the deflated ruble is already down to fifteen against the dollar from the high of twenty-one. The town desperately needs the supply of heating oil and coal that is already loaded onto freighters and sitting in a distant port. It cannot be moved without an authorizing signature, which cannot be given with the government in flux and no money available for payment. The Koryak Region has pushed for even greater autonomy to avoid being so dependent on the center.

Tatyana has been in Palana for only a year, since her husband was elected to the regional Duma. She spent nine months of her last year on the Olyutor Peninsula without electricity, a "frightening way to live." People were burning pine—the only available wood—which burns quickly to a great heat and gives off resin, both a health and a fire hazard. With so many trees being cut, the ecology of the area will be permanently affected. She has seen the recent television report from Moscow describing how bad things were in Palana, but she knows from her prior experience how much worse things could be. Because

Palana is an administrative center, there will always be some money for utilities.

We meet the group from the helicopter, out for a leisurely morning walk. They take their time coming back to the hotel, and when the designated hour of ten o'clock passes, we succumb to paranoid jitters that they have flown off and left us. As we stand waiting on the hotel steps, chatting with Tatyana and Vera, a woman with long black hair sprints across the square and embraces Alexia. This is Larisa Georgievna Khalmoyina, a young Koryak woman who is the president of the local branch of the Association of Peoples of the North (*assotsiatsia narodov Severa*), a Russia-wide indigenous rights organization with its headquarters in Moscow. Alexia and Larisa had met a year or so earlier in New York at a conference organized by David Koester. Larisa had been at Raisa Avak's house when Tatyana's messenger arrived to say that we were in town. She had also heard us on the radio broadcast from Anadyr.

Larisa is bursting with agendas. She reminds Alexia about a doll in our collection that is attributed to the Chuvantsy people, a subgroup of the Koryak. The doll is evidence of historical depth in the ethnohistory of Chuvantsy, a people who have been attempting to establish themselves as a legitimate ethnic group in their own right. Larisa has written about the doll in the local Kamchatka newspaper. She would desperately like a photograph. She also wants us to publish a catalog of Siberian shaman material. She wants us to meet the local indigenous rights organization. She wants us to be interviewed for the local radio.

This encounter highlights our growing awareness that we have not been making maximal contact with our stated target audience, "the descendants of those who made the objects in our collections." The museums are most often headed by Russians. Otke in Anadyr and Nutalyugin here in Palana are exceptions. We should also be trying to connect with the indigenous rights organizations or with Houses of Culture that work closely with Native people, as in Esso. If only we did not have a helicopter to catch. We toy with the idea of booking tickets on the domestic flight back to Petropavlovsk. This will require rubles, and Palana is still exchanging at seven to the dollar, nearly as it was before the wild gyration began.

The Marina-ich party arrives and it is determined that they are going to the festival in Kovran. They will return to Palana to drop people off and pick people up between three and four in the afternoon. The boss gives us his solemn word. We say that we will be waiting. This is a positive turn of events. We can go back to the museum for a leisurely tea and conversation with Vera and Tatyana. Larisa will arrange a meeting with the indigenous rights organization for the early afternoon.

By now, we are very hungry since we have not had any breakfast. We contribute fifteen rubles and our two apples to the cause of tea. Tatyana had originally rejected our offer of the apples, saying that we might get stuck somewhere and be glad to have them, but this seems the appropriate moment. Vera buys cheese, cookies, and candy. The daily bread is not yet available at the store.

Tatyana talks about the consequences for the museum of the Koryak Region's succession from Kamchatka. After World War II the ten autonomous regions in Russia were subordinated to the provinces in which they were located; the Koryak Region was subsumed by Kamchatka Province. For years residents of the regions chafed under this arrangement, feeling that their interests were not adequately represented at the federal level. In 1992 when Yeltsin declared that all administrative territories, whether provinces or regions, would be equal members of the Russian Federation, the Koryak Region's autonomy was officially reestablished. The loss of the connection to Kamchatka Province was more than a financial loss. Museum people, library people, House of Culture people, and all manner of professional civil servants used to travel at least once every three months to meet with colleagues. They maintained professional contacts and conversations, even though they worked in relative isolation. Whenever any of them had special needs, such as a textbook or money for travel to a conference, Petropavlovsk would come through for them. Now Palana is its own center, with neither the resources nor the infrastructure to provide for the outlying villages. As elsewhere, Tatyana and Vera lament the loss of clout once wielded by the all-Russian organization that oversees cultural monuments and the preservation of museum collections, a group that could have helped them secure necessary resources, such as computers.

We talk about how the Internet might solve some of their problems, how it might be beneficial to join forces with all of the museums in their sphere and request a big grant that would put them into virtual contact with each other. We talk about their current projects. They have a small grant from the local veterans' organization to videotape and document the oral history of World War II from local veterans. The results are sometimes amazing. The person who lives next door is someone you take for granted, Tatyana says, until you start interviewing them about their experiences during the war. Tatyana and Vera are becoming adept with the video camera.

They had a recent photographic exhibit documenting Palana from 1936 to the present. They used the familiar but effective gambit of juxtaposing old images with familiar contemporary shots of the same places. Older people came and commented on the materials on the wall, giving researchers a new perspective, including the old names of streets. We ask if they work with Koryak people. Not exactly. Some of the veterans are, of course, Koryak. Tatyana and Vera would like to do an oral history project with elderly artisans about traditional knowledge of patterns and techniques.

Larisa has summoned a car to take us to the meeting at the Institute for Teacher Development. The institute, as Larisa explains, is concerned with the revitalization of the language and culture of the Koryak, Even, and Itelmen.

Figure 34. Koryak girls weaving baskets, c. 1900. Several examples of exquisite Koryak basketry are in the collection of the American Museum of Natural History. No longer a practical necessity, and in the absence of either state subsidy or a stable market, the preservation of Native handicrafts is a precarious enterprise today. (AMNH Library 1576)

To this end, the staff develops teaching materials for schools and language classes. They have also developed an ethnography program for schools that covers the cultural history of the Itelmen, Even, and Koryak. They have recently begun to research the ritual life of these peoples. As elsewhere, they once had money for expeditions and for turning their findings into teaching materials, but now there is none.

The room fills with about half a dozen people—Native scholars, activists, a woman from the radio station with a tape recorder, and a newspaper reporter. Klavdia Nikolaevna Khaloymova, a specialist on Itelmen language and customs who has worked with the German anthropologist Erich Kasten, gives Alexia a warm embrace. They met at a conference in Berlin the previous winter.

Larisa introduces us, reminding everyone that she visited the American Museum of Natural History in New York and saw our collections. Mikhail Ivanovich Popov, the acting director of the institute, leads off the questioning.

He is a thin, intense older man with gray hair, a respected Native intellectual who holds a Ph.D. in pedagogy and was a delegate to the Supreme Soviet. Mikhail Ivanovich's first question is surprisingly specific. He knows that the preservation of reindeer hair can be problematic, and how do we deal with it? We talk about our conservation and storage facilities, and our conservators' expressed desire to learn more about local methods. He tells us that his sister visited AMNH some years back and that he and his colleagues are anxious to advise us regarding our collections. He would also like to know what percentage of the population of the United States is interested in our collection and in the Koryak people. To what degree do Native Americans see this collection as relevant to themselves? We answer as best we can, citing our recent experience with the international conference held to celebrate the centenary of the Jesup Expedition and the conversations that took place at that time between scholars, including Native scholars, from both sides of the Bering Strait. We can also report that although most Americans are ignorant of the Koryak, many thousands of visitors to the American Museum of Natural History receive a basic introduction to the Koryak through exhibits that use materials collected by the Jesup North Pacific Expedition.

Lyudmila Hilol, a young Koryak activist and member of the indigenous rights group, takes over and asks far more barbed questions. What use is the CD to them? Why did we bring it in that format? Will the local museum be capable of preserving the disk in working condition? Will the museum let Native people have access to it? Yes, the museum can preserve the disk, and, yes, the museum has assured us that the community at large can access it. (After we return to New York, we will send the indigenous rights group their own copy of the disk.)

Galina Urkachan, an Even newspaper reporter, asks, "Can the Native peoples of Kamchatka request the return of collections, just as American law now permits the repatriation of collections to Native American communities?" The inevitable question. Laurel's answer will be standard, cautious, but sincere. "The law only covers Native American collections. As to the rest, ownership is a lawyer's question. I am not the one who can give you an accurate answer. What I can talk about is how you can use the collection, even from this distance, and about what we might do together in the future." Galina also asks why so many American researchers are coming through Kamchatka. Have we exhausted the subject of Native Americans? We talk about the resumption of American anthropological interest in the region that began one hundred years ago and was disrupted during the Soviet period.

Through all of this, Tatyana and Vera sit very quietly on the sidelines. We're sorry we've brought them into an uncomfortable situation, but maybe this is a constructive experience for them. They heard an airing of Native peoples' concerns regarding museums and collections, while we took the heat. We've anticipated these sorts of questions and are not naive participants in this dis-

Figure 35. After our formal meeting at the Institute for Teacher Development, we are invited to tea. The loaf of bread, just purchased from the bakery kiosk, was so fresh that it emitted a curl of steam when it was cut. From left to right, Vera, Tatyana, Klavdia Nikolaevna, Larisa, and Mikhail Ivanovich. (Photo by Laurel Kendall)

cussion. The group's challenges are a prelude to a more constructive dialogue. At least, this is the positive gloss we choose to put on our afternoon.

When the session is over, Larisa presents us with a large and fragrant bundle of dry smoked fish, and we present Mikhail Ivanovich with a copy of the catalog of *Drawing Shadows to Stone*. As this was Larisa's party and she had been moderating throughout, Laurel mistakenly points the catalog in her direction, but Alexia quickly and effectively steers it into Dr. Popov's waiting hands. Had Laurel been thinking in Korean, she would not have blundered. There would have been no question: the distinguished elder scholar should receive our gift.

We all have tea with more delicious smoked fish. Dr. Popov darts outside and returns from the bakery with a loaf of baked bread so fresh that a curl of steam escapes from the loaf when it is cut, provoking exclamations of delight. We contribute the big box of chocolates that Madame Otke had given us as one of her many parting gifts. The chocolate is surprisingly good with the smoked fish and fresh bread.

Larisa tells us not to worry, that she will get a car to meet us at the hotel across Lenin Square so that we can make our appointment with the helicopter. Having thus assured us, she settles back into tea and fish and is still there, leisurely chatting, twenty minutes later when Alexia goes to find her. A car is found, and we are on our way to our rendezvous with the Marina-ich party.

Tatyana and Vera accompany us to the helipad, pointing out that we are getting away while they are stuck here. They are thinking of other departures, of Christina who has already gone back to the United States, of Alex who will depart very soon, and of the many Russians who have left the North to improve their lot in the 1990s. They ask if we think Alex and Christina will ever come back to Palana. It is hard for Russians in the North, they tell us. In the past, their children had certain educational priorities within the Soviet system, but in the Koryak Region, Russian children are the lowest priority. From their comments, we cannot help but wonder if these two energetic women will join the exodus out of the North.

Alexia complements Vera on her silky quilted jacket and asks, "Is it from China?" This is an innocent faux pas. They gently observe that "Made in China" now describes shoddy goods churned out for the Russian market in factories along the Amur River. In the past, of course, China's state-run factories produced lovely thick wool garments. Tatyana says the current products are good for children, who outgrow things quickly.

The helipad is a grassy field surrounded by a barbed-wire fence. We see a knot of other people waiting, although it is not yet clear to us that we are all waiting for the same helicopter. We recognize the man who manages the restaurant next to the hotel. We had met him the previous night when he was greeted like an old friend by both the pilots and the Marina-ich group. A fair-haired young woman and two small children are with him. Two men in hunting gear stand by a heap of small canvas body bags.

The helicopter arrives. On cue, Tatyana, Vera, and Alexia cover their heads and huddle by the barbed-wire fence. Laurel is new to Northern travel and slower to protect herself from the turbulence created by the helicopter landing. She is showered with dust and dry grass stirred up by the spinning rotor blades. The force of air is so violent that Tatyana's canvas bag, marked "tropical beach" in English, is ripped from her grasp and lands on muddy ground. Laurel's own suitcase is whipped over the fence and lands in a mud puddle beyond the enclosure.

The Marina-ich party is buoyant from their day at the festival in Kovran. Lidia and Sergey are tenderly carrying the bunches of wilted tundra flowers they received as tribute from local fans. Galina, the poetic judge's wife, demonstrates Native dance gestures and shows off a carved wooden mask purchased from a Native artisan at the festival. They have also bought a framed portrait of Ekaterina Gil, the lead dancer who had performed with the Esso troupe in New York. We have a sense of a circle closing.

Cargo is shifted from this to another helicopter, and we are on our way, but only to Esso; Petropavlovsk is fogged in. The passengers have expanded by two American hunters, Mel and John, and a fair-haired young mother with what will prove to be two of the world's most attractive and well-behaved children. The restaurateur, who seems to have a finger in many pies, was the local agent for Mel and John's hunting trip. The fair-haired young woman is the restaurateur's sister, Sveta. This little family will be immigrating to Australia with Sveta's boyfriend, who has a computer degree. Sveta has a degree in economics, but she suspects that she will have to settle for any available job, most likely as a nanny.

The hunters have paid $20,000 US for their trip and are delighted to have bagged two bears and four mountain sheep (the contents of the body bags). They consider this trip a bargain relative to the high cost of permits for killing a single bear or wild sheep in the United States and Canada. Overall, they say, the hunting is not significantly better in Kamchatka, but the price is right. Their tour provided them with a crew of four, including an interpreter, guides, and a cook. In their real lives Mel runs a foundry and John is in utilities; they have known each other since high school. Alexia's skill as an interpreter is welcomed by these American boosters of the local economy, and perhaps this is why we continue to be part of the party when we learn, at the heliport in Esso, that Lyudmila's place is full up with new guests.

The director's wife, Lena, is on the telephone, making arrangements, and warmly tells us that they will "take care" of us. We are to go with the group to spend the night at a hot spring resort in Anavgay, then fly back with them tomorrow to Petropavlovsk, weather permitting. In the middle of a rainy field, with no other prospects, we sink into the grateful passivity of members of a guided tour.

In the fading light, we fly to a resort area conveniently situated around a helipad. In an almost barracks-like lodge, we share a room with Sveta and her children. Sveta cannot believe that Laurel is fifty years old ("My mama is fifty!" she says in English).

We get into our bathing suits and go to soak in the very warm spring water with the rest of the party, testing particularly hot rocks with our feet and swimming some laps in the large tank. Here we are, in the pitch-dark night, splashing in the water with this diverse assortment of friendly nodding acquaintances. Afterward, it is like a jolly banya scene, with all of the women soaping and shampooing themselves. Laurel loses the backing to her earring, everyone helpfully searches the wet floor, but it has disappeared. Olga, the young blond, suggests using a bit of rubber band as a substitute, observing, "Russians are resourceful." Laurel recalls Ingrid in Kamchatka opining that "Russians can fix anything" and knows that she will forever after back her earrings with bits of rubber band while thinking of the Mir space station. A rinse under the bath hut's scalding tap of spring water makes us feel much better about the prospect of a night in an unheated dormitory room. We are further warmed when we emerge from the bathhouse and the go-fer greets one and all with a tumbler of vodka and some bread and sausage. And when we return to our room, the heat seems to be on. What more could one ask for?

Eventually, a midnight feast is served with lots of vodka and bottles of white wine. The wine is intended for the ladies and, like cheap Korean champagne, it tastes like bubblegum, but the thought is nice. We feast on a hash of meat and fried potatoes and an abundance of salmon roe caviar and fresh bread. There are innumerable toasts. The sonorous-voiced judge declaims some of his own poetry and celebrates the diversity and international character of our group. He emphasizes the word *rossiane*, meaning "citizens of Russia," as opposed to *russkie*, Russians. It is fitting that the judge is invoking the new marker for an ethnically diverse Russian Federation, an imagined community struggling to be born amid breakaway republics and ethnic strife. From our side, Mel offers a toast, declaring that he has been doing business in Russia since 1977 and thinks that things have improved a great deal since then. He offers encouragement, sees the federation as moving "along the right road." This is a good toast; Russians like to hear this sort of thing and the metaphor of a road is often invoked in reference to the direction the country might take. Lidia makes a long tribute to Marina-ich, the company that meets the needs of all kinds of people: artists, scholars (our slot), hunters, businessmen, mothers. Back in New York, we will share the story of this encounter with fellow anthropologist Igor Krupnik. He will laugh and tell us that this is all "really very Russian," that you can read about this sort of thing in old novels. We have been scooped up into the entourage of the traveling prince.

And then, inevitably, Lidia Nebaba sings her romantic ballads once more. The cook rests her plump arms on the kitchen counter and sobs without restraint. Eventually, we find ourselves all dancing in a line around the long table. A little later, we are sleeping more deeply than would seem possible in the crowded room of a resort dormitory.

The next morning, Laurel sits in the dormitory room, trying to catch up on her notes; Alexia is reading a local newspaper. We have given Sveta's children colored markers from our stash of gifts and they draw with quiet concentration. There is some confusion about where we are going next, talk of more stops at hot springs, and quiet grumbling among ungrateful hitchhikers impatient to get back to Petropavlovsk. Alexia provides clarification for the non-Russian speakers. Petropavlovsk is still fogged in but with a clearing anticipated for the early afternoon. The hot spring stop is to kill time. We are served a hearty breakfast of potatoes fried with meat, more lovely orange fish roe, and fresh bread.

With some confusion and more delays to confirm weather in Petropavlovsk, we are eventually up in the air and down again in a very isolated mountain spa that seems to be accessible oniy by helicopter. We are in the middle of a wide field surrounded by some newly constructed wooden shacks. The men and women change clothes in separate huts behind screens of vinyl and submerge in separate pools of hot water. It is very pleasant, despite the fact that the tank is filled with huge leafy algae-like plants that are slimy to the touch. Galina, a physician, says that the Japanese have been importing great quantities of this aqueous weed for its healing properties when applied to a wound. We all help her gather a supply and she fills a plastic bag. We think of Yura at the beach in Providenia. Here is one more instance of Russian resourcefulness, carrying a plastic bag with the idea of gathering nutritious or useful substances whenever the opportunity might present itself.

We visit a medicinal spring in the forest and pick berries on the way back to the plane. In the field, once more, the meal is vodka, bread, and sausages. Once again, the silver-haired jurist poet declaims a verse and sings a song. There is some good-natured but impatient grumbling, even among the Russians. We are all beginning to wonder if we will ever get to Petropavlovsk.

During this informal picnic we realize that Vladimir Kolegov, the Koryak representative in Petropavlovsk who arranged this helicopter mystery tour for us, has joined the party. He had gone up to Esso by bus to ensure that the only man who has the right to authorize the unloading of coal in Palana was safely on a helicopter bound for Palana. It gives us pause to imagine the man responsible for heat in the capital of the Koryak Region relying on travel arrangements as precarious as our own. We snap pictures of Kolegov as he snaps his own picture of Olzhebay Kasenovich, the Kazakh fisher king.

We have picked up yet another passenger, an old man who hitchhiked by helicopter to the spa in the hope of treating a medical condition. He had collapsed and required a medivac. We touch down in some unidentified place on the way back where an ambulance is waiting for him.

We are jammed into the body of the helicopter, which struggles and lurches just a bit before it is airborne. The flight is bumpy. A few of the passengers are quietly sick.

The sky is clear in Petropavlovsk when we land, clearer than it had been at any time during our previous stay. The spectacular snow-capped volcanic cones are unveiled, a veritable ring of Mount Fujis all around the city. The helipad is far from anywhere, including the airport where we must retrieve our checked bag. We are anxious to call the hotel and secure a room. We are chafing at having been passive travelers for the past twenty-four hours.

Olzhebay invites us to ride with him and his wife to where we can join the van that is transporting the Marina-ich group's luggage to Petropavlovsk. Lena drives us, which is rare in Russia. We ask Olzhebay if he would be interested in changing rubles for dollars. He obligingly pulls out his cell phone and learns that the going rate is twelve rubles to the dollar. It is coming back to a more reasonable rate; the crisis has been ameliorated for the present.

It is immediately evident that we and our luggage will not fit into the already crammed van. We decline the offer of a lift. Olzhebay, ever the gracious host, persists. We are to collect our bag and the van will come back for us. At the bag check we see row upon row of luggage racks stacked with reindeer antlers, a Kamchatka moment. The baggage attendant seems amused by our amusement.

Now we are stuck waiting for the van to return. We enjoy the spectacular volcanic scenery and Alexia tries to find a rooftop from which to photograph it. After a good hour, assuming that our driver has succumbed to unforeseen complications or forgotten good intentions, we find a cab. It is well after seven when we finally get back to the Oktyabrskaya Hotel, which now seems extremely luxurious. The cab ride is an extravagance, but we are in better shape than had we tried to struggle back on the bus with all of our bags. Indeed, with all of those dips in hot springs, we are in terrific shape, but very much in need of solitude. We opt for a quiet dinner in the hotel café, where we encounter the van driver, who asks us why we did not wait for him. We apologize. He is accompanied by one more American "friend" in need of translation and conversation—the last thing we need. Alexia brushes him off with polite apologies and the two men leave. We drink a lot of cheap Russian champagne, a brand that does not taste like bubblegum.

Chapter 9

Again Petropavlovsk

Packing up and tidying loose ends, the inevitable end of a journey, was magnified for members of the Jesup Expedition both by the volume of material they handled and by the complications of shipping from the Russian Far East. Laufer, concerned with the high cost of freight, would ship boats, sledges, and other big articles to New York via Suez, with a shipment of smaller objects sent via Vancouver. Some of the wonderful fish skin robes that had been a passion of his collecting would be damaged by water in transit. Laufer wrote to Boas from Yokohama, Japan, on December 28, 1899, begging for a respite to recover from the rigors of fieldwork:

I have not finished repacking and shipping my collections until today. . . . I beg you . . . to grant me kind permission to prolong my stay till the 26th of January, when the next steamer of the C.T.R. line leaves. . . . I could not yet get rid of a bad skin eruption I brought from Siberia. . . . I think, since I am . . . in Japan, it might be best to make use of hot springs. I dare say you will not have any objection to my staying in such a place for a week or two. Please charge the expenses of this trip to the amount of my salary kept there after return.

Jochelson was wrapping up his Koryak research when he wrote to Boas from Kushka on July 21, 1901:

We also made a very successful journey in two boats to the mouth of the river Nayukan [Naukan], where we came upon 61 Tungus tents. It was a great opportunity for ethnographic work, unfortunately, I couldn't stay there long. . . . Before leaving Gizhiga I have a lot to do still. The second collection I have to register and pack, I have to close all my accounts, and I have to get the equipment for the long and difficult journey over the Stanovoi mountains. . . . If you will receive this collection long before my arrival in New York, which is unlikely before fall 1902, it would be good to open the boxes. Please see to it that the labels don't get mixed up as I have detailed notes for each number. . . . Please pay special attention to box 33 which contains models of a Reindeer Koryak family traveling with a narta [sled] and dogs. These models are very artistically made and should be the special attraction of the Koryak collection. The artist, Fletscher, is half Koryak (father) and half Tungus (mother). His parents were baptized and russified, he himself has learned to read and write. Naturally his work cannot be considered aboriginal Koryak art, unlike the other models in the ethnological collection, since he must have been influenced by illustrated magazines.

Figure 36. Tungus on reindeer back crossing the River Naukan. Jochelson regretted that he was not able to spend more time with this community. (AMNH Library 1590)

Jochelson would conclude that although he had made four trips to reindeer Koryak villages, "one winter is not enough for long journeys in these areas, and ethnological work shows much better results when working more or less at a fixed site."[1] In fact, the ethnological expedition was a brief moment in the early history of American anthropology. For most of the twentieth century, "fieldwork" would be synonymous with work done for a long period in a fixed site. But despite his frustrations with the itinerant methods he had followed, Jochelson could report a huge success in meeting the tangible goals of the expedition: "we have 630 anthropometric measurements, 21 plaster masks, 595 photographs, 120 fairytales and myths, and 50 sketches of or by different Koryaks. The ethnological collection amounts to 1,440 artifacts. [There are also] phonograph cylinders with Koryak and Tungus songs, shaman incantations, and fairytales."[2] Most of the 630 measurements had been taken by Mrs. Jochelson, who requested permission to use them for her doctoral thesis at the University of Zurich. Permission was granted.

Sunday morning is overcast again, and a chilly breeze is blowing. It is Alexia's thirty-first birthday. We have an empty schedule, with an invitation to Lidia Nebaba's concert in the evening. We decide to visit the market where, at eleven in the morning, not all of the stalls are open, although by early afternoon the market will be bustling. The ruble has rallied overnight; some of the currency dealers in the market are trading at eight rubles to the dollar and some at nine.

All over Russia, old women sell hand-knit socks and caps in and near open-air markets, and the Petropavlovsk market is no exception. The women say that they knit by hand but the patterns themselves are standard, recognizable from vendor to vendor, suggesting piecework rather than individual handicraft; Alexia has seen nearly identical knitware in many other markets. We do see one old lady at work at her stall who makes a creative use of color. By now, Laurel's feet are very cold and she buys a pair of warm socks for forty rubles. Alexia buys a supply of baby booties and mittens for friends' new offspring, a soft gray goat-hair lap blanket for her mother's Christmas present, and a tuxedo-style black suit with a shiny satin collar, probably made in Turkey. She will wear the suit to the performance tonight.

Laurel is taken by the fur hat vendor's wares, in particular by a great pouf of white fur tipped in velvety brown. They call this fur *haryuk*. "Skunk fur," Alexia translates, but this is the classiest fate that a skunk could hope for. The hat would cost the equivalent of $70 US, a major purchase for a bargain shopper. The vendor insists that Laurel really ought to buy a soft brown sable hat, obviously a better investment, even at nearly three times the price. In the vendor's view, quality speaks for itself and the American traveler can well afford the better fur. Laurel cannot bring herself to tell the vendor this is a novelty purchase intended for those rare New York winter days when the temperature slips into the teens, not the everyday necessity that fur hats are for those who live in far Northern latitudes. Even so, the sable is also very nice. The vendor in the adjoining stall joins the discussion, urging Laurel to buy the sable. Passersby get into the act, telling Laurel that she would be crazy to buy the cheaper fur. Overwhelmed, Laurel leaves, hatless. On Tuesday morning, when the market is quiet, she will slink back to purchase the skunk fur hat and savor the possibility of telling people that she is wearing "Siberian *haryuk*."

There are dollar signs all over the market, more and more of them as the day progresses. Alexia sees a young tough wearing a dollar sign pinned to his shirt and asks him jokingly if he is for sale. He takes this without humor and asks if we are from Alaska. Everyone in the market seems to think that we are from Alaska.

Most of the clothing in the stalls is from Turkey, but a great many things are from Korea and China. One stall boasts large tiger-print chiffon scarves; the fabric has a stringy, spiky finish, like hairy legs. These are Korean products, an artifact of that outrageous overstated style sense that Koreans call *yahada*, "too, too much." Such a scarf would appeal to a successful Korean shaman when in Western dress, a fast-talking Seoul real estate woman, or an aggressive professional matchmaker. Laurel wonders about the women who might buy them in the Russian Far East.

We find Koreans selling *panch'an*, spicy food for side dishes, in little plastic tubes. The young woman vendor seems to understand Laurel's Korean and smiles with happy recognition at the Korean food names. She responds, quite naturally, only in Russian. We surmise this is how she communicates with her parents and grandparents. We select a couple of varieties of pickled vegetables to eat with instant noodles in our hotel room. The vendor gives us several more packets; business must be slow. The meal will leave us redolent with garlic, covertly chewing spearmint gum throughout the evening concert.

Alexia gets into a jolly conversation with two young and animated confectionery vendors who tell us their stock is much depleted but that when the last boatload of Japanese tourists was in town their shelves had been full and the visitors bought like crazy, then had their pictures taken with the vendors. The two women are reluctant to see themselves as "businesswomen" since they buy from a middleman and make only a small margin of profit. Here, again, is the ambivalence about entrepreneurship that we encountered in Providenia. The women tell us that during the financial crisis we weathered over the past week they felt as though there was no government in Russia. They think that they can sustain their business but wonder how they are going to ever make enough money to educate their children. Alexia tells them how we had been unable to change money and had been short of cash for days. "Now you know what it is like to live like Russians," they tell us affably.

At the concert, we sit with our former traveling companions, Olga the blond travel agent and Olessya, the quieter brunette, the daughter of the poetic judge and resourceful doctor. Olga's husband, a handsome navy officer, sits elsewhere. These are not down-home average Russians; they honeymooned in Spain and Portugal and will go to France. Olga's mother went to law school with the poetic judge; she is the link between Lidia Nebaba and Marina-ich.

Again, we endure Lidia's romantic ballads and enjoy Sergey's guitar solos. Alexia is called to the stage to receive a CD of Lidia's music, and other presentations are made to other members of the audience. Throughout the concert, young and old, male and female go forward and bestow bouquets of flowers. We learn after the concert, when Olzhebay asks loudly if Lidia appreciated the bouquets, that Marina-ich provided every last flower.

A banquet follows in the Lau Kai, the best Chinese eatery, perhaps the best restaurant in Petropavlovsk. We are part of Olzhebay's party, which dominates the restaurant. The only other patrons on this Sunday night are a table of well-dressed high school students who are celebrating a birthday on their own. They brazenly smoke cigarettes and drink champagne throughout the evening. Our meal begins with elaborate cold seafood dishes as at a Chinese banquet. The main course is in Russian mode, an excellent red fish, one of many varieties found in Kamchatka, There is abundant drink and there are endless toasts that go on until the small hours. Again the diversity of the gathering is celebrated, that the group includes people from all over the former Soviet Union, even Ukrainians (company employees) and scholars from the United States.

For our toast, we present Olzhebay and Lena with a copy of the *Drawing Shadows to Stone* catalog, describing the American Museum of Natural History's collections as a part of Kamchatka's past, which brought us here. We express thanks to our host and hostess for introducing us to Kamchatka's present and future. We say that as museum workers we are deeply appreciative of their support of local culture. Unstated, we hope that in the future their generosity might also help some of the museums we have visited.

There is dancing, and all ages are in motion, including the high school students from the adjoining table. Olessya toasts Alexia's birthday, and Olessya's mother, the doctor, slips a ring from her own finger and gives it to Alexia as a birthday present. It is well after two in the morning when we return to the Oktyabrskaya feeling no pain.

Monday morning arrives, clear and brisk. We are up at eight but feeling a bit groggy. We hope to leave on a scheduled weekly flight today although we are booked to leave on Thursday. We have accomplished most of what we hoped to accomplish and the more distant communities are closed to us owing to the irregularities of air transport in the foggy autumn weather. After several telephone calls, we can get on the flight, but because it is with a small Alaskan line, we cannot transfer our Alaska Air tickets. We decide that it is a better bargain to stay on, even at the higher hotel rate. The Alaska Air representative in Petropavlovsk warns us that their Thursday flight is heavily booked with "hunters and fish people" and advises us to check in early.

As if in validation of our decision to stay, we are finally able to reach Viktoria Petrasheva, the scholar-activist who has worked with our anthropologist friend David Koester. Viktoria is delighted that we are in town and makes a date with us for Tuesday. Alexia gets a call through to Alexander Slyugin, the director of the Esso museum, who tells us he rushed back to Esso to meet us only to learn that we had already gone off to Palana. We feel a stab of guilt; had we broken away from the fisher king's party at the Esso airport, we might have made this contact. (We would also have been stuck in Esso over Sunday and bouncing back to Petropavlovsk on the microbus today.) But on Saturday, we had not realized that Slyugin was around because we had never made direct telephone contact with him, and he had seemed, as a consequence, so very elusive. Slyugin tells us that he has an e-mail account care of the Esso library but cannot remember his address. We assume that he does not use it often. We give him ours and the conversation ends with mutual promises to stay in touch.

Out on the street, our first task is to secure more rubles to pay for our hotel room. The exchange in the G.U.M. still has none. Again, we go to the bank and, on the cashier's advice, wait until there is sufficient money in the bank to change $700 US, by our calculation a safe cushion until our departure on Thursday. While we sit and wait for nearly two hours, an émigré man, who, judging by his American accent, must have spent considerable time in the United States, wanders back and forth, muttering in English, probably for our benefit, "Again we have lines in Russia." The bank is now paying 9.7 rubles to the U.S. dollar but buying at 13. The Oktyabrskaya calculates our room at the

13 ruble rate, but we must pay with rubles bought at the 9.7 rate, a sleight of hand that inflates the cost of our room to $110 US a night.

We find the local Korean restaurant tucked away beside the market. The soup is hybrid, much influenced by Russian borscht. None of the restaurant staff seems to be Korean, but a Korean-language plaque over the cash register proclaims, "This house is filled with Jesus." Locally, this restaurant is known as an organized crime hangout. Later we hear from Nelson Hancock, our colleague from New York, that non-Koreans in Petropavlovsk often suspect the widely successful Korean businesses, particularly restaurants, of laundering money. These accusations could just as easily be leveled at any New Russians, but the Koreans, a successful minority, are an easy target.

Although the market is shuttered tight on Mondays, the berry and mushroom vendors have again set up their impromptu displays along the sidewalk. We buy some blueberries and some fresh morels, which we will have to boil to preserve them for transport. As we walk back through the empty market, a couple of drunken youths suddenly appear from nowhere and grab Alexia by the arm. Alexia lets loose a few of the Russian expletives she learned from Lyudmila, the navy cook, and they let her go, stumbling and laughing with liquored breaths. We spend the rest of the day working on our notes, dining on cheese, bread, blueberries, and the single crisp carrot a market vendor bestowed upon us as a spontaneous gift.

Tuesday morning, Viktoria meets us in front of the Petropavlovsk Pedagogical Institute; hers is a bright, familiar face. She takes us to her cozy apartment, full of books and artifacts. Something in the arrangement of her shelves and the quality of autumn sunlight spilling through the windows reminds Laurel of a Berkeley apartment. Viktoria likes the sentiment and repeats it to the guest who drops by later in the day.

At Viktoria's apartment, we also meet Dr. Watanabe, the Japanese scholar from the Abashiri Museum of Northern Peoples in Hokkaido who had been remembered in Palana for his immense backpack. Watanabe is researching the history of Japanese fishermen in the area. Viktoria has taken him to local museums and villages, and he has spent a great deal of time comparing fishhooks and harpoon points. They went as far as Tigil, in northwestern Kamchatka, where he saw a Japanese lacquer box that had been passed as an heirloom across generations of Itelmen. To his eyes, Itelmen like the sparkly eyed Viktoria look Japanese.

Viktoria serves us a hefty "tea" (by our reckoning, brunch) of scrambled eggs, mushrooms, potatoes, and slabs of bread spread with thick orange fish roe. She talks about her work at the local Institute of Ecology and Nature Management. She is pleased that her job gives her the time to work on projects with the nonprofit organization Kamchatka Ethnos, which she founded to address issues affecting indigenous Siberians in Kamchatka. Viktoria shares her concerns about commercial hunting in Kamchatka. The hunters only take large animals, fully grown bears and mountain sheep. This leaves the young in jeopardy and may ultimately lead to extinction. We ask if hunting might not be a mixed blessing, as it does bring money into the area. The issue, she says, is where the money goes. It is not going into the Native communities. Those who organize commercial hunting are outsiders.

We ask about poaching. When bears' gall is taken for the East Asian medicine market, are the culprits not local? Viktoria tells us that in Karaga, in northeastern Kamchatka in the Karaginsk District, she saw six bear corpses spread out on the ground with only the medicinally valued gall bladders taken. Native people would use the entire bear. She blames "newcomers," Russians and Ukrainians who have no such traditions. In Native eyes the amoral newcomers have landed here with no sense of respect for either the elders or the environment.

Viktoria is also concerned about the recent harvesting of reindeer antlers, another important item in the East Asian pharmacopoeia. As on Chinese reindeer farms, herders periodically cut the antlers and allow them to grow back. This was never done in the past, she says. People say that this harvesting diminishes the deer's strength. She has noticed that in the Northern herds, all of the animals are smaller than in the past. In Chukotka we had also been told that the herd sizes are diminishing at an alarming rate.

Land rights are a central issue in Viktoria's world. Most Native people rely heavily on hunting, fishing, and gathering berries and mushrooms as a means of subsistence; privatization means restricting access to these resources. Contests over natural assets are further intensified by an imbalance of power between newcomers and indigenous peoples such as the Itelmen, Koryak, and Even. As privatization proceeds, indigenous groups are not just sharing resources with newcomers; they are now sometimes denied access to the fishing waters and hunting and gathering areas as these are rented out to the highest bidder.

Viktoria also sees a positive side to the economic pressures brought on by the market transition. In her recent travels, she was heartened to see garden plots and greenhouses around Anavgay, just outside Esso. The Even and other Native peoples expected to be taken care of through the state stores, she says, and it has been difficult for them to learn self-reliance. This perspective is often voiced, although not always with the same tone of empathy, by those doing relatively well in the market transition. Alexia is reminded of a conversation she had with a young Evenk merchant in central Siberia who was vehemently against any form of social assistance to her relatives and friends in the Native villages. She said that they needed to learn how to work. Alexia cannot help but think that from this perspective, the people who relied on a system of governance and redistribution are blamed for the consequences when the government system itself has radically altered.

Viktoria buys handicrafts from local artisans to encourage them in their work. With her numerous contacts, she has become a middleman, with artisans bringing things directly to her. She has become very active in promoting their work, using her apartment as a sort of informal gallery. She even has the paintings framed. She tells us that the shops and commercial vendors take 10 to 15 percent of the purchase price. She, herself, takes no commission, but since this work is consuming more and more of her time, she wonders if she will soon be forced to do so.

Viktoria is impatient with the museums in the North, which she sees as inactive, short on initiative, and not doing enough to promote local heritage. She is guardedly respectful of Margarita Ivanovna at the Petropavlovsk museum but is suspicious of her as a non-Native collector who could take advantage of local artisans. In general, she thinks that museums take advantage of Native people, purchasing handicrafts for a pittance. When we ask her, Viktoria cannot think of any "good" museums in the Russian Far East. She tells us that she was amazed by how popular museums are in New York and so pleased that there are no old ladies yelling at the visitors. Then she recalls the small but very active museum in Tigil in northwestern Kamchatka, a community now without heat and electricity, where only indigenous people remain. But the museum persists. It reminds her of the small museum she had visited a few years ago in Homer, Alaska, a museum with a warm, welcoming atmosphere. The Tigil people are building an open-air museum and ask her for photographs of traditional structures. Ironically, the director, Klavdia Yegorovna Banakanova, has a surname that means "lazy" in Itelmen; Viktoria jokes that perhaps she is so energetic to compensate. Bogoras had passed through Tigil on his way back to Mariinsky Post in 1901 and had done some collecting in the region. It had been on our initial overly ambitious itinerary, abandoned when we confronted the unpredictability of travel in the Russian Far East. On hearing Viktoria's description, we feel more than a little regret.

We look at photographs from the 1992 Conference for Indigenous Peoples of the North that Viktoria helped organize. This was just after the collapse of the Soviet Union, and in that optimistic moment, there were workshops on such topics as "the market" and "indigenous rights." Viktoria's conference included cultural activities, a visit to an artist's studio, and an event in the museum in Petropavlovsk. Viktoria considers these excursions particularly important: "Native peoples could see how they were perceived and represented."

She believes that the right combination can bring crowds through the door. Old photographs in the House of Culture in Elizovo were a big draw. When they had an exhibit for the fiftieth anniversary of a popular local artist, people poured in. There had been an opening ceremony with dances—her granddaughter had been one of the dancers—and the performances gave life to the paintings.

She encourages us to send a small version of the *Drawing Shadows to Stone* exhibit to Kamchatka. The simple fact that such an expedition was made one hundred years ago would help Native people see the value of their own heritage. She recalls that when David Koester showed local people copies of Jochelson's photographs, an old woman responded, "That's my grandmother!" The pictures rekindled an interest in a history that had been devalued for much of the twentieth century. A museum is not just a place where things are stored but a repository of memory, she says, and this leads her back to a very personal story.

On September 7, just a few weeks ago, she arrived in Tigil. On September 9, 1932, her grandfather had been shot in Tigil for "counterrevolutionary" activities. She had located the execution order in an archive. On the ninth, she went to a place overlooking the river and thought about this man, an excellent hunter with a good dog team. He was only thirty-three years old when he died. One of his two children was Viktoria's mother. She shows us a copy of *The Itelmen* by the Russian ethnographer Alexander Pavlovich Volodin. They had been together at a conference dedicated to indigenous cultural heritage in the region when she showed him her grandfather's order of execution. As a tribute to the memory of Viktoria's grandfather, and because he viewed the order as an important symbol of what happened to the Itelmen during Stalinist repressions, Volodin included the execution order in his monograph.

A balding man in thick glasses with a quiet smile arrives to transact some business with Viktoria. This is Igor Fyodorev, formerly head of an indigenous rights organization whose goal is to preserve indigenous people's access to hunting and fishing. Most of the fishing out of Petropavlovsk in Avacha Bay is done from small boats, but these fishermen feel threatened by the presence of the large fishing companies. It is difficult to sustain the work of the fishing rights organization now, he tells us. Because of the government's instability, there are no funds for it.

Igor Fyodorev is a Kamchadal, a group that claims both Itelmen and Russian ancestry. "Kamchadal" was a Russian term used to refer to the "Itelmen," or "us" in their language. When the Soviet government began officially designating ethnic groups in the 1920s, it did not recognize a southern group as Itelmen since they no longer spoke the language; they were viewed as assimilated Russian. Owing in part to this lack of official recognition, this group developed an identity distinct from the larger population of Itelmen. Today the Kamchadal are seeking official recognition as an ethnic minority, which would entitle them to certain legal protections and privileges, including rights to land claims and hunting and fishing rights. Official recognition can also be advantageous in securing international scholarly and commercial connections, as well as access to higher education.

Igor Fyodorev has a sweet tooth and is uncommonly interested in the chocolate we have brought to Viktoria. It is rare for a man here to be unabashedly fond of chocolate; this is generally considered a feminine trait. He confesses that because his father was involved in trade, provisioning government-run

Figure 37. Kamchadal girls, c. 1900. The term "Kamchadal" is used today for native Kamchatkans who claim both Itelmen and Russian ancestry. It was used more broadly at the time of the Jesup Expedition, when Bogoras was delighted to find "Kamchadal" who had not been effectively assimilated. Today, the Kamchadal are trying to gain recognition as a distinctive ethnic group. (AMNH Library 260463)

stores, he always had a supply of chocolate as a child, and now he craves it. Viktoria teases that he will even take chocolate from his own children.

Our conversation turns to the recent economic crisis. Igor Fyodorev reflects that the currency crisis was "produced" because the government was in debt and needed funds; to bail out the government, the people suffered. The crisis, he opines, serves the interest of Russia's American, Japanese, and other trade partners. Laurel contradicts him, saying that stability is in American businessmen's interest, but Igor decries Russia's dependency on foreign goods. He speaks of the selling of Kamchatka's forests to Japan and its metals to India. Viktoria qualifies this; the pace of pillage has slowed, there is more cognizance of negative effects. She cites some of the consequences, describing a river valley that was overlogged and is now badly eroded. People thought they could just jump into capitalism, but they lacked a solid basis for protection, she says. It was all tied to politics, and it became corrupt. Organized crime moved in. There is little support for small businesses, less now than in the early 1990s. The banks have all been centralized in Moscow, and without local banks, small businesses have no access to credit.

By Korean analogy, Laurel asks about informal rotating credit associations, the foundation of many a Korean enterprise in the homeland and in the

United States. That's what people from Dagastan and Tadzhikistan do, Viktoria says. She envies the businessmen who have come to Kamchatka from Central Asia. They don't drink (being Muslim), and they have a tradition of rotating credit. The Itelmen and other Native people sometimes drink their profit rather than reinvesting. Viktoria reflects that from the perspective of Native people, Soviet times were relatively good times. Ethnic groups were not forced to compete for scarce resources. Like the woman we met in the microbus on the way to Esso, Viktoria separates a history of repression that had touched her own family from a more generalized "Soviet" experience that sometimes contrasts favorably with the present moment.

Igor Fyodorev leaves after accepting Viktoria's invitation to dinner tomorrow night. It will be our farewell dinner, and Viktoria urges him to bring fish for a feast. We ask Viktoria if we can borrow a pot to blanch our mushrooms for transport. While the mushrooms cook, Viktoria brings out her better handicrafts. She shows us some scrimshaw by the Koryak carver Yegor Chechulin. She respects him for passing up a secure position in a state workshop as a master artisan on the grounds that all they did there was sit around and drink tea. He does his own work, has apprenticed himself to master artisans in Chukotka, and in the summer travels up and down the east coast of Kamchatka salvaging walrus tusks that have washed up on the shore.

Viktoria shows us the ornate beaded headband that she takes to cultural events. Children can be photographed in it for five rubles. This exquisite piece is not for sale. Last year she had just received a substantial paycheck and settled her debts with money to spare when an artisan came by needing 500 rubles for an air ticket. The artisan offered her the headband as security and was surprised that Viktoria valued it enough to buy it outright.

Laurel purchases, on behalf of the American Museum of Natural History, a wonderful worked piece of black velvet with huge beaded flowers, one of a pair Viktoria had originally intended for the tops of her boots. The other cuff is currently in circulation as a demonstration piece. She also buys a headband with a lime-green background and a pattern of jagged points that Viktoria describes as "traditional." Viktoria hates to see this piece go, but the Koryak artisan wants to sell it, so what can she do? It had been made for her granddaughter who had replaced it with another band. Before entering into these negotiations, Laurel tells Viktoria her philosophy on museum collecting. Laurel explains that she has no intention of purchasing old things that cannot be replaced; those things ought to stay in Kamchatka. The purchase of contemporary handicraft brings evidence of living traditions back to New York, while encouraging Kamchatka artisans to continue their work. Viktoria says that she agrees with this completely.

When the mushrooms are done, Viktoria takes a handful to make into a soup with instant Japanese noodles, tomatoes, potatoes, dill, and powdered soup. She tells us, "If you watch closely you will see how an Itelmen woman

Figure 38. The scholar and activist Viktoria Petrasheva models beadwork she helps the local artisans sell. We later provided her with a CD of objects in the AMNH collection to use in her workshops with the artisans. (Photo by Laurell Kendall)

makes something absolutely wonderful out of nothing." We eat this delicious soup with dark bread and fish roe.

After nine hours of steady conversation, we leave Viktoria. Although it is eight in the evening, the Northern sun is still bathing the streets with bright light, but the market is shuttered tight. The sight could not be more at odds with Laurel's experience of the newly revived markets in China and Vietnam that carry on until all hours. The hotel café is filled with students from Moscow en route to Japan. That morning Alexia had placed a special order for blini, and we have these delivered to our room.

Wednesday is cool and clear. The ruble is now trading at 6.7 to the dollar. We have come full circle. We find Margarita Ivanovna working over a ledger in her office, warmed by a space heater. She cannot talk for long, she tells us, because there is a big tour boat of Japanese in the harbor, and she will have to give them a tour of the museum. She wants to know if we managed to meet her artisan friends in Esso and Palana. Her contact in Esso was at the festival in Kovran, and as for Palana, we explain our difficulties with transportation. She tells us what we already know, that we have barely scratched the surface, that we have not allowed for nearly enough time in Kamchatka. We agree emphatically. We tell her that we would like to work with her in the future. She is enthusiastic but also tells us frankly that she has not been in good health and is contemplating retirement. Also, she reminds us, the good artisans are already quite old. We leave her with warm feelings and also some concern for her future.

We have an appointment with Vladimir Kolegov, the Koryak representative to the Kamchatka provincial government, who arrives in his car. His intention is that we should eat lunch in his office cafeteria, but we plan to treat him to lunch at the Kazakh restaurant we had noticed in the market. At first he demurs on the grounds that this hole-in-the-wall is "too expensive," but we are emphatic. He tells us that as it turned out, we had flown out of Palana on the first and last good flying day; had we stayed on we would still be there. Kolegov missed Lidia's concert because he had been franticly harvesting potatoes. A third of his potato crop had been stolen out of the ground, and he had hastened to bring the rest in over the Sunday holiday.

Over a lunch of spicy noodles, *manty* (steamed wheat buns stuffed with piping hot ground lamb), and tea, we learn that Kolegov used to deal in reindeer antlers and bones, the former for Chinese medicine, the latter as a favored substance used in culturing more perfect pearls from oysters. He has been in China several times for business, traveling to Harbin and other Manchurian points, but he says that one "needs connections" to do that kind of work. He gave it up because he had no stomach for involvement with organized crime.

He got into politics by campaigning for the governor of the Koryak Autonomous Region. After her victory, the governor asked him to be her special representative in Petropavlovsk. It's an interesting job, but the pay is minimal. He tells us that when the workday is over, he spends every spare minute hustling carrots and potatoes to feed his family. If the governor will release him, he plans to leave the job next spring and open a fishing business. Alexia asks him about the risks in this enterprise. He tells her that since he intends to treat his employees fairly, he does not foresee any problems.

He describes himself as loving the outdoors, whereas his Russian wife and thirteen-year-old daughter are stay-at-homes. He would like to take us to a scenic spot where he also hunts bears. Would we be expected to hunt? Hunting is serious, Kolegov tells us. He does not go hunting with women. We ask about relations between indigenous groups and museums and he says we will continue the conversation in his office. Away from the public ear, we think.

In Kolegov's office there is a map of Kamchatka on the wall with a bold red border slicing off the Koryak Autonomous Region. The designated area consumes two-thirds of Kamchatka's territory but none of the major ports and communication centers. Was the succession such a good idea?

Seated behind his desk, Kolegov asks us if we remember the man who was medevacked from the spa on Olzhebay's charter flight. "His problem was drink," he says, "a common problem with indigenous people." There aren't any effective rehabilitation programs, but the problem is more basic than this. He speaks, as others have, of the infantilism of Native peoples in a system that until very recently always provided for their needs. His own experience was more positive because although he was sent to residential school, he spent long summers with his grandfather on the taiga. Now, when he tries to bring business opportunities back to his community he is frustrated. People will not stay with a fishing venture through the two to three weeks of intense activity; they drift off after only a few days. (This does not bode well for his plans.) He speaks of a lack of drive, a lack of experience, a susceptibility to deception. It is a standard rap, blaming the very people who suffer the most from the failing social system. "But how, then, can things change?" we ask. "People need to be told flat out that the government is no longer there as their uncle who will take care of them. The people who are accomplishing things in the region all come from somewhere else." Kolegov flourishes a glossy magazine probably intended for business promotion in the region. There is a piece on Kazakh businessmen engaged in successful enterprises in Kamchatka, including, of course, Olzhebay Kasenovich. Kolegov is concerned that resources are being drained from Native communities, a process compounded by the weak concept of private property in the Russian Federation. Although the region is rich in fur, platinum, and gold, all the profits go to Moscow, or at least to regional authorities, not local villages.

We realize that we are getting Kolegov's basic take on Kamchatka, such as he might give to any journalist or sympathetic researcher. We steer the conversation back to the subject of museums. His outlook is similarly bleak. Kolegov asserts that among the Koryak and Even, few are really drawn to their heritage. Native people are not attracted to museum work. They feel that what they need, above all, is money, and cultural work is not profitable. Native people have no time to enjoy museums. Even he, with his relatively secure position, is constantly under financial stress. How could he find the time to visit museums? And he, at least, respects his heritage, while the "young people" do not (we would be surprised if he is more than forty years old).

Kolegov is constantly being summoned to the telephone, and we decide to leave. Before we can exit he insists that we see the governor's office with its impressive desk and chair.

On our way back to the hotel, we pass through the market. Laurel buys her skunk hat, although one of the old ladies in the adjoining stall is still insisting that she buy the sable. We buy jars of orange fish eggs and stock up on vodka and Russian champagne to take home. We buy a bottle of Georgian wine to take to Viktoria's dinner party.

We are very tired. Alexia dozes on the bus. Laurel dozes in the hotel and Alexia goes to the three grocery stores in the vicinity of the hotel in an unsuccessful search for the cooking oil that Viktoria has asked us to bring. One of the shopkeepers tells her that there may be some in the remaining government store next to the market. We stop by on our way to Viktoria's. We stand in a long queue to make our purchase and stand in another long queue to procure the requisite chit, dealing everywhere with gruff cashiers. Back on the street, a bottle of oil and a couple of oranges in hand and heaving huge sighs of relief, Alexia tells Laurel, "I'm glad you had that experience," a lingering relic of Soviet life.

Viktoria's apartment is full of activity. We assist with the cutting and chopping, joining forces with a Japanese researcher who has lived here for two years after studying the Koryak language in Japan. Viktoria says that local people respect her for having lived with them through bad times. Watanabe arrives with beer. He laments that the Korean restaurant, his favorite spot in town, had been closed by the tax police (*nalogovaya inspektsia*) when he and Viktoria went there today for lunch. Viktoria grumbles that the tax police like to close down anything that's good. Igor Fyodorev, who provided Viktoria with the ample supply of fish that now fills her bathtub, paws around her cabinet looking for the remains of yesterday's chocolate. He filches a large hunk with a quiet, guilty smile, and the teasing ensues.

Even aside from the dinner party, Viktoria's apartment is a hub of activity. She is on the telephone arranging for someone to deliver more fish roe for us to purchase. A Japanese professor's wife, active in furthering the relationship between Petropavlovsk and its sister city of Kushiro, arrives to buy a bundle of necklaces and leather pouches since she is leaving on the boat for Japan tomorrow and needs a supply of omiage to make requisite gift presentations back home. A photographer of local scenery and his wife, leaving on a trip to their native Ukraine, deliver a plant and samples of his work for Viktoria's tending. As usual, there are many, many toasts to friendship and solidarity all over the world.

Toward eleven, Viktoria calls a friend who has a car and persuades him to drive us home, but first he joins the party for awhile. On the way home, we drive by the harbor and Igor points out his three boats, two for fishing and one for transport. He asks how the men in our lives put up with our travel, and tells us that he wouldn't let his woman run around. We tell him that we bring our men nice presents, and that if he let his women travel they would probably bring back lots of chocolate.

Thursday, September 17, is chilly. There are gray clouds in the sky, but it is clear enough for parting glimpses of snow-clad volcanoes. On our last morning, we take a bus to the outskirts of town for a quick tea with the Even dancer

Ekaterina Gil. She meets us at the bus stop wearing the red, white, and blue parka she bought in New York when she performed with the Nulgur troupe from Esso at the American Museum of Natural History the previous year. On the way to her apartment, we stop by the grocery store to buy things for tea. Ekaterina indicates the near-empty shelves and tells us that this is a consequence of the hoarding that took place during the crisis. Odd things remain. One shelf is crammed with several varieties of Cinzano, and Pringles are in good supply. Ekaterina buys simple cookies and Pringles for our tea and some juice for her grandchild. She will not let us pay. We supplement her purchases with one of the German chocolate bars Alexia bought yesterday while she was searching for Viktoria's cooking oil and an apple from breakfast. "Real live apples!" Ekaterina remarks.

Ekaterina's apartment is in a gray concrete block in a neighborhood of gray concrete blocks. We are greeted by Ekaterina's fair-haired daughter and handsome toddling grandson, a child at the jolly age of peek-a-boo and purposeful motion. "Hit the Road, Jack" is playing in the background. The walls of Ekaterina's apartment testify to a cosmopolitan performing life: local art, a black-and-white *Mona Lisa* clipped from a magazine, a Montmartre painting that Ekaterina bought in Paris during a dance tour, and a charcoal sketch of her own face done by a Paris street artist. One bare corner is decorated with autographs in multicolored paint by various visitors. Of course there are several posters from the Mengo dance troupe's performances. One of these features an enlarged head of the younger, very beautiful Ekaterina floating above the other performers, a relic of the time when she was the young star married to the brilliant choreographer.

Ekaterina tells us that when she returned last winter from performing at the American Museum of Natural History, she and many other members of the group gave television, radio, and newspaper interviews. They spoke of how well their cultural heritage is preserved within the museum and how happy they were to be given access to the objects in storage. We savor this. Museums are not often so appreciated by Native people. We tell Ekaterina about the CD we have left with the Petropavlovsk museum and our hope that local artisans will be able to use it. Ekaterina knows Margarita and assures us that access will not be a problem. Ekaterina tells us that she made pencil sketches in the museum of particularly compelling beadwork decorations and shared them with her artisan sister. This method works well enough for her sister, who is older and closer to the tradition, but for the younger artisans it will be much better to have the precise photographic data.

Although Ekaterina no longer dances with Mengo, she is extremely loyal to the troupe that is so strongly identified with her late husband's work, and with whom her son now dances. She gives us a colored brochure that includes pictures of dances and a portrait of her husband, an artistic and sensitive-looking Russian. "Mengo" means "hands" in Koryak. While Mengo is billed as a Koryak dance troupe, it performs representative dances from all of the peoples of Kamchatka and Chukotka. "A Chukchi legend" features a masked figure in the guise of the Chukotka mascot, the Pelikan figure.

Back at the hotel, we complete our packing and collect Watanabe at his hotel. Viktoria is with him and we make a stop by her home for the knit vest and letter she wants us to deliver to mutual friends in New York. We are happy to be part of her global network.

On the way to the airport, Alexia realizes that we are riding in a black Volga, not in the best condition. In the 1930s, black Volgas were often used to pick people up for possible execution, the official car of choice. This one has been renovated since its glory days; it sports a Toyota radio and a Mazda glove compartment. This now thoroughly hybridized artifact is a most appropriate vehicle for our last ride in the Russian Far East.

Epilogues

Laufer returned from Siberia early in 1899. In 1901, he was able to fulfill his dream of working in China, a land he had studied from afar. As the leader of another American Museum of Natural History expedition, he would boldly proclaim to Boas, who had appointed him: "I shall conquer China . . . [for] the anthropologist. China, no longer the exclusive domain of travelers and Sinologues, both narrow-minded and one-sided in their standpoints and researches, China to all who have anthropological interests."[1]

In 1908, Laufer began a long career at the Field Museum in Chicago where he filled several vaults with an eclectic array of antiquities and ethnographic objects from China and Tibet while writing up his omnivorous scholarly interests. In 1934, stricken with a fatal illness, he took his life by leaping from a tall building.

Bogoras returned to St. Petersburg in 1901 to write up the results of his research. The first volume of his monumental work on the Chukchi appeared in 1904, but in 1905 his dormant political passions were awakened by the possibility of revolution. Boas urged his younger colleague not to abandon his research, but Bogoras insisted on the necessity of social engagement at a time when "blood is flowing, the blood of the country, and no result is to be seen so far."[2] The Revolution of 1905 was aborted. Bogoras was arrested in Moscow and released on bail after two weeks in prison. His scholarly activities resumed, with Boas's encouragement, and by 1909, all three volumes of *The Chukchee* had been published.

After the Revolution of 1917, Bogoras headed the Institute of the Peoples of the North. His students would become the cohort of educators and activists whose early ethnographic efforts, and general respect for Native peoples, were so fondly recollected in our conversations with Native culture workers. Despite the vicissitudes of U.S.-Soviet relations, Bogoras would maintain a lifelong friendship with Boas, sometimes describing himself as Boas's student. At least one distinguished Soviet-trained anthropologist affirms that this line of transmission persisted despite the subsequent Stalinist purges and ideological control of the Communist Party: "The core of Siberian anthropological research during the entire Soviet era remained primarily evolutionist in its spirit and Boasian in its focus and content." In other words, he and his colleagues were all subterranean Boasians, and Russian and American anthropology share deep ancestral affinities.[3]

The Jochelsons traveled home in 1902 by way of Yakutsk, far to the west, where they collected clothing, tools, shaman paraphernalia, and large wooden basins for fermented mare's milk from the horse-riding Sakha people. A stunning diorama in the Hall of Asian Peoples at the American Museum of Natural History uses some of this material to portray an entranced Sakha shaman, about to fly off and capture his patient's soul. On returning from the field, Dina Jochelson-Brodskaya completed her degree in medicine at the University of Zurich, using the copious head and body measurements that she had made during the expedition as primary data for her dissertation. The couple made one more expedition to the Russian Far East, from 1909 to 1911. In 1912, Jochelson became curator in the Museum of Anthropology and Ethnogrpahy of the Russian Academy of Sciences. In 1922, the Jochelsons became permanent exiles in the United States, living on meager support from the American Museum of Natural History and the Carnegie Institution. For this reason, Jochelson's important works on the Koryak, Yukaghir, and Yakut (Sakha) have only recently been translated into Russian. His Yukaghir monograph has the distinction of a bilingual translation into Russian and the endangered Yukaghir language. Preparing the publication in 1996, the Yukaghir scholar Gavril Kurilov, whose shaman grandfather had been one of Jochelson's subjects, came to the American Museum of Natural History to study the collections and photographs made by Jochelson. This is one more example of the bonds of scholarship and heritage that stretch between the Russian Far East and New York, the link between the ethnographic labors of one hundred years ago and the urgent work of Native activists and scholars in the present moment.

These ties drew us to the Russian Far East and have continued after our journey. Both Vladimir Bychkov, the creative and resourceful director of the Providenia museum, and Natalya Pavlovna Otke, the imperious Chukchi director from Anadyr, have visited us in New York. Vladimir came for an extended study of the collections; Madame Otke was part of a cultural exchange delegation. Madame Otke's time was short, but on a whirlwind tour of our galleries, she managed, true to form, a nonstop critique. In 2002 we were able to carry out a project inspired by our conversations with curators in the Russian Far East. In March and April 2003, then-postdoctoral fellow Nelson Hancock took eight crates, each containing a mini-exhibition of Jesup Expedition photography, from the American Museum of Natural History to eight local museums in the Russian Far East, an act of "visual repatriation."[4]

From Nelson and other friends who work in the area, we have heard that conditions in the Russian Far East are much as we observed them in the sum-

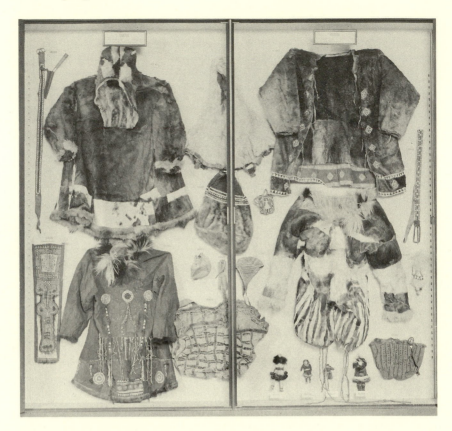

Figure 39. Siberian artifacts from the Jesup Expedition on display at the American Museum of Natural History in the early twentieth century. This installation predates the current Hall of Asian Peoples. (AMNH Library 31002)

mer of 1998. Civil servants now receive their pay on a regular basis, a vast improvement over the crisis moment of our visit, but air travel is even more limited. At the time of this writing, the Russian government is in the process of closing additional remote villages in Chukotka and Kamchatka and consolidating their residents in the towns, a major movement of peoples that in some quarters "has rekindled memories of the forced resettlements under Stalin when minorities, such as Chechens and Jews, were moved at the regime's will."[5]

How have our friends and fellow curators fared? Vladimir Bychkov, relieved of his job by the unpopular new governor of Chukotka, has enrolled in business school in Alaska, a serious loss to the museum world. Margarita Ivanovna Belova has retired from her long years of work with Native artisans in Kam-

Figure 40. A group of Even pose during the winter festival at Anavgay, near Esso, in March 2002. Framed photographs from the Jesup Expedition have been hung on the tent behind them. (Photo by Nelson Hancock)

chatka. Tatyana Volkova was on hand at the Palana museum to receive and mount our "exhibit in a box." Viktoria Petrasheva, the Itelmen scholar-activist in Petropavlovsk, maintains her lively salon as an international hub of art and scholarship. She uses one of our CDs in training workshops with Native artisans. The future of cultural life in the Russian Far East is in the hands of Viktoria and others like her. The rich cultural legacy witnessed and recorded by the Jesup North Pacific Expedition is being claimed and put to use by the descendants of those who were its subjects.

Notes

Preface

1. Unless otherwise stated, citations of Jesup Expedition correspondence are from the Archives of the Division of Anthropology, American Museum of Natural History.

2. Works by and about the Jesup North Pacific Expedition are included in the list of selected sources at the end of this volume.

3. Paul Fussell, *Abroad: British Literary Traveling Between the Wars* (Oxford: Oxford University Press, 1980), 39.

4. Boas to Bogoras, April 6, 1905, AMNH Division of Anthropology archive, # 1902–20.

5. Fussell *Abroad,* 39.

6. Mary Louise Pratt, *Imperial Eyes: Travel Writing and Transculturation* (London: Routledge, 1992), 148.

7. Cited in Fussell, *Abroad,* 40.

8. Mary Louise Pratt, "Fieldwork in Common Places," in *Writing Culture: The Poetics and Politics of Ethnography,* ed. James Clifford and G. E. Marcus (Berkeley: University of California Press, 1986), 27–50.

9. Claude Lévi-Strauss, *Tristes Tropiques* (New York: Atheneum, 1974), 4.

10. Pratt, "Fieldwork," 33.

11. James Clifford, *Routes: Travel and Translation in the Late Twentieth Century* (Cambridge, Mass.: Harvard University Press, 1997), 66.

Chapter 1. Across the Bering Strait and Through the Looking Glass

1. Waldemar Bogoras, *The Chukchee: The Jesup North Pacific Expedition,* vol. 7: *Memoir of the American Museum of Natural History, New York,* Ed. F. Boas (New York: G. E. Stechert, 1904), 53–65.

2. Patty A. Gray, "Tan-Bogoraz and the *Narodovol'tsy* under Alexander III," unpublished manuscript, 4; Nikolai Vakhtin, "Franz Boas and the Shaping of the Jesup Expedition Siberian Research, 1895–1900," in *Gateways: Exploring the Legacy of the Jesup North Pacific Expedition, 1897–1902,* ed. Igor Krupnik and William W. Fitzhugh. Contributions to Circumpolar Anthropology, 1 (Washington, D.C.: Smithsonian Institution, 2001), 71–92.

3. Gray, "Tan-Bogoraz," 4.

4. Bogoras to Shternberg, November 4, 1895, Russian Academy of Sciences Archives, St. Petersburg Branch, Waldemar Bogoras Collection, cited in Vakhtin, "Franz Boas," 79.

5. Vakhtin, "Franz Boas," 77.

6. Ibid., 80.

Chapter 2. Chukotka

1. Bogoras, *The Chukchee*, 23.

2. Ibid., 271.

3. Lyudmila Bogoslovskaya, "List of the Villages of the Chukotka Peninsula (2000 B.P. to the Present)," *Beringian Notes* 2, no. 2 (1993): 2–14.

4. Bogoras, *The Chukchee*, 442–43.

Chapter 3. Magadan

1. Jochelson cited in Boas, "The Jesup North Pacific Expedition," 107.

2. Ibid.

3. Boas, "The Jesup North Pacific Expedition," 108.

4. Ibid., 109.

Chapter 4. Anadyr

1. Bogoras to Boas, September 26, 1901, Anthropology Archive, AMNH, 1901–54. Bogoras's field report is summarized in Boas, "The Jesup North Pacific Expedition," 109-15.

2. Dramatic policy swings and their consequences for indigenous Siberians are also documented in Bruce Grant, *In the Soviet House of Culture: A Century of Perestroikas* (Princeton: Princeton University Press, 1995).

3. For discussions of this issue, see Alexia Bloch, *Red Ties and Residential Schools: Indigenous Siberians in a Post-Soviet State* (Philadelphia: University of Pennsylvania Press, 2003), and Piers Vitebsky and Sally Wolfe, "An Uncivilized Landscape of No Interest to Women: The Separation of the Sexes Among Siberian Reindeer Herders," in *Sacred Custodians of the Earth? Women, Spirituality, and the Environment*, ed. Alaine Low and Soraya Tremanye (New York: Berghahn Books, 2001), 81–94.

Chapter 5. Khabarovsk

1. Kenneth Lattourette, "Berthold Laufer, 1874–1934," *National Academy of Sciences, Biographical Memoirs* 18 (1936): 43–68.

2. Ibid.

3. Boas, "The Jesup North Pacific Expedition," 93–94.

4. Laufer to Boas, April 20, 1899, Anthropology Archive, AMNH, 1900–12.

5. Ibid.

6. Ibid.

7. Ibid.

8. Laufer to Boas, November 2, 1899, Anthropology Archive, AMNH, 1900–12.

Chapter 6. Petropavlovsk

1. Cited in Boas, "The Jesup North Pacific Expedition," 108–9.
2. Jochelson to Boas, December 3, 1900, Department of Anthropology, AMNH, 190 1–70.
3. Cited in Boas, "The Jesup North Pacific Expedition," 113–14.
4. Ibid., 114. Bogoras's reports quoted in this source.
5. Jochelson to Boas, December 3, 1900, Department of Anthropology, AMNH, 1901–70.

Chapter 7. Esso and the Way There

1. Waldemar Jochelson, *Tales of the Yukaghir, Lamut, and Russianized Natives of Eastern Siberia.* Jesup North Pacific Expedition, vol. 9, Memoirs of the American Museum of Natural History. Leiden: E. J. Brill, 1926.

Chapter 8. In the Entourage of the Fisher King

1. Jochelson to Boas, December 3, 1900, Department of Anthropology, AMNH, 1901–70.
2. Ibid.
3. Ibid.

Chapter 9. Again Petropavlovsk

1. Jochelson to Boas, July 21, 1901, Department of Anthropology, AMNH, 1901–70.
2. Ibid.

Epilogues

1. Laufer to Boas, August 12, 1903, Anthropology Department Archive, AMNH.
2. Bogoras to Boas, April 22, 1905, Anthropology Department Archive, AMNH.
3. Sergei Arutiunov, "The Post-Jesup Century of Research in Prehistory of Northeast Siberia," in *Constructing Cultures Then and Now: A Centenary Celebration of Franz Boas and the Jesup North Pacific Expedition,* ed. Laurel Kendall and Igor Krupnik. Contributions to Circumpolar Anthropology 2 (Washington, D.C.: Arctic Studies Center, National Museum of Natural History, Smithsonian Institution, 2003), 259.
4. This project was supported by the Trust for Mutual Understanding and the Ogden Mills Fund of the Department of Anthropology, AMNH.
5. "Russia to Relocate 600,000 from the Frozen North: World Bank Backs Scheme to Help Poor," May 2003, http://www.guardian.co.uk.

Selected Sources

The Jesup North Pacific Expedition in the Russian Far East

Boas, Franz, series ed. 1898-1930. *Jesup North Pacific Expedition, Memoirs of the American Museum of Natural History.* 11 vols. New York: American Museum of Natural History.
———. 1903. The Jesup North Pacific Expedition. *American Museum Journal* 3 (5): 69-107.
Bogoras, Waldemar. 1901. The Chukchi of Northeastern Asia. *American Anthropologist* 3: 80-108.
———. 1904-1909. *The Chukchee.* Vol. 7, Jesup North Pacific Expedition, Memoirs of the American Museum of Natural History, vol. 11. Leiden: E. J. Brill; New York: G. E. Stechert. Reprint 1975, New York: AMS Press.
———. 1913. *The Eskimo of Siberia.* Vol. 8, Jesup North Pacific Expedition, Memoirs of the American Museum of Natural History, vol. 12. Leiden: E. J. Brill; New York: G. E. Stechert.
———. 1917. *Koryak Texts.* Publication of the American Ethnological Society, vol. 5. Leiden: E. J. Brill; New York: G. E. Stechert. Reprint 1974, New York: AMS Press.
Freed, Stanley A., Ruth S. Freed, and Laila Williamson. 1988. Capitalist Philanthropy and Russian Revolutionaries: The Jesup North Pacific Expedition (1897-1902). *American Anthropologist* 90 (1): 7-24.
Jochelson, Waldemar. 1908. *The Koryak.* Vol. 6, Jesup North Pacific Expedition, Memoirs of the American Museum of Natural History, vol. 10. Leiden: E. J. Brill; New York: G. E. Stechert.
———. 1926. *The Yukaghir and the Yukaghirized Tungus.* Vol. 9, Jesup North Pacific Expedition, Memoirs of the American Museum of Natural History, vol. 13. Leiden: E. J. Brill; New York: G. E. Stechert. Reprint 1975. New York: AMS Press.
———. 1926. The Ethnological Problems of the Bering Sea. *Natural History* 26 (1):90-95.
———. 1928. Peoples of Asiatic Russia. New York: American Museum of Natural History.
———. 1933. *The Yakut.* Anthropological Papers of the American Museum of Natural History 33 (2):35-225.
———. 1933. *History, Ethnology, and Anthropology of the Aleut.* Washington, D.C.: Carnegie Institution of Washington.
Kendall, Laurel, and Igor Krupnik, eds. 2003. *Constructing Cultures Then and Now: Cele-*

brating Franz Boas and the Jesup North Pacific Expedition. Contributions to Circumpolar Anthropology, 4. Washington, D.C.: Smithsonian Institution, Arctic Studies Center.

Kendall, Laurel, Barbara Mathé, and Thomas Ross Miller. 1997. Drawing Shadows to Stone: The Photography of the Jesup North Pacific Expedition, 1897-1902. New York: American Museum of Natural History with University of Washington Press.

Krupnik, Igor, and William W. Fitzhugh, eds. 2001. Gateways: Exploring the Legacy of the Jesup North Pacific Expedition, 1897-1902. Contributions to Circumpolar Anthropology, 1. Washington, D.C.: Smithsonian Institution, Arctic Studies Center.

Laufer, Berthold. 1900. Preliminary Notes on Explorations among the Amoor Tribes. American Anthropologist. 2:297-338.

———. 1902. The Decorative Art of the Amur Tribes. Vol. 4, Jesup North Pacific Expedition, Memoirs of the American Museum of Natural History, vol. 7. Leiden: E. J. Brill; New York: G. E. Stechert.

Shternberg, Lev. 1999. The Social Organization of the Gilyak. Edited by Bruce Grant. Vol. 82. Anthropological Papers of the American Museum of Natural History.

The Russian Far East Since the Jesup North Pacific Expedition

Balzer, Marjorie Mandelstam. 1996. "Flights of the Sacred: Symbolism and Theory in Siberian Shamanism." American Anthropologist 98 (2): 305-318.

Black, Lydia. 1973. The Nivkh (Gilyak) of Sakhalin and the Lower Amur. Arctic Anthropology 10 (1):1-110.

Cruikshank, Julie and Tatiana Argounova. 2000. Reinscribing Meaning: Memory and Indigenous Identity in the Sakha Republic (Yakutia). Arctic Anthropology 37 (1):96-119.

Czaplicka, Marie A. 1914. Aboriginal Siberia: A Study in Social Anthropology. Oxford: Clarendon Press.

Fitzhugh, William W., and Aron Crowell, eds. 1988. Crossroads of Continents: Cultures of Siberia and Alaska. Washington, D.C.: Smithsonian Institution Press.

Forsyth, James. 1992. A History of the Peoples of Siberia: Russia's North Asian Colony, 1581-1990. Cambridge: Cambridge University Press.

Grant, Bruce. 1995. In the Soviet House of Culture: A Century of Perestroikas. Princeton: Princeton University Press.

Kasten, Erich, ed. 1998. Bicultural Education in the North. New York: Waxman Publishing.

Kerttula, Anna. 2000. Antler on the Sea: The Yup'ik and Chukchi of the Russian Far East. Ithaca: Cornell University Press.

Kolarz, Walter. 1969. The Peoples of the Soviet Far East. Hamden, Conn.: Archon Books.

Kotkin, Stephen, and David Wolf, eds. 1995. Rediscovering Russia in Asia: Siberia and the Russian Far East. Armonk, N.Y.: M. E. Sharpe.

Krupnik, Igor. 1997. Survival and Contact: Asiatic Eskimo Transition, 1900-1990. Washington, D.C.: Smithsonian Institution Press.

———. 1993. Arctic Adaptations: Native Whalers and Reindeer Herders of Northern Eurasia. Translated and edited by Marcia Levenson. Hanover, N.H.: University Press of New England.

Kuoljok, Kerstin Eidlitz. 1985. The Revolution in the North: Soviet Ethnography and Nationality Policy. Stockholm: Alqvist and Wiksell.

Levin, Maksim, and Leonid Potapov, eds. 1964. The Peoples of Siberia. Trans. Scripta Technica and Stephen Dunn. Chicago: University of Chicago Press.

Okladnikov, Alexei. 1981. Art of the Amur: Ancient Art of the Russian Far East. New York: Abrams.

Pika, Alexander, ed. 1999. *Neotraditionalism in the Russian North: Indigenous Peoples and the Legacy of Perestroika.* Edited by Bruce Grant. Seattle: University of Washington Press.

Rethmann, Petra. 2000. *Tundra Passages: History and Gender in the Russian Far East.* University Park: Pennsylvania State University Press.

Slezkine, Yuri. 1994. *Arctic Mirrors: Russia and the Small Peoples of the North.* Ithaca: Cornell University Press.

Stephan, John J. 1994. *The Russian Far East: A History.* Stanford: Stanford University Press.

Vakhtin, Nikolay. 1994. Native Peoples of the Russian Far North. In *Polar Peoples: Self-Determination and Development,* Pp.29-80. Minority Rights Group International Report 92/5. London: Manchester Free Press.

Vitebsky, Piers. 1992. Landscape and Self-determination Among the Eveny: The Political Environment of Siberian Reindeer Herders Today. In *Bush Base: Forest Farm: Culture, Environment, and Development.* Edited by Elizabeth Croll and David Parkin. Pp. 223-246. London: Routledge.

Vitebsky, Piers, and Sally Wolfe. 2001. An Uncivilized Landscape of No Interest to Women: The Separation of the Sexes Among Siberian Reindeer Herders. In *Sacred Custodians of the Earth? Women, Spirituality, and the Environment.* Edited by Alaine Low and Soraya Tremanye. Pp. 81-94. New York: Berghahn Books.

The Post-Soviet Era Beyond the Russian Far East

Anderson, David. 2000. *Identity and Ecology in Arctic Siberia: The Number One Reindeer Brigade.* New York: Oxford University Press.

Balzer, Marjorie Mandelstam.1998. *The Tenacity of Ethnicity: A Siberian Saga in Global Perspective.* Princeton: Princeton University Press.

Bloch, Alexia. 2003. *Red Ties and Residential Schools: Indigenous Siberians in a Post-Soviet State.* Philadelphia: University of Pennsylvania Press.

Doi, Mary Masayo. 2002. *Gesture, Gender, Nation: Dance and Social Change in Uzbekistan.* Westport, Conn.: Bergin and Garvey.

Essig, Laurie. 1999. *Queer in Russia: A Story of Sex, Self, and the Other.* Durham: Duke University Press.

Golovnev, Andrei V., and Gail Osherenko. 1999. *Siberian Survival: The Nenets and Their Story.* Ithaca: Cornell University Press.

Humphrey, Caroline. 1999. *Marx Went Away but Karl Stayed Behind (Updated Edition of Karl Marx Collective: Economy, Society and Religion in a Siberian Collective Farm).* Ann Arbor: University of Michigan Press.

————. 2002. *The Unmaking of Soviet Life: Everyday Economies After Socialism.* Ithaca: Cornell University Press.

Koester, David. 1997. Childhood in National Consciousness and National Consciousness in Childhood. *Childhood* 4 (1): 125-142.

Lemon, Alaina. 2001. *Between Two Fires: Gypsy Performance and Romani Memory from Pushkin to Post-Socialism.* Durham: Duke University Press.

Levin, Theodore. 1996. *The Hundred Thousand Fools of God: Musical Travels in Central Asia (and Queens, New York).* Bloomington: Indiana University Press.

Nazpary, Joma. 2001. *Post-Soviet Chaos: Violence and Dispossession in Kazakhstan.* London: Pluto Press.

Pesmen, Dale. 2000. *Russia and Soul: An Exploration.* Ithaca: Cornell University Press.

Pilkington, Hilary, ed. 1996. *Gender, Generation, and Identity in Contemporary Russia.* New York: Routledge.

Ries, Nancy. 1997. *Russian Talk: Culture and Conversation During Perestroika*. Ithaca: Cornell University Press.

Ssorin-Chaikov, Nikolai V. 2003. *A Social Life of the State in Subarctic Siberia*. Stanford, Calif.: Stanford University Press.

Guidebooks and Travel Accounts of the Russian Far East

Azulay, Erik, and Allegra Harris Azulay. 1995. *The Russian Far East*. New York: Hippocrene Books.

Bergman, Stan. 1927. *Through Kamchatka by Dog-Sled and Skis: A Vivid Description of Adventurous Journeys Amongst the Interesting and Almost Unknown Peoples of the Most Inaccessible Parts of This Remote Siberian Peninsula*. London: Seeley, Service.

Dodwell, Christina. 1994. *Beyond Siberia*. London: Hodder and Stoughton.

Kennan, George. 1871. *Tent Life in Siberia, and Adventures Among the Koryaks and Other Tribes in Kamchatka and Northern Asia*. London: Low and Marston.

Krasheninnikov, Stepan Petrovich. 1972. *Explorations of Kamchatka: Report of a Journey Made to Explore Eastern Siberia in 1735-17, by Order of the Russian Imperial Government*. Translated by E. A. P. Crownhart-Vaughan. Portland: Oregon Historical Society.

Noble, John, et al. 1996. *Lonely Planet: Russia, Ukraine and Belarus*. Hawthorn, Australia: Lonely Planet.

Taplin, Mark. 1997. *Open Lands: Travels Through Russia's Once Forbidden Places*. South Royalton, Vt.: Steerforth Press.

Thubron, Colin. 1999. *In Siberia*. New York: HarperCollins.

Index